Modernist Crisis and the Pedagogy of Form

Modernist Crisis and the Pedagogy of Form

Woolf, Delany, and Coetzee at the Limits of Fiction

Matthew Cheney

BLOOMSBURY ACADEMIC
NEW YORK • LONDON • OXFORD • NEW DELHI • SYDNEY

BLOOMSBURY ACADEMIC
Bloomsbury Publishing Inc
1385 Broadway, New York, NY 10018, USA
50 Bedford Square, London, WC1B 3DP, UK
29 Earlsfort Terrace, Dublin 2, Ireland

BLOOMSBURY, BLOOMSBURY ACADEMIC and the Diana logo are trademarks
of Bloomsbury Publishing Plc

First published in the United States of America 2020
This paperback edition published in 2021

Copyright © Matthew Cheney, 2020

For legal purposes the Acknowledgements on p. viii constitute an extension of
this copyright page.

Cover design: Eleanor Rose
Cover photograph: Two curious boys look on as Miss Ethel Gabain
paints a scene showing air raid damage for the Ministry of Information,
during the Second World War, 13th November 1940, UK. Photographer:
Reg Speller / Stringer © Hulton Archive / Getty Images

All rights reserved. No part of this publication may be reproduced
or transmitted in any form or by any means, electronic or mechanical,
including photocopying, recording, or any information storage or retrieval
system, without prior permission in writing from the publishers.

Bloomsbury Publishing Inc does not have any control over, or responsibility for,
any third-party websites referred to or in this book. All internet addresses given in this
book were correct at the time of going to press. The author and publisher regret any
inconvenience caused if addresses have changed or sites have ceased
to exist, but can accept no responsibility for any such changes.

Library of Congress Cataloging-in-Publication Data
Names: Cheney, Matthew, author.
Title: Modernist crisis and the pedagogy of form :
Woolf, Delany, and Coetzee at the limits of fiction / Matthew Cheney.
Description: New York : Bloomsbury Academic, 2020. |
Includes bibliographical references and index.
Identifiers: LCCN 2019025910 (print) | LCCN 2019025911 (ebook) |
ISBN 9781501355912 (hardback) | ISBN 9781501355929 (epub) |
ISBN 9781501355936 (pdf)
Subjects: LCSH: Modernism (Literature) | Fiction–Authorship–Psychological aspects. |
Fiction–Social aspects. | Crises in literature. | Critical pedagogy. | Woolf,
Virginia, 1882–1941–Criticism and interpretation. |
Delany, Samuel R.–Criticism and interpretation. | Coetzee, J. M., 1940—Criticism
and interpretation. Classification: LCC PN56.M54 C539 2020 (print) |
LCC PN56.M54 (ebook) | DDC 809/.9112–dc23 LC record available at
https://lccn.loc.gov/2019025910 LC ebook record available at
https://lccn.loc.gov/2019025911

ISBN:	HB:	978-1-5013-5591-2
	PB:	978-1-5013-7316-9
	ePDF:	978-1-5013-5593-6
	eBook:	978-1-5013-5592-9

Typeset by Integra Software Services Pvt. Ltd.

To find out more about our authors and books visit www.bloomsbury.com
and sign up for our newsletters.

In memory of Elizabeth W. Cheney
(1946–2018)

Contents

Acknowledgments		viii
Note on Punctuation and Editions Cited		x
Abbreviations		xiii
1	Introduction	1
2	Here and Now: *The Years*	39
3	Into Crisis: "The Tale of Plagues and Carnivals"	73
4	Improper Arts: *The Mad Man*	107
5	Away from Crisis: *Elizabeth Costello, Diary of a Bad Year, Summertime*	135
6	Conclusion	173
References		182
Index		194

Acknowledgments

Some paragraphs and sentences in Chapter 1 are also included in my essay "The Reader Awakes: Pedagogical Form and Utopian Impulse in *The Years*," published in *Woolf Studies Annual* volume 24, copyright ©2018 Pace University Press, and reprinted with permission. Anonymous reviewers for that essay asked provocative questions that shaped my reading of *The Years* both there and in this book, and I am grateful to them, to Mark Hussey, editor of *Woolf Studies Annual*, and to Robin Hackett, co-editor of the special section on Jane Marcus for which my essay was a contribution.

The staff of the Howard Gotlieb Archival Research Center at Boston University welcomed and guided my work with the Samuel R. Delany Papers, and this book would have been vastly weaker without their support and knowledge. (The Delany papers have since moved to Yale University's Beinecke Library.)

This book would not exist without years of intellectual support provided by colleagues, staff, and professors at the University of New Hampshire, particularly Sandhya Shetty, Rachel Trubowitz, Delia Konzett, Siobhan Senier, Janine Wilks, and especially Robin Hackett.

Numerous friends and family members provided me with conversation, distraction, snacks, money, laughter, refuge, and sympathy throughout the process of researching and writing this book. While Samuel R. Delany the byline is a subject of my writing and research, Chip Delany the man is a friend who made much of it possible; his trust in me and his enthusiasm for my work (even, or especially, when our interpretations are utterly different) are one of the great blessings of my life. Jason Burbank and Nilupa Gunaratna provided me with food, shelter, and friendship during my work at the Gotlieb Center at Boston University. Kenneth James, Ron Drummond, and Henry Wessells provided key information at important moments. Keguro Macharia gave me life-saving tips, and his enthusiasm for some of the ideas herein kept me going at crucial times.

Anonymous reviewers of the manuscript offered detailed critique that was a model of generous thinking. Many of their suggestions and questions proved revelatory, and even the suggestions which I ignored and questions I deliberately chose not to answer helped shape the book's final form. I also owe greatest of thanks and gratitude to Katherine De Chant at Bloomsbury Academic, whose enthusiasm for the book from the beginning is why it exists at all. She shepherded it through every stage of the publishing process, and her thoughtfulness toward both the material and the book's potential audience affected each page herein.

During the research for and writing of this book, my life was sustained by my parents, Elizabeth Cheney and Ann Thurston; my grandparents, aunts, uncles, and cousins; and numerous friends, some of whom I'm sure I will inadvertently neglect to mention here: Eric Schaller and Paulette Werger; Ann and Jeff VanderMeer; Cinthia Gannett and John Brereton; Luke Dietrich, Sherrard Harrington, Michael Haselton, Mary Grace Elliott, Jin Lee, Jeremy Parker, Stephen Roxburgh, Kristin Stelmok, and Elizabeth Sheckler; many faculty and staff at Plymouth State University, particularly Liz Ahl, Robin DeRosa, Hannah Hounsell, Cathie LeBlanc, and Ann McClellan; Nora Cascadden; Morganne and Steve Freeborn; and Seth Willey.

My mother died on November 3, 2018, while this book was undergoing peer review. It was her library card that, when I was young, allowed me, when I was in high school, to first read Virginia Woolf and Samuel Delany (Coetzee I would discover later). Her support kept me working toward my PhD, my dissertation was dedicated to her, and our last conversation of any depth involved her questions about what she had read of it. As I have revised that material into this book, I have kept her always in mind, because though she was not a scholar, she was exactly what Woolf meant by a common reader: someone who reads thoughtfully and inquisitively for both pleasure and knowledge, and someone who deserves to read writing that is clear, careful, and not patronizing. This book is for her. I miss her more than words can say.

Note on Punctuation and Editions Cited

Ellipses, Italics, and Titles

Because both Virginia Woolf and Samuel R. Delany employ ellipses frequently, throughout this book I use brackets around ellipses to indicate when I have cut any text. This prevents a preponderance of "ellipsis in original" notes, but still maintains accuracy.

Italics should be considered original unless otherwise noted. Delany is especially fond of italics, and having to note every "emphasis in original" would be distracting for the reader and tedious for the writer. The occasional added emphasis is explicitly noted.

Regardless of length, where a work has been published on its own as a book or pamphlet, I have italicized the title; if it was published as part of another book, I have put the title in quotation marks. However, in quotations, if a writer's own usage differs from my own, I have kept the formatting of the original writer rather than change it. This leads to occasional discrepancies—for instance, Samuel Delany typically italicizes the titles of "The Tale of Plagues and Carnivals" and "Atlantis: Model 1924," while I do not, since neither has been published separately as a book of its own.

Texts and Editions Cited

I benefitted from working with Samuel Delany's archives at Boston University's Howard Gotlieb Archival Research Center and have occasionally referred here to unpublished material with Mr. Delany's permission. Specific archival citations would be meaningless for most readers, and so I have avoided them; for researchers, I have provided as much contextual information as seemed reasonable for locating the material, which is now well catalogued at Yale University's Beinecke Library.

In the cases of Virginia Woolf and Samuel R. Delany especially, a plethora of published versions for some texts makes it important to explain the choice of editions for citation. Most of Coetzee's works are remarkably consistent, sometimes to the extent that the same page plates are used not only through all editions within one country, but even transnationally, particularly with US and UK editions (which explains the use of British spelling and punctuation in some US editions)—though notably *not* with South African and Australian editions.

My general rule for all references has been, wherever possible, to cite the most accurate and authoritative US edition that is also generally available to everyday readers. For Woolf, this means choosing the Harcourt/Harvest annotated paperback editions over the Cambridge editions. Though the Cambridge editions are the most authoritative, they are also priced well beyond the means of most common readers, thus likely only to be found in large academic libraries. In the case of every novel except *Between the Acts*, the textual differences between the Cambridge editions and the Harcourt/Harvest annotated editions are of no consequence for my purposes.

Samuel R. Delany's books pose the greatest challenge for citation. Many of his early novels have practically countless US editions, and some books such as *Dhalgren* not only have multiple editions with textual differences, but also have textual differences between individual printings. Generally, I have favored the most recent print editions that Delany himself considers the most accurate, as determined by his public statements and communication with me. (For print errata, see Kevin Donaker-Ring's official Delany errata website at www.oneringcircus.com/delany_main.html.) My one deviation from using the print editions is *The Mad Man*, for which I cite the ebook in its Kindle version published by Open Road Media. Though the novel appeared in various (textually different) hardcover and paperback editions throughout the 1990s and early 2000s, all editions of *The Mad Man* were published by small presses, are currently out of print, are not included in many libraries, and sell now as collectors' items. It makes most sense, then, to cite the ebook, which is readily available at an affordable price and is the writer's own preferred text. The reader should be able to search through the text easily to find referenced passages, but I have also included Kindle location numbers. Though some guidelines argue against listing Kindle location numbers for in-text citations, the book does not have small chapters or other section indicators; it is broken into five large sections (plus a beginning "Proem" and an appendix), the ebook edition does not include page numbers, and citing quotations by section would be useless. Since Kindle is the most popular ebook format and Kindle location numbers are (for now) consistent from user to user, this seems like the best solution, for though individual readers may find it easiest simply to search the document for the reference they seek, including location numbers allows the reader of this book a certain sense of the relative location of passages to each other, which may be information of interest.

As I stated above, Coetzee's editions mostly pose no problems, given the uniformity of US and UK editions (though it is important to note that the Australian edition of *Diary of a Bad Year* is differently paginated, a fact that has a real effect on the text, given the importance of page layout to that novel). There is one exception that has bearing on this study: *Summertime*, which has been published both as a book on its own and in the omnibus collection *Scenes from Provincial Life*. I have chosen to cite the latter in its US paperback edition, as it is the most recent and includes a slightly revised text.

Abbreviations

It is common in studies of Virginia Woolf to refer to the published volumes of her diaries, essays, and letters by the initial and then the volume number. I have followed that convention throughout this book, thus:

D 1–5   (1977–84), *The Diary of Virginia Woolf.* Edited by Anne Olivier Bell and Andrew McNeillie. 5 vols. New York: Harcourt Brace Jovanovich.

E 1–6   (1986–2011), *The Essays of Virginia Woolf.* Edited by Stuart N. Clarke and Andrew McNeillie. 6 vols. London: Hogarth Press.

L 1–6   (1975–80), *The Letters of Virginia Woolf.* Edited by Nigel Nicolson and Joanne Trautmann Banks. 6 vols. New York: Harcourt Brace Jovanovich.

1

Introduction

While correcting the proofs for *The Waves*, her most ethereal novel, Virginia Woolf felt unsettled, unsure of herself and her writing. It was August 1931. The world and its events pressed in on her. She read newspapers regularly, her friend John Maynard Keynes kept her up to date on the international financial crisis, and she and her husband Leonard had long been involved with policy committees of the Labour Party, which for the moment was in power, though both Woolfs were as aware as anyone that internal and external pressures threatened the party's ability to govern. By the end of the month, Prime Minister Ramsay MacDonald had resigned and formed a coalition government to circumvent Labour's leftists, who adamantly refused to support a 10 percent cut in unemployment benefits. Woolf wrote in her diary that "the country is in the throes of a crisis. Great events are brewing."

What was a writer to do? Woolf wondered: "Are we living through a crisis; & am I fiddling?" (*D* 4: 39).

The fear that creative work is little more than playing a fiddle while the world burns around you is one that has haunted artists at many times and in many places. One strategy for making art during crisis is for that art to take a stand, to become committed, proselytizing, didactic. (In the twentieth century, the novels of Upton Sinclair are one particularly obvious example, but committed art is not always so inelegant.) For writers committed to an idea of artistic autonomy, though, adding a political commitment may challenge the freedom of the writing. Woolf felt the peril deeply and expressed it most clearly in an essay she wrote for the Communist Party's *Daily Worker*, "Why Art Today Follows Politics." It is not one of her best essays, but it clearly illustrates her struggles and frustrations at the time. Woolf first tries (unconvincingly) to equate writers and visual artists and to say that the art of the past tells us nothing about history and material conditions. She then moves to a discussion of the artist's relationship to the audience in times of crisis, and her position becomes both more personal and more clear.

Artists, she says, need two things from an audience: money and attention. But neither can be provided under dictatorial circumstances—the artists must be free to create in whatever way their sensitivities lead them. Woolf separates artists out from other people because "it is a fact that the practice of art, far from making the artist out of touch with his kind, rather increases his sensibility. ... Perhaps, indeed, he suffers more than the active citizen because he has no obvious duty to discharge." Here and throughout the final third of "Why Art Today Follows Politics," Woolf seems to be speaking of her own situation as she struggles to figure out her place in the contemporary era, to reconcile her anxiety (and even terror) at the state of the world with her work as a novelist. She says that the artist's studio, which used to be a place of peace and refuge, is now "besieged by voices, all disturbing, some for one reason, some for another." The voice of the audience declares it can no longer afford to pay for frivolous things like art; the audience is "so tortured and distracted" that it can no longer find pleasure in art; and meanwhile there is the ceaseless voice pleading for help, time, money, something: "Come down from your ivory tower, leave your studio, it cries, and use your gifts as doctor, as teacher, not as artist." A voice tries to get the artist to be useful to the state or else to shoot guns and fly airplanes. And one last voice "proclaims that the artist is the servant to the politician,"—Woolf portrays this voice as especially malevolent: "You shall only practise your art, it says, at our bidding. Paint us pictures, carve us statues that glorify our gospels. Celebrate Fascism; celebrate Communism. Preach what we bid you preach. On no other terms shall you exist" (*E* 6: 77).

The cacophony of all these voices paralyzes the artist, Woolf says. How can anyone remain at peace in such circumstances? The artist is forced into political organizations, forced to advocate and proselytize—how could one not when faced with suffering or even extinction? "Two causes of supreme importance to him are in peril. The first is his own survival: the other is the survival of his art" (*E* 6: 77).

These two causes, survival of self and survival of art, continued to feel imperiled to Woolf as fascism swept through Europe and then the Second World War began. In August 1940, Woolf wrote multiple drafts of a letter to Vita Sackville-West's son Benedict Nicolson, then serving at an anti-aircraft battery in Kent (*L* 6: 398n1), who had expressed criticisms of Bloomsbury that were similar to those of other people of his generation: he intended to be an art historian and art critic who would educate the masses and thus bring about social change. In her reply, Woolf tried to articulate her thoughts about art, education, politics, and society, but she struggled. None of Woolf's other extant letters show as much work and revision. The importance and difficulty of the subjects for her seemed to defeat her, leaving her unsatisfied with her words. "My puzzle is," she wrote in an unsent draft, "ought artists now to become politicians? My instinct says no; but I'm not sure that I can justify my instinct" (*L* 6: 420). In the letter she sent, which is overall much more concise than the drafts, she developed this idea more fully:

> What puzzles me is that people who had infinitely greater gifts than any of us had—I mean Keats, Shelley, Wordsworth, Coleridge and so on—were unable to influence society. They didn't have anything like the influence they should have had upon 19th century politics. And so we drifted into imperialism and all the other horrors that led to 1914. Would they have had more influence if they had taken an active part in politics? Or would they only have written worse poetry? (*L* 6: 421)

She expresses support for him, apparently not wanting to destroy his idealism with her doubts—"I hope you will be able to [change the attitude of the masses]. It would solve many problems. Anyhow I think you've made a good beginning if you hate people who sit on the floor and despise humanity" (*L* 6: 422). But she ends the letter with a description of events that put all of the young man's ideals into question, as if asking him how an art critic could possibly help anyone overcome the bare, brute facts in their own backyard:

> Here a young man from the War Office interrupts; about putting up a pill box in our field. Also there is an air raid on. So excuse this very inadequate letter. Last Sunday we had five raiders almost crashing into the dining room. Then they machine gunned the next village, and apparently went on to Sissinghurst. (*L* 6: 422)

There is no indication here of how hard Woolf worked on the letter. She gives Nicolson the impression that she was just dashing it off, and in the writing was interrupted by a soldier. War creates inadequacy of communication, inadequacy of art. There are machine guns in the villages.

What is art to do in the face of such reality?

Questions of art and politics are not academic for writers during moments of crisis. For writers who believe to some extent or another in the autonomy of art from socio-political determinism, the immediate question becomes: If they are not to abandon art and become pamphleteers or activists (as did the Modernist poet George Oppen), how—and why—are they to write?

This study will explore how three novelists, each committed to Modernist ideas of art for its own sake (the survival of art), developed one particular strategy when faced with socio-political crisis that created personal crisis: they pushed fictionality toward and beyond its limits, but did so without their work becoming propagandistic and without themselves assuming the role of the preacher. They achieved this by providing readers with an experience congruent with the goals of critical pedagogy, an experience that avoids an authoritarian mode of communication—one that sees the writer's job as communicating a message to a passive reader—by requiring any successful reader of the novel to be an active interpreter of the texts' forms, contents, and contexts. Such active interpretation is a familiar feature of Modernist experimentation, but at these moments of crisis, the pedagogies Virginia Woolf, Samuel R. Delany, and J.M. Coetzee infused into their novels were not merely aesthetic or psychological, not limited to the quotidian (vital as it is), but also aimed toward an engagement with the world beyond the text.

I examine Woolf, Delany, and Coetzee in different relationships to moments of crisis: before, during, and after. A sense of impending crisis requires the writer to consider how and why to address the crisis as it gains form and momentum; the onset of crisis makes the writer's desire for response immediate, and that desire then shapes the writing in new ways; the diminishment or even resolution of crisis may allow the writer a new creative freedom, but it is a freedom inevitably shaped by the experience of crisis. These positions also affect the kind of intervention the writer considers: before crisis, the writer may think of the writing as an attempt at preventing the worst of what may come; amidst crisis, there is a sense of desperation and triage; after crisis, new moments of reflection and reconsideration emerge.

For Virginia Woolf, the crisis of European fascism brought new thinking about how facts and fictions work together, and what a novelist might offer the world. For Samuel Delany, the beginnings of the AIDS crisis brought an immediate threat to his life as a sexually active gay man in New York City, and in the midst of the crisis he grappled with the role of fantasy in fiction to an extent he never had before. J.M. Coetzee lived through the crisis of the apartheid era in South Africa, an era that shaped much of his life and career. His later work reflects on both the life and career (and necessarily the crises he lived through) while opening up new relationships to fictionality, relationships that circumvent conventional, received ethical stances in favor of making ethical thought unavoidably active for the reader.

Modernism

Questions of the artist's role in society have bothered both artists and society at least since Plato banished poets from his *Republic*. Where Romantic poets may have thought of themselves as the "legislators of society," and social-realist novelists may have sought to tell stories that would change society's views on such issues as women's rights and child labor, canonical Modernism inherited many of the assumptions of late-nineteenth-century Aestheticism—assumptions of the art object's autonomy from the grubby cares of the world, its value and purpose being only its own beauty, for its own sake.[1] Furthermore, even if Modernist writers didn't associate themselves with a puritanical aestheticism, their interest in subjectivity and psychology could make their work seem remote from the world. This was a particular peril for novelists, because the serious novel in English had, by the early decades of the twentieth century, grown to be associated with a sense of social purpose. Psychology, personal sensations, and Woolfian "moments of being" seemed, to many readers and critics, trivial in comparison. W.L. George's 1920 review of books by "Neo-Georgians" (Woolf, Joyce, Wyndham Lewis, Romer Wilson, Dorothy Richardson, and May Sinclair) is hardly unique in its contempt for writers who, George says, were able only to

> abandon illumination, and prove themselves unfit to fulfil the high function of the novel, which it took up a hundred years ago: to dispel error by exhibiting

---

[1] Andrew Goldstone's *Fictions of Autonomy: Modernism from Wilde to de Man* (2013) is an important study for any consideration of the relationship between Modernism and ideas of autonomy, and one of Goldstone's key insights is that "autonomy" has not only had many meanings throughout philosophical and literary history, but that it had numerous meanings for Modernists, because the term is transitive, its meaning dependent on what its user is claiming autonomy *from*. Benjamin Kohlmann's exploration, in *Committed Styles* (2014), of autonomy as conceived by writers in the 1930s is also useful, particularly via his discussion of the way writers used the word "integrity" and of what he calls, with an homage to Fredric Jameson, the era's "apolitical unconscious." In contrast to Goldstone and Kohlmann's complex, nuanced explorations of the word "autonomy" (and related concepts), my use of "autonomy" throughout this study is narrow and pragmatic, keeping the idea of an autonomous work of art synonymous with the (admittedly vague) idea of art having value for its own sake. That this definition can be unpacked and proved inadequate is obvious from Goldstone's and Kohlmann's works, but its packed form is adequate to my purposes.

the period in which it flourishes, to use the battleaxe of understanding upon the thickets of prejudice and folly, to cut a trail through the foolish forests of the present, along which to drive the chariot of the future. (Majumdar and McLaurin 1997: 84)

In a 1971 issue of *New Literary History*, Lillian S. Robinson and Lise Vogel denounced Modernist art, literature, and criticism as unengaged with socio-political concerns and divorced from history:

> Modernism ... seeks to intensify isolation. It forces the work of art, the artist, the critic, and the audience outside of history. Modernism denies us the possibility of understanding ourselves as agents in the material world, for all has been removed to an abstract world of ideas, where interactions can be minimized or emptied of meaning and real consequences. Less than ever are we able to interpret the world—much less change it. (198)

A year later, in *The James Joyce Quarterly*, Maurice Beebe declared: "Modernist writers refuse to take sides; they would rather straddle a fence than mount a soap-box" (1972: 180).

The idea that Modernism is apolitical, ambiguously political, or reactionary in its politics is one that has been stated by some of its practitioners and acolytes, and by most of its detractors. Yet while the idea itself has (some) basis in (some) statements by (some) inescapably Modernist writers, scholarship since at least the 1990s has complicated and contradicted the assumption that Modernism's fragments, streams of consciousness, and aestheticism were ever primarily autonomous from historical, political, or social concerns. This scholarship has shown that the idea of an unworldly, ahistorical Modernism is an idea constructed to suit specific ideological desires: whether a desire among the Marxist followers of Lukács to condemn such work or among the New Critics to praise it. The New Modernist Studies has not only expanded the idea of what "Modernism" means (and who gets to be a "Modernist"), but also added evidence to the insights of earlier feminist scholars of Modernism, demonstrating that canonical Modernists sought ways to square the circle of autonomous art and socio-political commitment.[2] Aesthetic attention is undeniably central

---

[2] The history of Woolf studies demonstrates the peril of seeing all historicist, materialist, and political reading of Modernist writers as dating from the arrival of the New Modernist Studies alone. Feminist scholars historicized and politicized Woolf from the early 1970s onward, and it was their intervention that saved Woolf from being viewed as a marginal figure within Modernist studies. The New Modernist studies certainly opened up new ways of conceptualizing various modernisms, but historical and political analysis of Woolf predates New Modernism's arrival by decades.

to Modernism, but a commitment to aesthetics and a belief in the art object's having an inherent value of its own do not require a disengagement from politics or history, nor did writers such as Woolf believe they did. What Woolf and many artists (Modernist or not) feared was not political engagement, but the reduction of art to propaganda.

Certain assumptions of Modernist aesthetics are shared by Woolf, Delany, and Coetzee, who each see questions of form as vital to their work, and who are strongly suspicious of propagandistic tendencies within fiction. Each of these writers is, in their own way, a formalist. But not only a formalist. None of the three show much belief in a binary that separates art and politics or art and history. Such separation is not the dilemma that crisis creates for them. Rather, the dilemma is one of immediacy and fictionality: At what point is fiction a kind of fiddling in the fires? Does the imaginative distance that constitutes fiction betray the immediacy of the threats to life and liberty that crisis creates? How direct must the writer's address be, and what form of writing will at least do no harm?

There are no simple answers to these questions, and the evidence I present is not for the purpose of creating a formula for how to write in crisis. I don't believe such a formula exists. Rather, my purpose is to show how the works these writers produced are responses to crisis in both their form and subject matter. These texts are not eternal exemplars of how to respond, but instead evidence for the kind of open, serious, committed, and experimental thinking that life-and-death crisis demands. New writers will find new ways to write before, during, and after crisis; the examples of Woolf, Delany, and Coetzee show that such work is far from futile.

My approach builds from feminist and New Modernist perspectives on political commitment, but starts from aesthetics, looking less at the *what* of the engagement and prioritizing the *how*. (In practice, the two are, like form and content, often inseparable.) Before the advent of the New Modernist Studies, Toril Moi called for a critical approach to Woolf that would "refuse to accept this binary opposition of aesthetics on the one hand and politics on the other" and would instead locate "the politics of Woolf's writing *precisely in the textual practice*" (1985: 16). Moi's call was heeded by some writers and abjured by many more. For a few decades, questions of Woolf's aesthetics were devalued in favor of political, psychological, biographical, historical, and sociological interpretations, until a relatively recent return to aesthetics as textual politics (e.g., in such works as *Politics and Aesthetics in the Diary of Virginia Woolf* by

Joanne Campbell Tidwell and *Virginia Woolf and the Politics of Language* by Judith Allen). Though made over thirty years ago, Moi's call for locating the politics in the aesthetics remains a productive approach not only for Woolf, but also for many writers, including Delany and Coetzee, and it helps us see how they avoid the didactic in favor of the pedagogical.

A brief note on terminology: For nearly as long as it has been in use, the word *modernism* as a descriptive label has been contested and denounced, often by the people using it. Malcolm Bradbury and James McFarlane's influential 1976 anthology begins with a chapter expressing regret that the very word of their title, *Modernism*, is now settled in critical use despite its vagueness and ambiguity. In his massive 2005 anthology, Lawrence Rainey devotes most of his introduction to a genealogy of the term, concluding only, "Whatever literary modernism was, it was impatient with or overtly hostile to received conventions of fiction" (2005: xxv), and even in a "Note on the Selection, Texts, and Order of Presentation" he evades defining his terms. In 2015, Bloomsbury launched their New Modernisms series with Sean Latham and Gayle Rogers' *Modernism: Evolution of an Idea,* a book that begins:

> What is modernism? This question has now beset, driven, and often befuddled generations of students and scholars alike. It is not, however, the question this book will answer. That's because there is no such thing as modernism—no singular definition capable of bringing order to the diverse multitude of creators, manifestos, practices, and politics that have been variously constellated around this enigmatic term. (1)

This is true. And yet, if we are to have an object of study, we must be able to set some boundaries and find a way to describe not only what the object of study is, but what it is not. It seems to me irrefutable that there are many modernisms. It also seems necessary for this study to choose a Modernism.

I capitalize *Modernism* to distinguish my approach (which sees Modernism as bounded in history and geography) first from critics of modernity generally, and second from the more free-floating ideas of ahistorical, global modernisms popular with some New Modernists. A critique of modernity is simply beyond the scope of my project. As for global/planetary modernisms, there are, I think, valid and exciting approaches to that topic, but I strongly believe they need to be informed by the methodologies of postcolonial studies and comparative literature, or else, for all their good intentions, they end up replicating imperial power structures via a colonizing gaze.

Susan Stanford Friedman has influentially offered in place of canonical definitions of modernism a rhizomatic "planetary modernism" that she believes can overcome the Eurocentrism of previous taxonomies. While I certainly feel the force of Friedman's critique of Eurocentrism, I differ with her in not seeing the need to collect so much within the realm of Modernism. At a definitional level, it's unwieldy and imprecise, but there's a further problem of intellectual imperialism. As a concept, at least, Modernism is a Western idea, and to speak, for instance, of "African Modernism" would be to apply concepts that indisputably arise outside of Africa to African texts.[3] I am skeptical that the European term *modernism* can ever be purged of Eurocentrism; a truly decolonizing approach would eliminate the word altogether, replacing it with terms and genealogies from beyond Europe and the United States. Furthermore, I am wary of extending Modernism too far beyond the Atlantic world not because I want to encourage Eurocentrism, Anglophilia, or American exceptionalism, but because I fear the flattening power of the deterritorialized label will render other sorts of texts invisible.

In discussing a term that will be important to this study, *metamodernism*, David James and Urmila Seshagiri defend their use of traditional dates (placing Modernism between the end of the nineteenth century and the middle of the twentieth century) not only because without such dates there is no way to talk meaningfully metamodernism, but most importantly because

> we need to retain periodicity not to shore up a canonical sense of when modernism began, the moment from which it cast its influence, but to establish a literary-cultural basis for charting the myriad ways that much twenty-first-century fiction consciously engages modernism through the inheritance of formal principles and ethicopolitical imperatives that are recalibrated in the context of new social or philosophical concerns. Contemporary literary fiction responds to modernism as an aesthetic venture that can certainly occur globally, in different cultures. For such writing, however, modernism also belongs in a temporally localizable moment that we should not overwrite in our eagerness—however politically well-intentioned—to impart a democratic sensibility to art long perceived as Eurocentric, metropolitan, and elite. (2014: 92–93)

---

[3] This is to ignore for the moment the productive encounters between Modernism and African writers, as Peter Kalliney has chronicled, and also to ignore the pre-postcolonial-studies tendency to describe and assess African writers according to limited, traditional ideas of Modernism (for an example, see M.M. Carlin's 1965 review of *Weep Not, Child* by Ngugi wa Thiong'o [James Ngugi], *Transition* no. 18, pp. 54–55). Both phenomena deserve attention, but they remain outside the scope of this study.

It seems to me a mistake to try to obscure the literary-historical force of a body of work (however loosely collected) that has, for better and worse, until recently been conceived, discussed, analyzed, and responded to *as* a body of work. Finally, Friedman's atemporal, planetary modernism too easily obscures how power works between literary communities, and risks portraying a fanciful world of equal exchanges.[4]

Rather than an amorphous Friedmanesque "planetary modernism," my approach is centered on a Modernism that began to cohere in Europe and Britain in the late nineteenth century (developing from Aestheticism and Symbolism), spread to the Americas, reached an apex of influence in the 1920s, metamorphosed into various tendencies afterward, and then came to an end with the conclusion of the Second World War. It is a Modernism of "make it new!" of cubisms and collages, of radically free indirect discourse, internal monologues, and streams of consciousness. It recognizes the canon-expanding moves of feminism, black studies, queer studies, and the New Modernist Studies but depends on demonstrable lines (not anxieties) of influence and communication. It maps easily to the year Woolf and Joyce were born (1882) and the year they both died (1941).

My insistence on a Modernism bounded (however fuzzily) in time and place allows us to talk about what Andre Furlani and James & Seshagiri have separately come to call *metamodernism*: the modernism-after-Modernism (as opposed to postmodernism) that learns from, responds to, challenges, and multiplies

---

[4] Jeesoo Hong's review of *Lily Briscoe's Chinese Eyes: Bloomsbury, Modernism and China* by Patricia Laurence quietly shows some of the pitfalls: "Laurence in many cases limits herself to eulogizing the Chinese and English intellectuals' attraction to the other's artistic vision. She admits at the end of the book that she has somewhat generalized each culture, particularly Chinese culture" (2004: 534–535). Laurence's ignorance of Chinese languages and her desire to show an equal cultural exchange lead her, in Hong's view, to replicate imperialist power structures in her interpretations: "I also find the author's reading of the letters in those archives too sympathetic. I can hardly agree that these materials, which I have also read in the course of my own research, buttress Laurence's argument that the artistic interchange between the Chinese and British intellectuals, unlike economic and political relations between the two nations, can be exempted from the imperialist model or that the intercultural practices between the two modernisms were reciprocal" (535). I cite these concerns not for what they say specifically about Laurence's book, but because they so clearly highlight some of the dangers in a planetary modernism that is not highly attuned to questions of power. This is not to discount, though, the productive insights gained from, for instance, applying Modernist reading protocols to works outside the traditional Modernist canon, as Berman does with Indian women's writing. Furthermore, a truly informed study of global modernity and literary texts is of significant value, as Steven Yao shows in advocating for "an approach to both canonical modernist Orientalism in particular and to transnational modernism more generally that takes into account the historical and cultural specificity of, as well as the interactions among, different sites within the part of the world now commonly referred to as the Pacific Rim" (2009: 7).

Modernist moves.[5] My approach also allows such fields as postcolonialism and queer studies to offer their own perspectives, as they need to do for Delany and Coetzee, neither of whom can be understood only as metamodernists. Similarly, while Woolf can, of course, be discussed primarily as a Modernist, queer and postcolonial approaches to her texts have proved to be some of the most insightful of recent decades. Even with an initial capital letter, Modernism is not a monolith.

Establishing a set of clear influences and positions for each of these writers is a straightforward task, as all three published dozens of essays on literature (in Woolf's case, hundreds of essays), and there is significant scholarly work on Woolf and Coetzee especially, including biographies. Woolf's letters and diaries have been published, and Coetzee's manuscripts have been well studied by David Attwell in his recent book *J.M. Coetzee and the Life of Writing: Face to Face with Time* and Jan Wilm in *The Slow Philosophy of J.M. Coetzee*. I have done my own work in Delany's archives, and have also talked with him about his literary opinions and sense of influence. While Coetzee has been reluctant to give interviews about his personal life, his interviews with David Attwell in *Doubling the Point* are comprehensive; similarly, Samuel Delany (who is not at all reluctant to talk and write about his personal life) has given significant interviews, many collected in *Silent Interviews, About Writing,* and *Conversations with Samuel R. Delany*. Such material allows us to establish a foundation of productive influences; we don't need to resort to biographical speculations about the texts or Bloomian anxiety-of-influence psychoanalysis, but it is important, I think, to say, "Here is the tradition the writers themselves find meaningful, the ideas and texts they say they are responding to."

Starting with these three writers, then, we can make some discoveries about Modernism itself—one of which is confirmation of the longstanding insight that there is no one Modernism, but rather various related modernisms. Even within the limits I am setting on period and geography, it is clear Woolf, Delany, and Coetzee draw from different Modernist strands. Woolf was a participant in and icon of Modernism, one of the writers without whom any definition of Modernism has been incomplete for the last few decades (the history of

---

[5] For the sake of consistency with Furlani and James & Seshagiri, I have chosen to refer to *metamodernism* rather than *meta-Modernism* or *Metamodernism*. This makes some sense beyond simply indicating my debt to previous scholars, as metamodernism is more of a stance than a movement, more a technique than a title.

her place within that definition could fill a book-length study of its own).⁶ By the 1930s, she was able to look back on what she had participated in and to evaluate some of her sympathies and influences, as well as to plan for future work. She struggled to understand her own writing in relationship to younger writers' aesthetics, for instance, remarking in September 1933 about Vera Brittain's *Testament of Youth*: "A very good book of its sort. The new sort, the hard anguished sort, that the young write; that I could never write" (*D* 4: 177). It seems to me that *The Years* bears traces of this diary entry, particularly in the novel's close attention to details of material and bodily life. Similarly, Woolf had a conflicted relationship to the works of D.H. Lawrence, but was reading books by and about him throughout the 1930s, and many elements in the form and substance of *The Years* could be read as a response to Lawrence.⁷ Her essays, diaries, and letters also show her frequently thinking about Henry James, Joseph Conrad, Marcel Proust, and James Joyce in relationship to her own work, and her partnership in the Hogarth Press helped her think not only about her contemporaries, but about the generation of writers who came after her own. By the 1930s, the Modernist archive was rich and settled enough for a writer like Woolf to become something of a metamodernist.

Just as Woolf in the 1930s was writing partly in response to an earlier moment of Modernism, so, too, are Delany and Coetzee's works written, to varying extents, in response to certain Modernist writers and ideas. Coetzee's primary Modernist influences are many, but most consistently Kafka and Beckett, as well as Ford Madox Ford, about whom he wrote his master's thesis. He has published significant essays on all of them, as well as on Robert Musil, D.H. Lawrence, Walter Benjamin, and others. Delany is as affected by Modernism as Coetzee,

---

6 Hugh Kenner, who could never forgive Woolf for disliking *Ulysses*, sneered as late as 1984 that Woolf is "not part of International Modernism; she is an English novelist of manners, writing village gossip from a village called Bloomsbury for her English readers (though cultivated readers; that distinction had become operative between Dickens's time and hers, and Bloomsbury was a village with a good library). She and they share shrewd awarenesses difficult to specify; that is always the provincial writer's strength" (57). This was a distinctly contrarian opinion by 1984, however. As early as 1936, Winifred Holtby, in the first book-length study of Woolf, took it for granted that Woolf should be compared with Proust and Joyce, as did David Daiches in 1942 (his study of Woolf was part of New Directions Books' Makers of Modern Literature series), and Bradbury and McFarlane included discussion of Woolf in their influential 1976 study of Modernism. Woolf's *centrality* to the field, though, is a development since the 1970s, largely the result of the efforts of feminist scholars, and Kenner's comments could be seen as a backlash against the early success of those scholars in making Woolf more important to conceptions of Modernism.
7 Anna Snaith writes that as Woolf "embarked on *The Pargiters*, she was reading D.H. Lawrence's *Letters* ... considering and discounting his views on incorporating social critique into fiction" (Woolf [1937] 2012: liv).

but by different Modernists—in his public writings, at least, he has shown no sustained interest in Kafka or Beckett, preferring poets (especially Hart Crane), Djuna Barnes (with *Nightwood* being the book he claims to have read more than any other in his life), and others.[8] Delany's interest is, then, not so much in Modernism generally as in a notably queer Modernism, although "Atlantis: Model 1924" also shows that his Modernism is inextricable from the Harlem Renaissance, and particularly Jean Toomer. ("Atlantis: Model 1924" is, further, an explicit work of metamodernism: Delany has said he wrote it "to see what it felt like to have the experience of writing such a work" as *Ulysses*, *The Waste Land*, or the *Cantos* [Delany 2013: 225].) Delany's own commitments as a writer of fiction are at least as much to the European novel of social realism embodied by the works of Flaubert and Balzac, which he has consistently referenced throughout his life, as to the experiments of the Modernists. This makes his metamodernism particularly interesting, as his aesthetic melds a queer black Modernist poetics to the representational and materialist commitments that many Modernists set themselves in opposition to. It is no surprise that in his work as a teacher particulary, Delany has had a sustained engagement with Woolf's *The Years*, which seeks to meld the poetic advances of *The Waves* with the social details of earlier modes.

Crisis and propaganda

Crisis is a word commonly used in discussions of Modernism and modernity: crises of meaning, of representation, of form, of tradition, of reason, of consciousness, of imagination, of legitimation, of sovereignty, of epistemology, of metaphysics, of ontology, and so on.

Crisis has been central to most definitions because of the idea of Modernism as a break or rupture, and numerous political, social, and economic events of the late nineteenth and early twentieth centuries contributed to the sense of crisis. I am drawing from this general sense of Modernism as inextricably associated with crisis, but my primary concern is with a specific type of crisis within the conception of Modernism for metamodernist writers particularly: an assemblage of crises, really, in which a (fundamentally personal) aesthetic

---

[8] Including Woolf—he has used *The Years* in his classes a number of times, and references to Woolf begin to appear in his published essays by 1979.

crisis arises in response to a socio-political crisis in the writer's world. It is this crisis that Woolf names in her diary and illustrates in her *Daily Worker* essay, a crisis of purpose that puts aesthetic ideals in conflict with lived realities. Such crisis is not inherently Modernist; it spans many eras, geographies, and styles. For artists of any sort, such moments can make art feel trivial and irrelevant. When life itself is jeopardized, artistic representations of life may seem too distant to be useful.

A desire to separate the work of art from political determination does not constitute Modernism, but it is strongly present within it because of the prioritizing of form that is one of the constitutive features of Modernism. The idea that propaganda, preaching, and didacticism are anathema to art is one Modernists and metamodernists take as a given, and critical analysis of the idea has been limited by what Mark Wollaeger identifies as "an intuitive sense that modernism and propaganda must be antithetical in ways that do not require much elaboration" (2008: xii). That sense is as old as Modernism itself—perhaps not surprisingly, since proaganda and Modernism "emerged concurrently as interrelated languages of the new information age. Propaganda has always existed, but modern propaganda, operating through techniques of saturation and multiple media channels, developed contemporaneously with literary modernism" (xiii).

In a 1933 article titled "Literature and Propaganda," Joseph Wood Krutch identified the propagandistic impulse of younger writers as one that returned to literary conventions the Modernists had pushed away: "young men are not, to be sure, on the side of the conventions, but they have taken up the position once maintained only by the conventional. They do, that is to say, insist that it is the business of literature to teach and they have nothing but scorn for any art which professes to be detached or neutral" (1933: 793). While Krutch says that propaganda is "not incompatible with literature; but it imposes on the work of art a heavy handicap" (797–798) and "a good three-quarters of all the attempts to define the function of literature have resulted in the conclusion that it does teach" (795), his idea of how to evaluate a work of literature is staunchly aesthetic, saying that "the thing which has made all books great" is "a delight in the thing itself, a contemplation of the struggle for its own sake, a determination to pass on to the reader an aesthetic experience" (802). A few years later, writing from a position more in sympathy with younger writers of Marxist and Communist inclinations, L. Robert Lind asserts that "there is no real need for avowed propaganda in literature. While it is rightly conceived of by those of the left as an instrument of great power in the class struggle, it is doubtful whether the openly propagandist writer achieves his purpose as fully as he might by allowing an *implicit* expression of the views he holds and the side he has taken to become clear in his work" because "heated argument has always been a notoriously poor way to convince; yet avowed propaganda is not far from heated argument" (1939: 202, 203). For all the apparent differences in their assumptions and tastes, Lind's position on the evaluation of literature ends up not far from that of Krutch: "literature as propaganda cannot be criticized merely as propaganda and thus dismissed; on the other hand, literature which has at the same time a propagandist purpose must first be discussed on the basis of its merits as literature," though he notes that the latter will be a task "difficult for critics to whom the slightest hint of propaganda is as a red rag to a bull" (199).

Both of these critics assume literature and propaganda to be separate modes of communication, and they then prioritize literature over propaganda, with their disagreement being only the extent to which propaganda weakens literature, not whether it does so at all. How much they assume these modes of communication are separate becomes clear if we reverse the infiltration and imagine how, to a politically committed critic like Lind who is not hostile to the idea of propaganda itself, *literature* might weaken *propaganda*. For all his political commitment, Lind shows no desire for literature to infiltrate propaganda; he does not, for instance, advocate for Soviet ideas of socialist realism, with literature's ambiguities, complexities, and artistry being seen as poisonous to the good and unambiguous exhortation that is propaganda. In all of these formulations of *literature/propaganda* and *propaganda/literature*, the two terms make each other possible. Hence, they must remain separate, and the artist, by definition, must always side with literature over propaganda while the political activist, by definition, must side with propaganda over literature. The opposition sets limitations, enforces roles, and creates impossibilities. If a third way is possible, it must exist outside this schema.

While it is difficult to imagine that Woolf, Delany, or Coetzee would ever want their fiction to be called *propaganda*, even in praise, the ways they experiment with social commitment and didacticism reveal some impulse toward undoing the opposition of literature and propaganda—less to redeem either than to unsettle the assumptions that construct those categories in the first place.

We have plenty of evidence for what Woolf, Delany, and Coetzee think about propaganda. For Woolf, propaganda limits the writer's freedom and simplifies the text, thus reducing its artfulness. In one of her last essays, "The Leaning Tower," she says that the novelist who can "shift from his shoulders the burden of didacticism, of propaganda" might, through such efforts, allow readers to "look forward hopefully to a stronger, a more varied literature in the classless and towerless society of the future" (*E* 6: 275). A propagandistic, didactic literature is for Woolf one that is weak and lacking variety, one that we know (from her *Daily Worker* essay) she considers a limitation on the writer, a violation of the imagination's freedom. Similarly, in a contribution to a 1984 "Forum" in *Fiction International*, Delany wrote that "the aesthetic bias I share with a lot of others is that the artist can't propagandize" (Ai et al. 1984: 12). For him, propaganda is "the ultimate aesthetic no-no" (Delany [1984] 2012: 141), though the "argument for the social value of art over propaganda" is one that easily becomes "tedious" and "familiar" (Delany 2011: 32).

Unlike Woolf and Delany, Coetzee (who contributed a brief statement to the same *Fiction International* "Forum") has hardly ever used the word "propaganda" in his writings, fiction or nonfiction, with one clear exception: his first book, *Dusklands*, where in the section titled "The Vietnam Project," Eugene Dawn is writing a report on propaganda methods for a boss named Coetzee. Dawn's report in *Dusklands* points to another reason *propaganda* is a negative term for these writers: its association with the violence of war, a violence Woolf and Coetzee address (and condemn) repeatedly. As Wollaeger (2008: 6–7) notes, before the First World War, "propaganda" and "information" were generally used interchangeably, but after 1917, neutral or positive references to propaganda became fewer and fewer. After the growing sophistication of both propaganda and advertising, after the rise of the Nazis (and especially Goebbels' Ministry of Propaganda), and after the propaganda saturation of the Second World War, the word became, for the English-speaking public at least, inevitably linked to ideas of lying and manipulation. While it's not difficult to find essays published in the 1930s arguing about the need for propaganda in literature, after the Second World War, most discussions of aesthetics and politics include the word "propaganda" only as an insult, which is one reason why the word is more rare in Delany and Coetzee's writings than Woolf's.

Woolf tended to link the words "propaganda" and "didactic" (also "preaching"), and while a good case can be made for differences between the words, I will usually keep them linked in this study (partly to preserve my particular use of the word "pedagogy," as discussed below). Didactic texts exhort the reader toward specific stances and actions beyond reading. The writer's great hope for readers of a didactic novel is that they will close the book and then go out and change the world for the better.[9] The didactic text is an instruction manual for activism, and the propagandistic text seeks an audience that acquiesces to it. That's not what Woolf, Delany, and Coetzee want to use their novels for, nor the relationship they desire with their readers. Instead, each uses the novel form for ethical and epistemological purposes that are revealed via rhetoric that is too ambiguous to be called propagandistic. The rhetoric guides and questions, but it does not insist on a single path forward, a single way of thinking. By framing rhetorical choices within the metaphor of pedagogy, we are able to see how these texts address themselves to social and historical crises (and, indeed, sometimes take clear sides on crucial issues of the day) without their falling into the monological, authoritarian, one-way communication of propaganda.

One of the important rhetorical moves common to these texts is that of destabilization. "Rhetoric," Wayne Booth claims, "is employed at every moment when one human being intends to produce, through the use of signs or symbols, some effect on another—by words, or facial expressions, or gestures, or any symbolic skill of any kind" (2008: xi). We must ask, though, what becomes of rhetoric when the effect that it seeks to produce is not only obscure but also dependent on significant choices made by the reader when reading. We will see this destabilizing effect in works by Woolf, Delany, and especially Coetzee, an effect that is significantly different from that of didactic/propagandistic rhetoric, which as a necessarily stable text seeks to limit a reader's choices as fully as possible and to avoid whatever ambiguities are avoidable, because the didactic text fears nothing so much as the reader missing the point or thinking wrong thoughts. The risk that Woolf, Delany, and Coetzee all allow their readers is the risk of being in conflict with the text itself.

It is my contention that Woolf, Delany, and Coetzee each created destabilizing texts, and they did so with similar strategies. By strengthening the idea of Modernist pedagogy—the text teaching the reader how to read it—and then by pushing fictionality to (and sometimes beyond) its limits, these writers created texts that are pedagogical and often essayistic but not didactic in the sense of

---

[9] The most famous example from the twentieth century is Sinclair's *The Jungle*, which led to changes in food safety regulation in the United States. This example shows the difficulty of controlling the response to didacticism, though: Sinclair's goal was not primarily to change meat regulations but to expose injustice and inspire readers toward socialism.

propagandistic. As I will show, the difference between *the pedagogical* and *the didactic* is brought to life through highly different assumptions about power and authority.[10]

Virginia Woolf, Samuel R. Delany, and J.M. Coetzee

Woolf, Delany, and Coetzee are not writers typically linked together, but it is my contention that doing so allows significant insights about the writings of each while also providing insights about fiction, aesthetics, and artists' responses to crises in their worlds. Though drawing from different sources within Modernism, these three writers express, to varying degrees, a belief in art's autonomy from political determinism, but the work of each demonstrates a commitment to aesthetic experiment in the face of crisis, a commitment that links these writers to Modernism's particular valuing of innovation and to critical pedagogy's valuing of new perspectives. Furthermore, in anticipating crisis, experiencing crisis, or recovering from crisis, each writer chose to interrogate fictionality and sought experimental structures with which to meld fiction and nonfiction. We can trace Woolf's unfulfilled desire for an essay-novel to Delany's fusing of fiction and nonfiction in "Tale of Plagues and Carnivals" and to Coetzee's inclusion of actual essays throughout *Diary of a Bad Year*. Even when keeping within the mode of fiction, each of these writers demonstrates a similar restlessness with conventional boundaries, a similar desire to take the settled expectations common to genres and remake those expectations into tools for readers' education and, perhaps, liberation.

Woolf wrote relatively traditional novels at the beginning of her career, then began overtly experimenting with the form in *Jacob's Room* (1922), and continued to experiment through *Mrs. Dalloway* (1925), *To the Lighthouse* (1927), *Orlando* (1928), and *The Waves* (1931), before then turning to what she called the "essay-novel" with a manuscript titled *The Pargiters*, parts of which would serve as

---

[10] Etymologically, *didactic* comes from either Greek (διδακτικός) or Latin (*didactica, didacticus*) words relating to teaching, learning, or instruction, and thus *didactic* is nearly synonymous with *pedagogical*. I have chosen to ignore this etymological similarity and use the words for different tendencies, with *didactic* more or less synonymous with *propagandistic*, a use that is mostly supported by Woolf, Delany, and Coetzee's own uses of the words. For my purposes, it is important to be able to distinguish between the propagandistic/didactic and the pedagogic. Nonetheless, there are inevitable, unavoidable slippages with these terms, and my hope is that specific examples keep my meaning clear in each case.

raw material for the novel *The Years* (1937) and the book-length essay *Three Guineas* (1938). What began as an experiment in unsettling fictionality ended up not doing so, but what remained was the pedagogy, as both *The Years* and *Three Guineas* require much activity from the reader, and activity of a particular sort. Woolf's final novel, *Between the Acts* (left mostly finished at her death and published posthumously in July 1941), experiments again with narrative, mixing the form of drama into novelistic narrative. Once again Woolf wrote a novel that does not problematize fictionality itself, but she also, and again, created a novel that so deviates from readers' expectations of what a novel is that it contains a pedagogy of reading—though not, it seems to me, a liberatory pedagogy on the scale of *The Years* and *Three Guineas*.

Delany began writing various sorts of novels as a teenager, and originally planned to have a career as a literary novelist, but he found he was able to sell science fiction when he was not able to sell his literary work, and his first novel, *The Jewels of Aptor*, was published when he was twenty years old in 1962. He quickly achieved success in the science fiction field in the 1960s, winning numerous awards for work that was often experimental, but not in a particularly overt way until 1975's *Dhalgren*, a behemoth that befuddled as many readers as it excited, yet also sold over a million copies within its first ten years. A year later came *Trouble on Triton* (originally *Triton*), which demonstrated that Delany was not going to go back to his pre-*Dhalgren* mode.[11] The publication in 1980 of *Tales of Nevèrÿon* initiated the Return to Nevèrÿon series of sword & sorcery stories and novels, which would continue with *Neveryóna* (1983), *Flight from Nevèrÿon* (1985), and *Return to Nevèrÿon* (1987, as *The Bridge of Lost Desire*). While generally more straightforward in

---

[11] In a vitriolic review in *The Magazine of Fantasy and Science Fiction*, Barry N. Malzberg said, "If professors of English get hold of *Triton* and discover it and *Dhalgren* to be the tenth-rate James Joyce pastiche they are then they will think less of science fiction for having produced and in the mass having admired such work; if they take it to be work of literary quality they will assign it to classes, write it up for *PMLA*, and render the painstaking attempts of certain of us to discipline our work laughable" (1976: 34). Spider Robinson pointed to the appendices in his review of *Triton* for *Galaxy*'s October 1976 issue. (His general evaluation was: "I'm happy to say that it isn't as opaque as *Dhalgren*, but I'm sorry to say that it too bored the pants off me" [130].) Robinson wrote that "if you go for appendices containing out-takes from the book in the context of what *seems* to have been meant as a discussion of the science-fiction novel as an art form, go to it—if nothing else, you'll learn the answers to exciting literary questions like 'is it orthodox to speak of a "metonym" rather than "metonymy"?' which had been keeping me awake at night" (131). Later, reviewing *Tales of Nevèrÿon* for *Analog* in May 1980, Robinson seems to believe the reports of the "Culhar' Fragment and Missolonghi Codex" in the book's appendix may be true. "By the way," he writes in a parenthetical comment, "I am no scholar of antique literature—for all of me, the whole Culhar' Fragment could be as much of a hoax as the 'date' and 'author' of the appendix" (171).

their storytelling than *Dhalgren* or *Triton*, the Nevèrÿon books highlighted Delany's interest in semiotics and poststructuralist philosophy through subtitles (such as that of *Neveryóna*: "The Tale of Signs and Cities"), as well as epigraphs from such writers as Ernst Bloch, Edward Said, Susan Sontag, Michel Foucault, Julia Kristeva, and other writers that the average reader of a paperback book of sword & sorcery stories in the 1980s was unlikely to have heard of. The philosophical qualities of science fiction had always appealed to Delany, but from *Dhalgren* onward, those qualities are often foregrounded.

After *Dhalgren*, Delany began to experiment more and more with melding fiction and nonfiction, first with faux-nonfictional appendices, then, finally, bringing an overtly nonfictional form into dialogue with overtly fictional narrative in "The Tale of Plagues and Carnivals" (which, though a section of the book *Flight from Nevèrÿon*, is the length of a novel). From the first, the Nevèrÿon books teased readers' interpretive strategies with prefaces and appendices by fictional scholars who explained the derivation of the tales from "an archaic narrative text of some nine hundred or so words (depending on the ancient language in which you found it), sometimes called the Culhar' Fragment and, more recently, the Missolonghi Codex" ([1979] 1993: 12). While the prefaces and appendices to the books are complex and sometimes bewildering, they're also easy enough to skip over, and the framing of texts as some sort of long-lost manuscript is a common technique to fiction generally, adventure and fantasy fiction particularly (e.g., the appendices to popular books such as *Dune* and the *Lord of the Rings* trilogy). "The Tale of Plagues and Carnivals" is a significant departure because it is the first and only Nevèrÿon tale to undermine its own fictionality within the text itself by interspersing apparently nonfictional diaristic writing about New York City in 1983/84 alongside a more typical Nevèrÿon story—one the diaries, amidst other subjects, chronicle being written.

"The Tale of Plagues and Carnivals" is an anomaly; subsequent Nevèrÿon stories return to the series' earlier forms and modes. After the final Nevèrÿon book (*Return to Nevèrÿon* [1987]), Delany struggled to write fiction for a few years, publishing only nonfiction until his major novel of the 1990s, *The Mad Man*, a pornographic academic novel that is also an exploration of the transmission patterns of HIV. While *The Mad Man* ends with an appendix reprinting an actual article from the British medical journal *The Lancet*, for the most part its overall fictionality and novel form are never in question. Much like

The Years, though, *The Mad Man* does offer a pedagogy of subversion/liberation to its reader, a pedagogy deeply connected to the development of the AIDS crisis after "The Tale of Plagues and Carnivals." In many ways *The Mad Man* can be read as a sequel to Delany's 1980s fiction (not just the Return to Nevèrÿon series, but also *Stars in My Pocket Like Grains of Sand*).[12]

Much of Delany's fiction before and after *The Mad Man* could be discussed as unsettling fictionality and/or offering a pedagogy of subversion and liberation, and works such as "Atlantis: Model 1924" are highly metamodernist, but I am concerned in this study only with the fiction that most directly responds to the AIDS crisis. The 2007 novel *Dark Reflections* may be seen as a coda to "The Tale of Plagues and Carnivals" and *The Mad Man* in that it tells the story of a black, gay male poet's life in the second half of the twentieth century, a man whose experience of the AIDS crisis is very much that of an outsider and observer because, unlike Delany's other characters, he is mostly celibate and not at all involved with any sort of gay community. This allows the book a view of the crisis as *not* a crisis for the lead character, and goes some way toward making that novel one of Delany's least subversively pedagogical and most accessible texts. (This is not a negative criticism, simply an observation. Indeed, for me *Dark Reflections* is among Delany's most satisfying works of fiction.[13]) In a certain sense, *Dark Reflections* is an inverse of *The Mad Man*, and the two could be read productively together. That, though, is a task for another time.

J.M. Coetzee's first book, *Dusklands* (1974), is a fragmentary mix of genres, but best described as two linked novellas that sometimes employ nonfictional techniques. After that book, his fiction and nonfiction stay separate until *Boyhood* (1997), the first in his ever-more-fictionalized trilogy of memoirs (followed by *Youth* [2002], which is similar in technique, and *Summertime* [2009], which is more overtly fictional, and will be discussed in this study).

---

[12] The idea of *The Mad Man* as the true sequel to *Stars in My Pocket* (the official sequel to which Delany never finished writing) is Damien Broderick's and is an idea Delany has shown some approval of in a letter he wrote to Broderick dated April 20, 1997, available in Delany's archives at Yale University's Beinecke Library.

[13] Though I don't think *Dark Reflections* is particularly subversive in its pedagogy, it would be a mistake to say it is not pedagogical—it is heavily so, but its dominant pedagogy is not aimed at a general audience, and is not designed for a Freirean liberation; instead, it is a novel that Delany has explicitly said he hoped would be informative to aspiring writers. In that sense, it is highly pedagogical, using the protagonist's life to illustrate and dramatize various principles Delany articulated in his 2005 essay collection *About Writing*. For more on this, and *Dark Reflections* generally, see my 2016 *Los Angeles Review of Books* essay on it.

With *Elizabeth Costello* (2003; partially published 1999 as *The Lives of Animals*) he brings the fictional status overtly into question by posing much of the novel as narratives of lectures given by the title character. He soon followed that with the metafictional *Slow Man* (2005), in which Elizabeth Costello appears as a character who might be writing the novel she is a part of, and *Diary of a Bad Year* (2007), which puts fictional frames around—or, literally, beneath—essayistic chapters. Since *Summertime*, Coetzee's novels have returned to a mode that doesn't unsettle their fictionality, but in their titles and content *The Childhood of Jesus* (2013), *The Schooldays of Jesus* (2016), and *The Death of Jesus* (2019) court allegorical readings, a type of fiction that has often been associated with Coetzee, and which Guido Mazzoni identifies as a pre-nineteenth-century form of culturally acceptable didacticism. This has led some critics to see Coetzee as becoming more didactic and less fictional, but it seems to me that if we can say that the recent novels evoke a feeling of allegory, it is nonetheless impossible to say with any certainty what they are allegories of or for. Such impossibility renders whatever didacticism we perceive in them into an aesthetic feature, more a tone than an argument, thus inescapably part of their fiction and form.

The limits of fiction

As with *modernism*, even the most complicated and hedging definitions of *fiction* tend to fall apart in contradictions, while precise definitions prove vague when analyzed. The basic definition of fiction as *that which is not true* or *that which is imagined* doesn't work as a description for a complete text of narrative prose (e.g., a novel) for reasons elaborated by Bakhtin at the latest and well explained by Richard Walsh in *The Rhetoric of Fictionality*: "Fictions are often not entirely fictional, and in principle may not be fictional at all. There are various circumstances in which nonfictional material, whether avowed (the historical novel), surreptitious (the roman à clef), or entirely adventitious, may inhabit a fictional narrative" (2007: 45). Alok Yadav points out that when reading a work of fiction "one often wonders whether a given feature of the narrative discourse is fictional or in some direct or oblique manner taken from the world of actuality. In fact, I might suggest that one constantly makes such judgments in the process of reading fiction" (2010: 192). Therefore, he says, "Any adequate account of fiction will need to recognize not only that fictional discourse is always a mixed discourse, a combination of fictional and nonfictional elements, but also that our reading of fiction engages many of the same protocols and considerations as our reading of nonfiction" (194).

Walsh and Yadav take a similar approach to fictionality, an approach that analyzes fictionality as a rhetorical act.[14] This is useful because it relieves us of the need to determine which textual features produce and/or constitute fiction, and instead allows us to see fictionality as a consequence of expectations created in the relationship between text, reader, and context. Walsh makes what may seem to be a radical claim: "fictionality has no determinate relation to features of the text itself" (45), but it is a claim that helps us consider what may, in fact, determine our sense that a given text is fictional. While certain narrative moves are more common to contemporary fiction than nonfiction—Walsh cites the representation of characters' thoughts—there are no moves that are exclusively fictional or nonfictional.

Similarly, false or counterfactual information is not itself a sign of fiction:

> If a narrative offered as historical is shown to be inconsistent with documented evidence, even to the point of reference failure (if it had interpolated a nonexistent character into the narrative, for instance), then precisely because this error or subterfuge is held accountable to criteria of historical falsifiability, it confirms that the text in question is not fiction, but compromised historiography (Walsh 2007: 45).

Walsh also points out that fictionality does not depend upon any particular features of the text:

> For example, fiction may very well do without the representation of thoughts; and nonfiction (a biography, say) may resort to it. The representation of mental discourse in a nonfictional narrative will probably strike contemporary readers as a liberty, but this does not make the text a fiction (in fact, it confirms their interpretative orientation towards it as nonfiction). For the same reason, the dissociation of fictionality, in principle, from any textual indicators may be extended to matters of reference. (Walsh 2007: 45)

---

[14] Walsh describes the differences between *fiction* and *fictionality* thus: "Fictionality (as a rhetorical rather than ontological quality) is almost inherently narrative, but it is not coextensive with narrativity, and still less with textuality in general. Not that fictionality should be equated simply with 'fiction,' as a category or genre of narrative: it is a communicative strategy, and as such it is apparent on some scale within many nonfictional narratives, in forms ranging from something like an ironic aside, through various forms of conjecture or imaginative supplementation, to full-blown counterfactual narrative examples. Conversely, much fiction serves communicative functions, of both non-narrative (essayistic) and narrative (documentary) kinds, which do not exclusively belong to the rhetoric of fictionality: think of the generalizing moral commentary of George Eliot, or the historical contextualizations of Scott. But the generic marker of all fictional narrative, literary or cinematic, is that the rhetoric of fictionality is the dominant framework for the communicative gesture being made, and therefore defines the terms in which it solicits interpretation" (7).

The contexts and paratexts that produce an idea of fictionality are ones that are often so obvious that most texts' status is unquestioned by readers: We assume a book is fictional because, for instance, we found it in the Fiction section of a bookstore and it says "A Novel" on the cover. Fictionality is not, Walsh maintains, an ontological category or a Platonic ideal existing outside the relationship between writer, text, and reader; rather, fictionality is a communicative relationship that produces a different kind of knowledge via fiction than nonfiction does: "The knowledge offered by fiction [...] is not primarily specific knowledge of what is (or was), but of how human affairs work, or, more strictly, of how to make sense of them—logically, evaluatively, emotionally. It is knowledge of the ways in which such matters may be brought within the compass of the imagination, and in that sense understood" (Walsh 2007: 36). Thus, "The distinction between fiction and nonfiction rests upon the rhetorical use to which a narrative is put, which is to say, the kind of interpretative response it invites in being presented as one or the other" (45).[15]

Rhetorical use here leads us toward seeing fictionality not as a quality but, as Wolfgang Iser has proposed, as an action or event. In *The Fictive and the Imaginary*, Iser says that the "accepted definition of fiction as something invented tells us nothing about its effects, let alone its achievements" (1993: 171). The effects and achievements are central to any consideration of why writers turn the act of fiction into a problem for readers. Seeing fictionality as rhetoric allows us to speculative productively on how the problematization of fictionality is valuable for nondidactic writers at moments of socio-political crisis. Such problematizing of fictionality changes the rhetorical use of the narrative and unsettles the easy interpretation of a text as fiction or a novel. When the immediacy of reality overwhelms the writer's desire to bring matters "within the compass of the imagination," the impulse toward didacticism becomes tempting: one wants to speak truth to power, not tell an imaginary story about an imaginary character speaking truth to power. For a text to have hope of being anything other than a bit of fiddling in a burning world, it must in some way activate the reader within the text/reader relationship. As decades of reader-response theory have shown

---

[15] For an example of the impossibility of locating fictionality within a text itself, see Jo Ann Beard's "Werner," which was reprinted in *Best American Essays 2007*, edited by David Foster Wallace. Having read "Werner" numerous times, I have found nothing in its text that would indicate it is not a work of short fiction. We read it as an essay because it is published as an essay. Though "Werner" is an extreme case, any theory of fiction and fictionality must be able to account for such a text if it is to be valid. Walsh's theory can; many others cannot.

us, all texts do this to some extent, but committed texts and texts responding to crisis do so with goals beyond entertainment or the contemplation of beauty.[16]

Iser formulates fictionality as a boundary crossing and fiction as a method by which reality and imagination are transgressed, with fiction giving form to the transgression. The act of fictionalizing "leads the real to the imaginary and the imaginary to the real, and it thus conditions the extent to which a given world is to be transcoded, a nongiven world is to be conceived, and the reshuffled worlds are to be made accessible to the reader's experience" (4). The writer in a given world affected by crisis must consider not only how that crisis affects the conception of the nongiven world (i.e., the imaginary elements of the story), but the extent to which crisis will affect the balance of the fictive and the imaginary, and how that balance will then affect the reader's experience. In crisis, reality gains mass to such an extent that imagination may not be able to balance it out, and the act of imagining therefore feels trivial, like placing pretty feathers on a scale to balance a hefty chunk of lead.

While for the purposes of this study *the novel* as a form is secondary in my interests to *fictionality* as a concept, it is no coincidence that Woolf, Delany, and Coetzee are all primarily novelists. Claire de Obaldia has summarized well the many scholars who have shown that the novel is a form especially hospitable to essayistic discourse: "If essayism connotes self-reflection and open-endedness, then the novel is without a doubt the most essayistic of genres: the most heterogeneous—with a capacity to combine the narrative, the lyric, and the dramatic, and to include entire essays—the most open-ended, the most reflective or self-critical" (1995: 239). This capaciousness is attractive to writers seeking to encompass something of the world in their work, but it also opens opportunities for writers to work within the form to challenge readers' ideas of what that form can and should be. By presenting such challenges, the writers teach the readers new ways of perceiving the novel genre, making it possible

---

[16] Though I will admit to finding many elements of reader-response theory useful, this study is not a work of such theory except obliquely, because my concerns throughout are primarily with the text *before* it reaches the reader, even though, of course, readers are fundamental to any reading or interpretive process, and writers themselves may be said to be the first reader-interpreter of the text. "The reader" herein is a speculative figure of potential. As we would begin to look at any pedagogy from the teacher's aspirations, intentions, and authority before looking at the effect of the pedagogy on students, so, too, do I focus throughout this study on the text before it reaches readers, but in a way that nonetheless imagines readers. That such an approach includes paradoxes is inevitable. For instance, when not quoting the writers themselves, I am either offering my own reading/interpretation or that of other people, which is all subsequent to the publication of the text and, thus, a reader's response. My interpretive position, though, is one that prioritizes an idea of the text before it reaches the reader.

for the reader to develop new expectations and assumptions not only about this novel that they have read, but also about the next novel they pick up to read.

Many readers, however, have no desire to perceive the novel differently. Coetzee's career demonstrates this vividly. Though my concern in this study is with the books he published between *Disgrace* and *The Childhood of Jesus*, it is worth noting that his most recent novels have been perceived by some reviewers in ways that suggest these reviewers' expectations of Coetzee have been permanently affected by the shift in his writing after *Disgrace*, a shift away from careful scenic structures, rich descriptions of landscape and objects, and other elements of conventional realistic fiction since the nineteenth century. The three *Jesus* novels are strange and elliptical, with more dialogue than description of landscapes or actions, and Coetzee does not create psychologically rich portraits of his characters, instead preferring to let them remain mostly inscrutable. These books court allegory even more stubbornly than Coetzee's early works, which were often read as allegories even as he objected to the term. The *Jesus* novels are not allegories in any traditional sense because it is impossible to say what their figures symbolize. They are, in that way, deliberate failures of allegory; or if not failures, then incomplete allegories: They allow readers to come to their own conclusions about the symbolic implications, and it is unlikely that any two readers would agree about those implications. But the same could be said of many novels, and there is nothing in these books that makes fictionality itself a problem. Similarly, it's difficult to call these books *didactic* because it's hard to say exactly what they're trying to teach, even though their characters engage in philosophical conversations.

Nonetheless, Elizabeth Lowry, reviewing *The Schooldays of Jesus* in *The Guardian* (2016), declared, "In his fidelity to ideas, to telling rather than showing, to instructing rather than seducing us, [Coetzee] does not actually write fiction any more." This is an extraordinary statement, one that suggests that philosophical material within a novel invalidates it as fiction, that the only real fiction is fiction that tells a good ol' story. (Woolf, I expect, would have some harsh words for Elizabeth Lowry.) Lowry's narrow conception of novelistic discourse is absurd and historically ignorant, but it is also a common one, and shows the sedimented conventions that Coetzee's work must overcome if it is to have acceptance from readers. At *Vox*, Constance Grady (2017) offered a similar view to Lowry's: "*Schooldays* is not a realistic novel. I would hesitate to call it a novel at all: It's closer to a Socratic dialogue on the relationship between reason and passion that is structured around a small child for reasons that are frankly beyond me. It aggressively disdains the idea of *story* in favor of the idea of *thought*." Here, too, an ahistorical and provincial idea of the novel form limits the reader's ability to enter the text, and likely forestalls the possibility of the pedagogy's success.

If fictionality is a type of rhetoric (a communicative act that sets up a relationship between a communicator and an audience), then we must admit that the limits of fiction cannot be determined by the text alone, and may not even be determined by writers of fiction who try to explore the borders, margins, and limit-points of fiction. The reception of Coetzee's later books vividly shows that some readers of fiction may disagree with the writer about where the border lies, and the distance between them may be unbridgeable. The limits of my fiction are the limits of my readers.

Pedagogy

Didacticism is not the only strategy for activating the text–reader relationship in a way that addresses crisis. Gayatri Spivak has proposed the idea that readers can learn to be "activists of the imagination" and that teachers can help their students liberate imagination "so that it can become something other than Narcissus waiting to see his own powerful image in the eyes of the other" (2014: 54). Such a liberatory approach is at the core of critical pedagogy (as developed by Paulo Freire, Henry Giroux, bell hooks, and others), and inspires my own analysis of nondidactic Modernist and metamodernist writers' strategies as types of pedagogy.

This is not a book about Woolf, Delany, and Coetzee as classroom teachers, though each had such experience; nor is it a study of their ideas about education. To a limited extent, that work has already been done or is in progress, particularly with Woolf.[17] My concern in this book is not with Woolf, Delany, and Coetzee's

---

[17] "'Tilting at Universities': Woolf at King's College London" by Christine Kenyon Jones and Anna Snaith (2010) adds important detail to our understanding of Woolf's own formal education, various essays by Beth Rigel Daugherty show how educational ideas fill Woolf's essays, and Natasha Periyan's *The Politics of 1930s British Literature: Education, Class, Gender* (2018) not only highlights how important pedagogical concepts were to writers in the 1930s, but also includes a valuable chapter on Woolf's critique of educational institutions in her 1930s writings. Delany worked for a few decades as a teacher of comparative literature and creative writing, and his approach to teaching can in some ways be gleaned from the essays in *About Writing*, as well as the material in *Letters from Amherst* (itself an interesting companion to the novel I discuss in Chapter 4, *The Mad Man*), but barely anything has been written about Delany himself as a teacher. Given the prevalence of teachers and students as characters in Coetzee's later fiction, numerous studies of what Gayatri Spivak calls his "scenes of teaching" exist. Little has been written about Coetzee's own work as a teacher; the most comprehensive coverage is in J.C. Kannemeyer's biography (see in particular pp. 475–481), though Jonathan Crewe's *In the Middle of Nowhere: J.M. Coetzee in South Africa* (2015) offers some interesting glimpses from a colleague.

own theories of education, nor with depictions of teaching and learning within their novels, but rather with how the forms these writers create open possibilities for how readers learn to interpret the texts. My interest is not with pedagogical subject matter, but rather with how the organization and structure of a novel itself may suggest, and perhaps even require, a pedagogy—a pedagogy of form. I have chosen the term *pedagogy* because it allows new possibilities for understanding the relationship between form and didacticism, while building on established concepts of the writer–reader relationship. Beth Rigel Daugherty has illuminated Woolf's own understanding of this relationship multiple times, and has linked that understanding to teaching and learning. Discussing Woolf's essay "How Should One Read a Book," Daugherty writes:

> Woolf removes reading from the giving of prizes, from competition, from hierarchy (grades?), and trusts students, if they simply keep reading, to recognize worth when they see it. She is also delighted that they will all define such worth differently. Woolf both respects and likes her readers for their abilities, questions, and common sense. Using self-fulfilling prophecy as a teacher might, Woolf assumes her readers can meet the expectations she has for them. We, in turn, can imagine being her readers, can *be* her readers. She thus creates the readers she wants. (1997: 166)

It is one thing to explore the creation of an idea of the reader for a work of nonfiction, a genre hospitable to philosophizing, instruction, didacticism, and even outright preaching. It is something else, though, to propose that fiction which eschews didacticism nonetheless promotes a pedagogy. The (imagined or real) construction and then shaping of an audience by an orator or writer is a central idea in rhetoric back to Aristotle, and Woolf herself asserted in the early 1930s that "Every writer has an audience in view" (*E* 5: 356). Having an audience in view suggests a desire to have an effect on that audience, a desire to lead readers through an experience made possible by the text. We need to look only to the many studies over the years of John Milton's seemingly lifelong quest for a "fit audience," an audience that "is not, in the prose tracts, simply something Milton finds already constituted; rather, his descriptions are an attempt to create the proper readers and interpreters of his tracts" (Shore 2012: 23). Milton is an especially useful example for our purposes here of an author thinking about audience, because in Milton we can see quite vividly how assumptions about agency and authority affect a writer's construction of a text. Milton before revolution has a somewhat different idea of human agency than after the restoration of the monarchy: "the scope of human freedom, either in setting out to find a responsive audience or in seeking a remedy for perceived ills, is much greater in works by Milton written amid the hopes of revolutionary transformation than in 'evil dayes' after the failure of the English Revolution" (Chernaik 2018: 129). For change to be possible, and for a writer's words to participate even in a tiny way, then the writer must assume a fit audience can not only be found, but can also be created, developed, and expanded. That assumption may affect any type of writing, poetry or prose, fiction or nonfiction. Woolf possessed this hope when she was writing *The Years* and *Three Guineas*, but it's possible the hope became extinguished by the time of her death. Delany's work, by contrast, shows a continuing hopefulness, a continuing sense that a fit audience may be cultivated, a better world may be created by human action. *The Mad Man* was published at a time when even many determined AIDS activists had been, like Milton after the return of the king, embittered by despair. *The Mad Man* is a violent, sometimes disturbing novel, but it is also still radiant with hope for humanity.

Daugherty's analysis of "How Should One Read a Book" is useful for thinking about how Woolf and other writers create any sort of text: by establishing expectations and assuming readers can meet them. Like a teacher creating a lesson plan, the writer while writing maps out, to some extent or another, an idea of what the experience of reading might be able to provide to a receptive reader.

The difference between *the pedagogical* and *the didactic* is crucial to critical/liberatory pedagogy, wherein the teacher is not an omniscient bestower of knowledge, but rather a coordinator for the production of knowledge and a facilitator of dialogue. The role of the writer and the role of the teacher are not exact analogues, nor are the roles of reader and student, but both teaching/learning and writing/reading are communicative events in which acts of language and imagination produce knowledge. A novel premised on a liberatory pedagogy is one that seeks to achieve within the writer–text–reader relationship what a liberatory pedagogy of education seeks to achieve within the teacher–classroom–student relationship. As such, the role of the reader must be heightened and cannot be passive. Freire writes: "In the learning process the only person who really *learns* is s/he who appropriates what is learned, who apprehends and thereby re-invents that learning; s/he who is able to apply the appropriated learning to concrete existential situations" (2005: 93). Didacticism, as I use the term, is anathema to critical pedagogy, because didacticism is both authoritarian and monologic, while critical pedagogy is premised on anti-authoritarianism and dialogue. This makes the novel an especially useful form for this textual pedagogy, given the dialogism that Bakhtin famously located as the core of the genre.

Of course, there is nothing that makes any individual novel inherently liberatory in its pedagogy.[18] Nor are didacticism and the novel necessarily opposed. For many types of novels throughout many eras of literary history, didacticism has been something of a requirement. In his *Theory of the Novel*, Guido Mazzoni locates the move away from didactic expectations with Goethe's *Sorrows of Young Werther*: "At the end of the eighteenth century [...] we witness a radical transformation: allegorism and moralism began to disappear from texts. This was not a sudden transition but a slow process that took many decades to complete" (2017: 188).[19] Mazzoni writes that while no one text demonstrates a decisive break from the didactic/moralistic expectation, Goethe's preface to *Werther* is a useful marker "because it shows that new moral attitudes toward stories and people were emerging. Vice and virtue, or what the work 'means' in a conceptual form, stopped being crucial issues; novels no longer presented themselves as secondary texts that gave form to an *exemplum* of something already known, but rather as primary texts recounting experiences irreducible to a preexisting truth" (191).

If the post-*Werther* novel is one that is itself a primary text of representations that are "irreducible to a preexisting truth," then the novel as a form can be particularly powerful for engaged pedagogy, because such pedagogy "produces self-directed learners, teachers, and students who are able to participate fully in the production of ideas" (hooks 2010: 43). A successful teacher, therefore, doesn't seek to simply transfer knowledge or information, but to create an environment in which everyone may be a creator or producer of knowledge. This type of pedagogy stands in sharp contrast both to a pedagogy that sees students as nothing but vessels to receive information and also to novels that assume readers are similarly empty vessels.

---

[18] Here, I am speaking of a pedagogy that is at least quasi-intentional and that can be reasonably discerned from the text. Much is unpredictable in the relationship between writer, text, and reader, and that unpredictability renders any novel potentially pedagogical for any one reader.

[19] For Mazzoni, the completion of the process of removing overt moralizing and didacticism from novels was inflected by class expectations: "Moreover, the bipartite structure of the modern narrative pace—divided between works created for specialists and those for a wider public—led to different escape velocities, because the novelists who wrote for middle- or lower-class readers never relinquished moral control" (188). The move toward a stance of art-for-art's-sake in the second half of the nineteenth century could be seen as part of this process for texts aimed at the cultural elite, while certain tendencies in popular culture (the rise of noir fiction, for instance, in the 1920s and 1930s) could be seen as part of a similar process for mass audiences. Didacticism is usually aimed at the masses; it is rare to encounter didactic art that seeks to change the ruling classes that support and consume it. Less educated and less wealthy audiences are usually the ones who get lectured and preached to.

Both the didactic novel and the novel that seeks a primarily passive reader are texts that *convey* ideas rather than *produce* them. The experiments of Modernist aesthetics with the novel form made the form itself less conventional, forcing readers into a more active relationship with texts, since generic expectations and assumptions were no longer necessarily useful. Not only did readers have to learn anew how to read novels, but learning to read one Modernist work did not guarantee that readers would now have the skills to understand and appreciate another, and so they either had to learn how to read each new novel they encountered separately or they had to develop reading strategies for common features of such texts. While such reading strategies are undeniably useful at first, any such strategy could lose its critical force through repetition. One of the insights of metamodernism is that Modernism developed its own conventions, so the reader who became experienced with, for instance, interior monologue and parataxis would be able to navigate further Modernist novels with nearly as much ease as they could navigate more traditional writing. These conventions entered the toolboxes of metamodernists, who then deconstructed, subverted, and detourned them, returning the novel form to newness.

Newness is a key idea within Modernism ("Make it new!"), but also to liberatory pedagogy, because liberation cannot be predicated on pre-processed truths and common sense if the assumed truths and common sense are part of an oppressive system. Outside of utopia, all assumptions, and all conventional knowledge, must be open to question. What Freire calls the "banking concept of education" wherein "the students are the depositories and the teacher is the depositor" ([1970] 2000: 72) is also in some ways the model for the traditional relationship between text and reader. Freire introduces chapter 2 of *Pedagogy of the Oppressed* by linking teaching and narration:

> A careful analysis of the teacher-student relationship at any level, inside or outside the school, reveals its fundamentally *narrative* character. This relationship involves a narrating Subject (the teacher) and patient, listening objects (the students). The contents, whether values or empirical dimensions of reality, tend in the process of being narrated to become lifeless and petrified. Education is suffering from narration sickness.
> The teacher talks about reality as if it were motionless, static, compartmentalized, and predictable. (71)

Freire's complaint about the teacher's narration of reality could easily fit within any number of Woolf's essays about conventional fiction, and the model of the narrating teacher and receiving (passive) students is one that resembles many Modernists' low opinions of the relationship between conventional art and its audiences.

Newness, then, is not about faddishness, nor is it a fetishization of idiosyncracy, but it is instead a key component for avoiding the kind of complacency that leads to oppression. If activists of the imagination are to produce new imaginings (a kind of new knowledge), then what is conventional, familiar, and commonsensical must be re-imagined, it must be made new. Within critical pedagogy, a crucial value of imagination is its ability to estrange the familiar. In one of the best manuals for English teachers seeking to practice critical pedagogy, Eleanor Kutz and Hephzibah Roskelly write that "'Making the familiar strange' can help any researcher or learner find new patterns of significance, new meanings in what had previously been taken for granted" (1991: 226). *Making it new* is a fundamental technique of teaching, learning, and imagining.

One pedagogy of liberation for the novel will seek to unsettle the passive traditional relationship between the depository (readers) and the depositor (writer or text) by unsettling the assumption of fictionality. Catherine Gallagher has argued that the novel as we know it, and the English novel in particular, arose alongside—and, indeed, dependent upon—a discourse of fictionality:

> In England, between the time when Defoe insisted that Robinson Crusoe was a real individual (1720) and the time when Henry Fielding urged just as strenuously that his characters were not representations of actual specific people (1742), a discourse of fictionality appeared in and around the novel, specifying new rules for its identification and new modes of nonreference. And it is on the basis of this overt and articulated understanding that the novel may be said to have discovered fiction. What Fielding had that Defoe lacked was not an excuse for fictionality but a use for it as a special way of shaping knowledge through the fabrication of particulars. (2006: 355)

Gallagher goes on to argue that the development of the novel through the nineteenth century and later was, simultaneously, a development of an ever-more-subtle discourse of fictionality. For Modernist writers to render the novel new, they would also have to render fictionality new. As we have seen from Walsh, any valid definition of fictionality must attend to contexts and paratexts, which means attending to readers and reception. If we accept Gallagher's account of novels, we must then recognize that in teaching readers new strategies for reading novels, Modernist texts also, unavoidably, teach new strategies for understanding fictionality.

Learning new reading strategies requires the reader to be active, and the kinds of strategies that I identify Woolf, Delany, and Coetzee building their pedagogies to teach are ones that require the reader's attention to move toward the relationship between the text and the world beyond the text (the reader's own world, the world presented by the text, etc.). By unsettling fictionality in the specific ways that they do (and by heightening the reader's awareness that the fictionality of the text cannot be taken for granted), these novels put readers into a position where they must always assess for themselves what they take to be the text's distance or closeness to reality. In doing so, readers must also assess what their own sense of reality is.

Aesthetics and ethics

While each of these three writers wrestles with fictionality in different ways and for different reasons, the effect on the status of each text's fictionality is similar. That effect shares a goal of making ethics, in particular, more obviously primary within the novel's remit and encouraging the reader not only to consider narrative, but to consider questions of how to live and what to believe. What links these texts are not their levels of fictionality, but the way they turn fictionality and the novel form itself into a tool for a certain pedagogy. These are works that avoid didacticism by foregrounding the reader's role in learning how to navigate the discourses each text puts into play, and they do so with a clear goal of inspiring readers to think about the relationship between writer and reader, text and world, politics and ethics. Each seeks to avoid what Jonathan Lear, in discussing Coetzee, has called "ersatz ethics": preconceived ideas and opinions that the text would simply reaffirm. Ersatz ethics are a particular danger for fiction writers, who may benefit from an aura of intellectual authority. In notes for a lecture on Olive Schreiner, Coetzee said, "Generally, it is not important that writers have good ideas. Rather, it is a matter of seeing a mimesis of intellectual engagement" (qtd. in Attwell 2010: 219). Such mimesis is anathema to authentic ethics, but at the same time, the rhetorical tools that produce such mimesis may be useful in provoking authentic ethical thought for the reader.

For many philosophers and writers, ethics and politics are separate realms. Jessica Berman notes that G.E. Moore's *Principia Ethica* was a significant book for many members of the Bloomsbury group, and that in it Moore "distinguishes the matter of ethics from that of politics (and from other metaphysical questions) by claiming that ethics is a science concerned with the question of defining the 'good' and distinguished from inquiry into the more complex notion of 'good conduct.'" Such an approach, she says, removes philosophy from "our practical understanding of conduct in society or for politics" (2011: 13). Berman writes that feminist philosophy makes a "rapprochement" between ethics and politics, and her discussion of Mulk Raj Anand's *Untouchable* suggests the same for anti-colonialism (and, by extension, postcolonialism). Queer philosophy obviously belongs with this mix, too, as another ethico-political philosophy of the personal-as-political (and the political-as-personal), and Delany's writings often have an ethical concern. He is fond of quoting Wittgenstein's statement that "Ethics and aesthetics are one" ("Ethik und Ästhetik sind Eins," *Tractatus* 6.421; see Collinson [1985] for discussion), as well as a statement he attributes to Lukács's *Theory of the Novel*, but which I have not been able to verify: "The novel is the only art form where ethics is the aesthetic problem" (qtd. in Delany 2013: 175). Much work in Coetzee studies focuses on questions of ethics, and his work has been of as much interest to scholars of philosophy as of literature. Though ethics as a discipline has not been as common a topic for analysts of Woolf and Delany, their work nonetheless frequently links ethics and politics, making some of the ethical discussions around Coetzee valuable for Woolf and Delany as well.

Ethics is never separate from form and genre in the texts I discuss, but this is not to suggest that these writers' ethics or forms remain static. The differences between each of the writers are important, but those differences are often clear; the differences *within* their own oeuvres are less obvious and more important for my claims about the texts' relationships to specific crises. In addition to exploring how Woolf, Delany, and Coetzee approach fictionality, it is important to look at how their approaches differ from previous forms they each employed. The "essayism" of Woolf's work in general has been a topic for a number of scholars (Randi Saloman in particular), but Woolf's conception of *The Pargiters* as an essay-novel from the beginning stands in clear contrast to the more integrated essayistic elements of her earlier fiction (and fictional elements of her earlier essays). Samuel Delany had previously been attracted to science fiction and fantasy as tools for exploring ideas in ways he didn't feel other sorts of fiction-writing allowed, and he had used nonfictional elements briefly in previous novels, but "The Tale of Plagues and Carnivals" is a significant break from his earlier writing in the way the novelistic narrative breaks into outright diaristic and essayistic material to such an extent that the reader is forced to consider whether they are reading fiction at all. Coetzee's *Dusklands* adds essayistic elements to its fictional form, but it remains primarily fictional rather than essayistic. All of his novels are in dialogue with Modernist and post-structuralist criticism, but it is not until *Elizabeth Costello* that he pushes the form to such a degree that many reviewers (including the Woolf biographer Hermione Lee) declared the book not to be a novel at all, even when it was not labeled as one. With *Slow Man*, Coetzee returned to a more obviously novelistic form, but he then upset that form by bringing Elizabeth Costello in as a character (she immediately quotes the novel's first lines to its protagonist). Because *Slow Man* inserts Elizabeth Costello into a less complexly fictional novel, and her presence there fits comfortably within the parameters of metafiction, my attention will mostly be toward the other two post-*Elizabeth Costello* books that put fictionality into play: *Diary of a Bad Year* and *Summertime*. With *Diary of a Bad Year*, Coetzee mixes novelistic and essayistic elements in a way similar to that dreamed of by Woolf when she began *The Pargiters*[20], while *Summertime* unsettles both fictionality and nonfictionality.

After they wrote these texts that push fiction to its limits, Woolf, Delany, and Coetzee each then returned to writing novels in which the fictionality is less problematized. Their work was no less bold or innovative, but having discovered and tested certain limits, they were then able to pull back and move in other directions (toward, perhaps, other types of limits, other borders and margins). In each case, though, their later work demonstrates significant difference from what they wrote before their fictionality-testing texts.

My goal is for this study not to be simply about three writers, important as they are to world literature. The New Modernist Studies of the last two decades has conclusively demonstrated that Modernism was never separate from the political sphere, but the scholarship has done so via one primary tactic: an insistence on the politics within what was seen previously as primarily aesthetic. I believe that case is on solid ground, and now it is time that we re-examine the aesthetic

---

[20] Woolf's plan for *The Pargiters*, and the drafts she managed to write, alternates essays with novel chapters. The two inform each other, however, as Anna Snaith points out: "In a metafictional move, the narrator, moving from essay to novel and back again, not only animates and particularises the historical material, but also enacts the transformation of data into fictional prose" (Woolf 2012: lv), with the later essay chapters incorporating more and more fictional discourse. *Diary of a Bad Year* includes essays ostensibly written by the protagonist, whose neighbors refer to him as Señor C, but as James Wood described in *The New Yorker* in 2007, the book "takes a daring form: Señor C's essays occupy the bulk of each page, more or less, but running beneath them, like the news crawl on a TV screen, are what read like short diary entries by Señor C and by Anya, which offer a running commentary on the developing relationship of employer and employee, and which convey the plot of the novel, such as it is. So a typical page is segmented like the back of a scarab beetle, and the reader must choose to read either one narrative strand at a time or one page at a time and thus two or three strands simultaneously. In practice, one does a bit of both—a gulp of essay, a snatch of diary—and the broken form usefully, but relatively painlessly, corrupts any easy relation to innocent continuity." Coetzee's approach is more visually ostentatious than Woolf's, positioning the essay and novel sections on the same page, but the spirit is generally the same, forcing the reader to speculate on the connections between the different modes.

choices affected by artists' social and political commitments. If we are to be able to talk about how and why art matters, we must be able to talk about how and why artists shape their art, and how that shape affects our interpretation of the work.

The chapters that follow attempt just such a conversation. Chapter 2 explores Virginia Woolf in the 1930s, primarily through her struggles to conceive and write *The Years*, a novel that began as an experiment in melding fiction and nonfiction, but which ended up as an experiment in exploding the conventional novel form from within. While there is a substantial body of literature on Woolf, war, and crisis, that literature is far more focused on the 1910s and 1920s than the 1930s, a period of Woolf's life and writing that, while far from neglected, has not received the same critical attention as the earlier years. Much of the attention the last decade of Woolf's life has received has been thoughtful and insightful, and I have attempted in the notes and references here to give some map to the critical writing I have found most insightful, while also attempting to show some of the critical assumptions that, it seems to me, may lead us to devalue and even misread Woolf's work after *The Waves*.

Chapters 3 and 4 are devoted to two of Samuel Delany's AIDS-related texts, first "The Tale of Plagues and Carnivals" and then *The Mad Man*. Though Delany's work is receiving increasing academic attention, that attention usually comes from science fiction studies and queer studies, not modernist studies. The secondary literature on Woolf is now likely more than any one person could read in a lifetime, and the secondary literature on Coetzee threatens to soon be nearly as vast; Delany is not (yet) so fully studied, and so it seemed necessary to allow more space for discussion of his work in this book, as many ideas could not be dispensed with through a quick citation of studies that provide more discussion and context, as is possible with Woolf and Coetzee. In addition, Delany is the writer whose work best illustrates my ideas of the pedagogy of form *amidst* crisis. Woolf's *The Years* is a work conceived in anticipation of crisis, while Coetzee's later novels are work created after crisis has passed and a new way of living (along with its own attendant crises) has begun. It might have been equally interesting to look at Coetzee's work during the apartheid crisis or Delany's work after AIDS had become less of a crisis in his community, but Coetzee's apartheid-era novels have been analyzed well by other writers, and it seemed to me necessary to analyze Delany's 1980s writings before moving on to anything later (though I have written at length about his 2007 novel *Dark Reflections* elsewhere).

Chapter 5 considers three books by J.M. Coetzee: *Elizabeth Costello*, *Diary of a Bad Year*, and *Summertime*. Each is a different sort of text, with *Elizabeth Costello* initiating his move toward a more abstract sort of fiction than he had written before, and then *Diary of a Bad Year* and *Summertime* both approaching questions of reality, genre, and ethics from different vantage points. *Diary of a Bad Year* uses nonfiction to press against the limits of fiction; *Summertime* uses fiction to undermine our assumptions about biography and memoir. As with the Woolf chapter, I am trying here to show how our assumptions about what literature is and should be, as well as our assumptions about writers themselves, affect our engagement with a text's pedagogy.

The final chapter returns to concepts initiated in this introduction and developed by the chapters, and seeks to apply the knowledge gained from the previous chapters toward new understandings of the relationship between critical pedagogy and narrative form. The conclusion seeks to embody some of what this book has analyzed, to open areas for speculation, and to allow you, the reader, to consider the implications of what we've explored in these pages.

It would be the height of hypocrisy for me to offer this book as a collection of answers. Certainly, I have my own opinions about form and crisis, aesthetics and politics, ethics and responsibility, imagination and reality, education and authority; ideas about what artists can offer a world that feels like it is falling apart, about the value of the humanities in a time of inhumanity. Some of those opinions will be clear, others more implied. But I am not convinced that it is my own opinions, or even the opinions of the writers I analyze, that matter. Instead, what I most hope you gain from this book is a sense that the contemplation of the questions is, itself, an activity of value.

In a 1918 essay about Chekhov, Woolf wrote, "There may be no answer to these questions, but at the same time let us never manipulate the evidence so as to produce something fitting, decorous, or agreeable to our vanity. Away fly half the conclusions of the world at once. Accept endlessly, scrutinize ceaselessly, and see what will happen" (E 2: 245–246). I went to these writers assuming they could be models; I came away from them having learned that they are, instead, inspirations. Chekhov himself, in an 1888 letter, wrote to his editor and publisher, "You are right to demand that an author take conscious stock of what he is doing, but you are confusing two concepts: *answering the questions* and *formulating them correctly*" (1973: 117).

With luck, I have formulated some questions correctly.

2

Here and Now: *The Years*

In a 1936 letter to her nephew Julian Bell, Virginia Woolf cautioned him against writing a novel ("such a long gradual cold handed business") and said that she wished he would "invent some medium that's half poetry half play half novel. (Three halves, I see; well, you must correct my arithmetic.) I think there ought to be a scrambling together of mediums now" (Woolf 1990: 374). During the time she wrote this letter, Woolf was working on final revisions of her novel *The Years* and had begun to formulate ideas for the long essay *Three Guineas*.

Woolf's desire for "a scrambling together of mediums now" was in keeping with her aesthetic goals from at least the time when she wrote "The Mark on the Wall" in 1917. When Clive Bell praised that story, Woolf replied: "its [*sic*] high time we found some new shapes, don't you think so?" (*L* 2: 167). Such a desire fit with Ezra Pound's famous Modernist command to "Make it new!"[1] By the 1930s, though, Woolf and other Modernist writers had created many new shapes, and the most canonical Modernist works had all been in print long enough for their writers to seem less like the avant-garde and more like the old guard. "In the eyes of many young left-wing writers," Benjamin Kohlmann writes, "the high modernism of the 1920s came to embody the kind of writing they were reacting against" (2014: 2). Furthermore, with the rise of fascism in Italy, the stock market crash in the United States, the growing threat of nazism in Germany, and political and economic instability in England, writers of various ages and aesthetics felt at least some pressure to shape their writing toward the crises of the day. That pressure came from their own sense of the world's peril as

---

[1] The historical accuracy of the statement being Pound's motto is explored (exhaustively) by Michael North in "The Making of 'Make It New'" (2013). I use it here, and add the exclamation point Pound himself did not use, because for metamodernists it is has come to be such an accepted slogan for Modernist imperatives.

well as from the younger generation of writers who considered the aestheticism of Woolf's literary generation, particularly as associated with the Bloomsbury group, to be not only undesirable, but anachronistic. As Kohlmann concisely framed it, much of the writing in the 1930s, and especially politically committed writing, was "writing against modernism, rather than simply after it" (12).

By the 1930s, Woolf was keenly aware of her own reputation. She had published her first novel, *The Voyage Out*, in 1915, had received much attention for *Mrs. Dalloway* (1925) and *To the Lighthouse* (1927), and hit the bestseller lists with *Orlando* in 1928. She had been publishing reviews and essays since before the First World War, and 1929's *A Room of One's Own* sold over 12,000 copies in England in the first six months of publication (Willis 1992: 154). As the founders, owners, and editors of the Hogarth Press, she and Leonard were at the center of the British literary community. She had established herself as a serious writer and a public intellectual, and by her fiftieth birthday in 1932, she was no longer a member of the younger generation of literary innovators. Like it or not, she was now part of the establishment that newer writers would rebel against. It was clear that the literary priorities of the era would not be sympathetic to the highly psychological and interiorized fiction she had mastered, despite the subtle and often complex socio-political inclinations within what she wrote. Subtlety is not much of a defense against a world in crisis, and Woolf feared that the younger generation of writers might be right that her aesthetic would prove irrelevant.

In October 1931, she wrote a letter to Goldsworthy Lowes Dickinson (the Cambridge philosopher who had first imagined the League of Nations), thanking him for his praise of *The Waves* and adding:

> Perhaps for me, with my limitations—I mean lack of reasoning power and so on—all I can do is to make an artistic whole; and leave it at that. But then I'm annoyed to be told that I am nothing but a stringer together of words and words and words. I begin to doubt beautiful words. How one longs sometimes to have done something in the world. (*L* 4: 397–398)

The doubt of beautiful words and the longing "to have done something in the world" would continue to haunt Woolf as she measured herself against the younger generation and against the demands of a world growing ever more chaotic. She had tested the limits of fiction ever since publishing the short story "The Mark on the Wall" in 1917, and after finishing *Night and Day* (1919)— which Katherine Mansfield called "a novel in the tradition of the English novel" (Majumdar and McLaurin 1997: 82)—Woolf moved away from "the novel of fact" until, having finished *The Waves*, that form began to attract her again: "What has happened of course is that after abstaining from the novel of fact all these years—since 1919—& N.&D. indeed I find myself infinitely delighting in facts for a change, & in possession of quantities beyond counting: though I feel now and then the tug of vision, but resist it" (*D* 4: 129). When she decided that her new manuscript would a novel of fact more than vision, she was doing so not only as the novelist who had written *Night and Day*, but as the novelist who had gone on to write *Mrs. Dalloway, To the Lighthouse, Orlando,* and *The Waves.*

It was in conceiving *The Years* that Woolf clearly became something of a metamodernist: the new generation of writers was now established and she had become an internationally prominent, best-selling writer. It was the arrival of one writer of the new generation, John Lehmann, to the Hogarth Press that moved Woolf toward ennunciating her view of her relationship to newer writers, a view that would be expressed through various essays and reviews, particularly "A Letter to a Young Poet" (1932) and "The Leaning Tower" (1940). Where her earlier essays about art and fiction were written from the position of someone innovating against an established order (exemplified, in her opinion, by H.G. Wells, John Galsworthy, and Arnold Bennett), a position from which she presented herself as a contemporary of (and even a competitor to) James Joyce and Dorothy Richardson, now she wrote from the position of someone well established, able to look back not only on more than a decade of successful work of her own, but on the entire aesthetic movement that would come to be called Modernism. After *The Waves*, which took Woolf's experiments with interiority and impressionism to an extreme of expression and comprehensibility, her challenge was not simply to extend the corpus of Modernism, but to write with an acknowledgment of how settled that corpus was becoming. Her Modernism was in crisis because it risked becoming repetitive, sedimented into a conventionalized genre of its own.

"Modernism" as a label was already becoming anachronistic; the type of writing it labeled was no longer new. After finishing *Night and Day* in 1919, Woolf could declare " ... I can't help thinking that, English fiction being what it is, I compare for originality & sincerity rather well with most of the moderns" (*D* 1: 259), whereas in 1933, reading Vera Brittain's *Testament of Youth*, she had a distinct sense that not only was she not part of the younger generation of writers, but that that generation was the one writing the "new sort" of book "that I could never write" (*D* 4: 177). If she was not able to write the new sort of book, then what was she to write?

Woolf's solution was to return to the novel form she had so conspicuously set herself against when she began her experimental work—to return, in some way, to the moment after she finished *Night and Day* and brought her aesthetic forward with the stories "The Mark on the Wall" and "An Unwritten Novel"—a moment she remembered in a letter to Ethel Smyth in 1930:

> I shall never forget the day I wrote The Mark on the Wall—all in a flash, as if flying, after being kept stone breaking for months. The Unwritten Novel was the great discovery however. That—again in one second—showed me how I could embody all my deposit of experience in a shape that fitted it—not that I have ever reached that end; but anyhow I saw, branching out of the tunnel I made, when I discovered that method of approach, Jacob's Room, Mrs Dalloway, etc— How I trembled with excitement; and then Leonard came in, and I drank my milk, and concealed my excitement, and wrote I suppose another page of that interminable Night and Day (which some say is my best book). (*L* 4: 231)

As she remembered it, that moment was the product of personal crisis. She explained the conventional form of *Night and Day* as a bulwark against insanity: "I wrote it, lying in bed, allowed to write only for one half hour a day. And I made myself copy from plaster casts, partly to tranquillise [sic], partly to learn anatomy" (*L* 4: 231). Whether this was, in fact, the actual development[2], it was how Woolf remembered the development more than a decade later, and the artistic metaphor she uses to describe her process shows that she saw the novel as both an apprentice work and something with which to stave off anxiety and madness. In this recounting, Woolf's Modernist form becomes her artistically mature way to capture the visionary experience that had previously threatened to annihilate her. By the 1930s, she was an accomplished artist, she had (to use the terms of her own metaphor) learned anatomy, she had no need to copy from plaster casts, but now she again needed to find a new way forward, to push against both her own limits and the limits of fiction, while also staying sane in a world itself moving toward what she perceived as a kind of global madness and chaos.

When she finally finished a first draft of *The Years* in September 1936, the novel had expanded and expanded, growing to an unwieldy 900 handwritten

---

[2] Woolf did not write a lot about *Night and Day* while she was at work on it, so its origins and development are somewhat murkier than for many of her later books. It was published in 1919. "The Mark on the Wall" was first published in 1917, then in a slightly revised form again in 1919; "An Unwritten Novel" was published in 1920. Woolf links the two sketches to the development of her next novel after *Night and Day* in her diary entry of January 26, 1920, where she says she has "arrived at some idea of a new form for a new novel" (*D2* 13).

pages that she knew required significant revision. She continued revising, dragging herself through the book until she finished a typed draft in April 1936 and then collapsed in exhaustion and anguish for months, her worst bout of mental illness in more than twenty years. After much rest, she rallied, and was back to work revising the novel in proofs at the end of July. The Hogarth Press published *The Years* on March 15, 1937, followed by a US edition from Harcourt Brace on April 8. It sold quickly and well, becoming, during her lifetime, her best-selling novel. She appeared on the cover of the April 12, 1937, issue of *Time* magazine in a photograph by Man Ray.

The April 13, 1936 cover had been a picture of Adolf Hitler.

Genesis of an essay-novel

John Lehmann was twenty-three years old when he was hired by the Woolfs as manager of the Hogarth Press in January 1931. He was a friend of Virginia's nephew Julian Bell, who had suggested Lehmann send a collection of his poems to the Woolfs. Lehmann did, and the Woolfs offered not only to publish him, but to give him a job. Lehmann only ended up staying until September 1932, when wanderlust and frustration with Leonard led him to flee to Europe, but he returned in 1938 as a partner, buying out Virginia's share, and stayed till the beginning of 1946. Within a year of his hiring, Lehmann began to influence the Press by bringing in younger writers such as his friend Christopher Isherwood. Lehmann was instrumental in the publication of the anthology *New Signatures* in February 1932, the first book to collect work by some of the foremost members of "the Auden Generation" (W.H. Auden, Stephen Spender, C. Day Lewis, Julian Bell, William Empson, and Lehmann himself).

Lehmann and Virginia Woolf talked frequently of poetry and new writers. Her 1927 essay "Poetry, Fiction, and the Future" had portrayed poetry as inadequate to the present moment and called for a new type of novel "written in prose, but which has many of the characteristics of poetry" (*E* 4: 435). She and Lehmann discussed these ideas, and he encouraged her to contribute to the new series of Hogarth pamphlets in which various intellectuals and writers penned essays in the form of letters. She said she would do so, and would use his name, and "then I'll pour forth all I can think of about you young, and we old, and novels—how damned they are—and poetry, how dead. But I must take a look into the subject, and you must reply, 'To an old novelist' … " (*L* 4: 381).

Woolf's "Letter to a Young Poet" was published in July 1932 and succeeded in annoying Lehmann and his friends, especially as Woolf quoted what she considered weak passages from their work and declared that no writer should publish anything before they were thirty years old. Her central complaint was that poetry was inadequate to the reality of the day and that the young poets were too obsessed with themselves, seemingly uninterested in other people. "That is your problem now," she wrote, "if I may hazard a guess—to find the right relationship, now that you know yourself, between the self that you know and the world outside" (*E* 5: 315). She defended some of her positions in a private letter to Lehmann, saying that the young poet "doesn't reach the unconscious automated state—hence the spasmodic, jerky, self conscious effect of his realistic language," and then added, referencing a common charge against her own work: "But I may be transferring to him some of the ill effects of my own struggles the other way round—writes poetry in prose" (*L* 5: 383).

Even in the letter, Woolf seems to recognize that she is not an ideal reader of contemporary poetry, and her recognition that the "Letter to a Young Poet" may be mis-addressed is astute. It is not especially insightful about the younger generation of writers, but it is highly revealing if read as a "Letter to an Aging Virginia Woolf."

Woolf began writing the "Letter to a Young Poet" just as *The Waves* was published and as she was reflecting more and more on the relationship of her writing to the world. For many years, she had thought about the connections between fact and vision—or, as she memorably put it in the 1927 essay "The New Biography," between granite and rainbow (*E* 4: 478)—and felt that her novels after *Night and Day* had been rainbow "novels of vision" rather than granite "novels of fact." After *The Waves*, fact called to her again. In November 1931, when she was in the midst of writing the "Letter to a Young Poet," she said that one day while in London she "was thinking of another book—about shopkeepers & publicans, with low life scenes" (*D* 4: 53). Certainly, as a novelist, Woolf had written about many sorts of people, but there was still a lingering sense for her that by surrendering so much of her work to vision, she had skated perilously close to the brittle ice covering an abyss of personal, even hermetic, language. Now, with the world economy crumbling, with governments falling and civilization itself seemingly in peril, it made no sense to her to continue along the lines she had followed for a decade.

The Years began as *The Pargiters*, the work that Woolf in November 1932 dubbed an "essay-novel" (*D* 4: 129). *The Pargiters*, though, began from a speech that in January 1931 Woolf conceived of as becoming a book that could be "a sequel to A Room of Ones Own—about the sexual life of women: to be called Professions for Women perhaps" (D 4: 6). The hybridity of the essay-novel was not a new concept for Woolf, for she had similarly first conceived of *The Waves* as a "play-poem" (D 3: 139), and few of her books after *Night and Day* lack generic mixing.

After Woolf's death, scholars' descriptions of *The Pargiters* manuscript suggested that Woolf kept the boundaries of the essay and novel forms clear: essay sections alternated with novel sections. Such a description is not accurate, and it fed an assumption that Woolf simply split *The Pargiters* into two books, with the revised novel sections providing the raw material for *The Years*, the revised essay sections for *Three Guineas*. This assumption affected the editing of the manuscript for publication. Editor Mitchell Leaska added genre-descriptive section headings (*First Essay, First Chapter, Second Essay, Second Chapter* ...) where Woolf usually only placed a doodle.[3] Grace Radin, in an influential study of the writing and revising of *The Years*, described the structure of *The Pargiters* thus: "After each scene of the novel, Woolf inserts an interpretive essay in which she analyzes the events she has just portrayed and relates them to their historical background, using facts and quotations gleaned from biographies and other documents" (1981: 14–15). This description is accurate in a broadly general sense, but it elides one of the most interesting attributes of *The Pargiters*: just how much trouble Woolf had keeping the genres separate, especially in the later pages. A careful reading of *The Pargiters* shows that the sections presented as novel extracts were intended to be exemplary parts from which the reader could extrapolate the whole and from which the narrator of the essay sections could expound ideas. What such a structure creates is not an "essay-novel," as Woolf hoped, but rather an essay that uses fictional examples to make its points, with the essayistic passages referring back to the novel passages for evidence. As the manuscript develops, it becomes clear to the reader (and likely became clear to Woolf) that while the novel pieces could not exist, except as fragments, outside of the essay structure, the essays' ideas could certainly be conveyed without the novel itself—as, indeed, many of those ideas were in various essays and *Three Guineas*.

Whatever her reasons for abandoning the essay-novel concept, the strategy Woolf chose in her revisions is quite clear: she assiduously removed narrative

---

[3] For instance, what Leaska titles "First Chapter" was titled by Woolf "Chapter Fifty-Six" to show that what she offered was only a small excerpt from the (imaginary) novel.

commentary and heightened the ambiguity in characters' motivations. As Evelyn T. Chan demonstrates particularly well, Woolf's move away from her original structure was motivated by a fear of didacticism: Chan notes that "a week before deciding to remove the novel-essay division," Woolf wrote in her diary, "I'm afraid of the didactic" (*D* 5: 145), but "Woolf may in the end have been fearful of not just the didactic, but also the wrong didactic in a form of writing that she wanted to convey an unimpaired truth" (2010: 612). Chan's idea of *the wrong didactic* helps show that the shift from *The Pargiters* to *The Years* was a shift in the effect Woolf sought to have on readers. Where her initial impulse had been to put readers into a position of needing to extrapolate missing chapters of a novel from information in essays and commentary that explain (at length) the meaning of social structures, psychologies, and behaviors, her final structure does exactly the opposite, providing a complete novel (if one filled with gaps) and conspicuously refusing to explain much of anything. What Chan calls "the pregnant emptiness of the published version" (613) is a text that demands a reader imagine much more than any dreaded "preachy" text does. The result of the revisions brings *The Years* more in line with Woolf's earlier novels, which Erich Auerbach described as having an effect "that we might call a synthesized cosmic view or at least a challenge to the reader's will to interpretive synthesis" (549). The strategy of *The Years* was to activate that will to interpretive synthesis, to put it to work.

The overall effect of the pattern Woolf originally established subordinates the novel passages to the essay passages, with the extracts from the (otherwise unwritten) novel as illustrations for ideas within the essay (rather than the essay passages as items within the novel), but from the beginning the text unsettles its nonfictional status. As early as what Leaska labels the "Second Essay," Woolf writes not as if the Pargiters are characters in a novel, but as if they are real people, and the narrative slips out of the expository mode she had established for the essay portions and into the narrative mode of the novel sections, for instance:

> The sight of the baby had stirred in each quite a different emotion. Milly had felt a curious, though quite unanalyzed, desire to look at the baby, to hold it, to feel its body, to press her lips to the nape of its neck; whereas Delia had felt, also without being fully conscious of it, a vague uneasiness, as if some emotion were expected of her which, for some reason, some vaguely discreditable reason, she did not feel; and then, instead of following the perambulator, as her sister did, with her eyes, she turned and came back abruptly into the room, to exclaim a moment later, "O my God," as the thought struck her that she would never be allowed to go to Germany and study music. (Woolf 1978: 36)

Woolf later revised that passage for the first chapter of *The Years*, expanding the moment significantly and replacing most of the description of feelings with more concrete details. What's particularly notable is that when she revised the material into a novel, Woolf didn't simply polish it, but instead changed the kind of information the passage provided and withheld. Radin notes that Delia's cry of "O my God" becomes, in *The Years*, unattached to any obvious motivation, and the girls' interest in the perambulator is unexplained, which to Radin means that the girls "seem to share a longing to marry" (19), but other readers could imagine different motivations. The key point is that readers can—must, if meaning is to be made—come up with their own interpretations of the characters' behavior and thoughts.

Woolf enjoyed *The Pargiters*' form at first, mostly because it was a change from the type of work she had done on *The Waves*. Though the writing and revision process continued on laboriously into 1937, with the manuscript changing its shape and focus many times, as early as April 1933 Woolf had imagined what *The Years* would ultimately turn out to be: a melding of her early "novel of fact" (*Night and Day*) with her recent "novel of vision" (*The Waves*). "I want to give the whole of the present society—nothing less: facts, as well as the vision," she wrote in her diary. "And to combine them both. I mean, The Waves going on simultaneously with Night & Day. Is this possible?" (D 4: 151–152).

In the middle of February 1932, Woolf began the process of removing the explicitly essayistic sections from *The Pargiters*, setting the manuscript on the long course toward becoming *The Years*. Why she decided her original plan would not work has been a subject of speculation for everyone who has written on *The Pargiters*, but it remains speculation, for though she chronicled the writing of *The Years* quite fully in her diary, she did not record her reasons for that particular decision.[4] Whatever the reasons, once she had decided on a new structure, one of her tasks when revising became to remove all traces of a

---

[4] Following Leaska, Radin, and Christine Froula (2005), Molly Hite speculates that "Woolf reached back to some of her most painful memories from childhood and early adulthood, and the persistence of the threats contained in these memories eventually prompted her to drop the sections of direct commentary in favor of a narrative riddled with gaps, which became *The Years*" (2017: 169). This is plausible, but the question of why Woolf abandoned the form of *The Pargiters* is unanswerable with current evidence. I am less neutral on Hite's later conclusion—indeed, the conclusion to her whole book—that Woolf's abandonment of *The Pargiters* was a failure of nerve, a fear of public criticism or ridicule. In the absence of evidence for why Woolf changed her approach, this speculation seems to me to say more about the idea of Woolf that Hite has imagined in her own mind than it does about the woman who went on to write *Three Guineas*. A question that deserves more analysis (or self-analysis) is why critics such as Radin and Hite feel the need to imagine such a Woolf, and what it is within *The Years* that so upsets them.

didactic narrator and to cut down on the characters' own statements of social and political opinion, increasing what more and more became one of the novel's dominant themes: the failure of words to communicate thoughts accurately and efficiently. After *The Years* was published, Woolf herself wondered if she had gone too far in cutting, for instance, what have come to be known as the "two enormous chunks": a section of the 1914 chapter and a complete episode based in 1921, both of which develop Eleanor's thoughts more fully.[5]

Though Woolf quite deliberately scraped any whiff of didacticism from the pages of *The Years*, her long work assembling the novel led to some of the concepts and conclusions in *Three Guineas*, for *The Years* required her not only to reflect on her own life and situation, but to research the lives and situations of many other people, particularly women, and to develop scrapbooks of relevant material.[6] That work, and the effort to bring it to life within her fiction, seems to have affected how she viewed the world outside her windows. With terrifying political and social crises filling the newspapers, and with her scrapbooks overflowing with material about patriarchy and fascism, she could not turn away from her terrors. As she edited *The Years* in preparation for publication, her emotions, imagination, and intellect found a new home in *Three Guineas*. *The Years* was the result of her work on the essay-novel; *Three Guineas* was the result of her work on *The Years*.

It is important to note, too, that *The Years* is not simply *The Pargiters* without the essayistic material. In *Virginia Woolf's Late Cultural Criticism*, Alice Wood looks carefully at each step of Woolf's laborious refashioning of the text, finding that in January 1933, when Woolf moved away from the essay-novel structure she originally planned, she "modernized her family saga by composing each chapter through a series of interlinking and resonant scenes in a manner typical of her experimental fiction" (2013: 44). Though she would continue to refine the form as she revised almost to the moment of publication in 1937, Woolf's goal of compacting her ideas and arguments into the text remained primary. In *Virginia Woolf: Public and Private Negotiations*, Anna Snaith shows how an

---

[5] See Radin Chapter V (80–89) for some discussion of the effect of these deletions on the novel. The cut passages are included as appendices in most editions of *The Years* now, including the Cambridge edition (2012), the Oxford World's Classics (1992) paperback, and the annotated Harcourt paperback (2008).

[6] For information on Woolf's research for *Three Guineas*, see Marcus's edition of the book, which reprints some pages from the scrapbooks; chapter 3 of Naomi Black's *Virginia Woolf as Feminist* ("The Evolution of *Three Guineas*" pp. 51–72); and Merry Pawlowski's "Exposing Masculine Spectacle." Also of interest are Rebecca Wisor's articles "Versioning Virginia Woolf" and "About Face."

examination of the manuscripts "clarifies that the idea of conflict between fact and fiction, in which fiction eventually triumphs, is a radically inaccurate version of Woolf's own conception of the process. The text is layered and palimpsestic rather than generically antagonistic" (2000: 94). Seeing *The Years* as "layered and palimpsestic" rather than a novel at war with itself is an important insight for understanding the reading strategies it requires.

Unlike some of Woolf's other writings, and unlike texts I discuss in later chapters, *The Years* does not overtly unsettle fictionality; it is not *Orlando*, nor is it, for that matter, *A Room of One's Own* or *Three Guineas*, both of which, though basically nonfictional, employ fictional voices, characters, and scenes throughout.[7] Much of Woolf's writing from *Orlando* through *Between the Acts* demonstrates the "scrambling together of mediums" that Woolf told Julian Bell she considered the most appropriate form for writers of the era, but this is less overtly true of *The Years* than any other novel she published after *To the Lighthouse*: *Orlando* is a mock biography, *The Waves* radically explodes novelistic conventions, *Flush* might be called a novel though it is at least equally a biography, and *Between the Acts* melds novel and drama. *The Years* in its final form displays the trappings of a conventional novel, and it uses those trappings for specific purposes of invoking certain reading protocols (which it will often frustrate and subvert). *The Years* is not an essay, nor is it an essay-novel; it is a novel that uses its genre and form to invoke readers' expectations about what a novel is and should be, and then to frustrate those expectations for particular purposes. The essayistic portions were removed early in the writing process, but *The Years* encourages us as readers to think essayistically about its form and subject matter. The novel creates a kind of imaginary shadow, and that shadow is an essay about novels, fiction, history, families, violence, class, and patriarchy. Though Woolf removed the sections of commentary, the spirit of those commentaries remains present within the novel's form (its genre conventions, juxtapositions, and gaps), and the reading strategies that find the most sense and coherence in *The Years* are strategies that provoke the reader toward thinking about the novel as the narrator of the commentaries might have.

The Years is in dialogue with its readers, and it truly *is* a dialogue, not Woolf's dreaded "preaching." What the reader brings to the text matters,

---

[7] For a particularly insightful discussion of the voices in *Room*, see Spivak, *Death of a Discipline* (2003: 39–44); for *Three Guineas*, see Jane Marcus's introduction to the edition she edited (2006).

and the text does not offer any clear answers to the questions it raises about time, society, history, or the novel form. We might say, then, that its dialogue is Socratic; in "On Not Knowing Greek," Woolf described the effect of one of Plato's dialogues: "as the argument mounts from step to step, Protagoras yielding, Socrates pushing on, what matters is not so much the end we reach as our manner of reaching it" (*E* 4: 46). With *The Years*, the "manner of reaching" was the novel form and the traditional expectations that form called forth from the reader.

Explosion from within

The finished novel comprises eleven chapters: ten given specific years for their titles, starting in 1880, and then the final, long chapter is titled "Present Day." These chapter titles alert us to the possible sub-genre of the book. Generational novels about families had been popular at least from the time of Zola's Rougon-Macquart novels; after the first decades of the twentieth century, though, they came to be seen as a rather dusty genre. Woolf herself contributed to that sense in various essays in the early 1920s that attacked writers of the generation before her own who wrote long novels of social realism and domestic life ("such stories seem to me the most dreary, irrelevant, and humbugging affairs in the world" [*E* 3: 432])—but as a writer obsessed with time and memory, she must have felt an inescapable attraction to the form's possibilities. Woolf was not the first or only modernist writer to attempt this (Gertrude Stein's *Making of Americans*, for instance, is subtitled "Being a History of a Family's Progress"[8]) but her approach was distinct.

Woolf was determined to make her own book into something more than a family chronicle, and in changing the working title from *The Pargiters* to *Here and Now*, she commented, "It shows what I'm after & does not compete with the Herries Saga, the Forsyte Saga & so on" (*D* 4: 176). Woolf sought to invite the reader to begin her novel with the expectation that it could be read as a family saga; and then, once the reading protocols of the genre were initiated, the text could challenge and retrofit them, training the reader toward a new way of reading and, with luck, of seeing the world.

---

[8] The Woolfs rejected *The Making of Americans* for the Hogarth Press in 1925, though they did publish Stein's important lecture "Composition as Explanation." See Willis (1992) pp. 125–127.

While it's a cliché now to say that a novel subverts this, that, or another convention, I know of no better way to describe what Woolf achieves in using the family novel genre. Conventions regulate readers' expectations, and the subversive writer invokes those conventions, then shapes them either to guide the reading experience toward new effects or to surprise (or frustrate) the reader into some new awareness. Readers may expect, for instance, that a novel of generations will make note of important historical events, and *The Years* does (British colonialism, the death of Charles Stewart Parnell, the women's suffrage movement, the death of King Edward VII, the First World War), but these events are often noticed only in passing, or their drama is muted, and many major events are skipped over altogether. Woolf's focus is on the everyday details of life, the steady changes of technology that affect how people communicate with each other and get around in the world, how money gets made and accounted for, who gets to go to school and who gets to go to work, and what sort of schools and what sort of work they go to. The private, quotidian world is emphasized, the public world radically de-emphasized, shifting what is assumed to be important in historical writing. Though it is a family novel, or at least a novel that depicts one family over multiple generations, *The Years* is skeptical of families. Families produce patriarchs, and Woolf is careful throughout the novel to link families to institutions that reinforce and reproduce patriarchal power (the military, schools, government, courts). She doesn't do so obviously, but the pattern becomes clear to any reader paying attention to who among the characters gets to do what. (The implied critique of families within *The Years* is explicit in *Three Guineas*, where an analysis of war and patriarchy sits alongside blistering attacks on traditional ideas of families and family structures, attacks that reflected Woolf's always-developing philosophy of the interrelations of oppression and social institutions.[9] In their force, these analyses are quite different from the narrative of *The Years*, but they are not different in substance.) The family saga sub-genre especially supports a normalizing discourse of *the family*, a discourse Woolf knew to be highly compatible with traditional novel form.

The Years is also stubbornly anti-heroic. Woolf knows that hero-worship is an easy trap to fall into, that society encourages its members to worship fathers, generals, and politicians; but for Woolf, that urge to worship heroes is one of the seeds of fascism. No character in *The Years* is without significant flaws,

---

[9] For a thoughtful exploration of Woolf and concepts of family, see Zwerdling, particularly chapters 6 and 7. For more recent scholarship, see Amidon, Saariluoma, and Suh.

and some of the characters we associate with political positions that appeal to us (and, in all likelihood, to Woolf herself) are among the most significantly flawed. This has been a trap for readers who want to read the characters as mouthpieces for Woolf herself, and so are taken up short by moments of sexism, racism, anti-Semitism, jingoism. *The Years* is not a tract against patriarchy or war or Hitler or Oswald Mosley; it is something more valuable: an exploration and, perhaps, inoculation against what Michel Foucault described in a different context as "the fascism within us all, in our heads and in our everyday behavior, the fascism that causes us to love power, to desire the very thing that dominates and exploits us." The questions Foucault says are addressed by Deleuze and Guattari's *Anti-Oedipus* are the very questions raised—dramatized—by *The Years*: "How does one keep from being fascist, even (especially) when one believes oneself to be a revolutionary militant? How do we rid our speech and our acts, our hearts and our pleasures, of fascism? How do we ferret out the fascism that is ingrained in our behavior?" (Foucault [1972] 2009: xiii).

In refusing to provide clear role models among its characters and in downplaying major historical events, *The Years* contradicts the desires of any reader seeking propaganda, but Woolf uses additional strategies as she seeks to create an immunizing text. One such strategy is repetition. Throughout *The Years,* particular phrases, colors, sounds, and objects repeat, but the repetitions are not obvious—the repetition of colors, for instance, does not fit a simple symbolic schema, but serves a more impressionistic purpose, linking events, characters, and images across the entire novel with, for the reader, an effect akin to old memories drifting just beyond conscious reach. This effect thwarts any literal-minded critic seeking to tally an allegory, because the repetitions don't add up to a message or moral; instead, they provide a texture to the whole.[10] The repetitions are not themselves highly meaningful, and only the most obsessive reader will note the majority of them, but because the repetitions are so many, anyone somewhat attentive to the text will notice a few and likely be vaguely conscious of others in a kind of penumbric effect whereby we sense that there is much more beyond our conscious understanding of the text. That sense is one motor for the engines of the novel's ethical action: we are haunted always by the feeling that something whispers just outside our range of hearing, and so we wonder and speculate

---

[10] In *Virginia Woolf: Dramatic Novelist*, Jane Wheare (1989) chronicles many of the repetitions, and what is little more than a list with brief explanations requires twenty pages.

what it might be. *The Years* offers no answers, but in raising the questions within its complex, reverberative narrative structure, it provides readers with tools to think and feel their way toward solutions of their own. It is, in that sense, a liberating text. But such a structure proves frustratingly slippery for a reader seeking propaganda, much as a class led by a teacher committed to critical pedagogy will prove frustrating to a student who simply wants to know which questions will be on the final exam.

The danger of Woolf's strategy was that many readers would simply interpret *The Years* as a failed family novel, even if they recognized its subversive intent. Phyllis Rose recognized many of the elements of what I am calling the pedagogy of *The Years*, but saw them as examples of the novel's failures: "The disturbing thing is that the static effect of *The Years*, its pattern of frustrating expectation and embedding the reader in inconclusiveness, seems to stem less from conscious design than from a perilous reticence in the author" ([1978] 1987: 215). Rose is simply wrong about this. As subsequent scholars have demonstrated, like it or not, the design of *The Years* was extremely conscious on Woolf's part. Similarly, Pamela J. Transue is able to acknowledge many of the anti-family-novel features of *The Years* and to identify its lack of didacticism, but still judge it a failure as a novel. Writing of the scene with the exhibitionist in the first section of *The Years*, Transue says: "In *The Pargiters*, Woolf uses Rose's experience as a nexus for a discussion of male sexual aggressiveness in general. In *The Years*, we are left, right or wrong, to our own conclusions" (1986: 152). The authoritarian desire is clear: Transue wants propaganda, a style of writing in which a reader is never given the opportunity to make interpretations different from those of the controlling didact. Critics like Transue demonstrate significantly less trust in and respect for readers than Woolf does.

Transue also disapproves of the demands *The Years* makes: "As the book rambles on through a period of about fifty years, the reader becomes increasingly lost. It is nearly impossible to keep track of all the characters, to remember who did what and when, or even to maintain a sense of distinct personalities" (1986: 164). She approvingly quotes Phyllis Rose's complaint that the book fails to provide a central character, fails to give shape to its narrative, and fails to sort through all the details it provides. These are the complaints of readers who expect a particular form for the novel as a genre, and perhaps who even expect *The Years* to be a family novel and are disappointed that it does not adhere more closely to those conventions. The novel's pedagogy failed to affect these readers because their preconceptions about what a "Woolf novel" is and should be overwhelmed their ability to learn from the text itself.[11] We will see Samuel Delany deal with similarly calcified readerly expectations when he moves away from writing science fiction and J.M. Coetzee when he does not repeat the form and style of *Disgrace*. (Indeed, it is exactly this sort of calcification-by-reputation that Coetzee combats via radical experiments with self-destructing authorial authority.)

The reception of *The Years* shows the hegemony of the discourse Clifford Siskin calls *novelism*, "the now habitual subordination of writing to the novel" so that "even when we want to separate the two ... we have trouble pulling them apart" (1996: 423). Novelism doesn't simply subordinate all unmarked prose writing to the novel—it promotes and polices a very specific idea of what a novel is and should be. (What that idea is depends on the era and literary culture, particularly the interpretive communities that evaluate and promote certain novels as successful models and others as failures.) From the complaints of Rose, Transue, and others, we can see what a "good Woolf novel" must be—Woolf's better-approved books of the mid-1920s (*Mrs. Dalloway*, *To the Lighthouse*), for all their innovations, still have trackable characters with distinct personalities and voices, narratives with easily noticed organizing principles, and details that clearly serve those principles. Perhaps more importantly, Woolf's "good novels" are overtly, even ostentatiously experimental—Transue calls *The Waves* "a unique literary creation, daringly experimental in style, structure, and theme" (127) and writes that "On almost every level ... *The Waves* is in part a comment on the limitations of the novel in its classic form" (144). For Transue, *The Waves* is successful in all the ways *The Years* is not. Such an evaluation fails, though, to read the books on their own terms, and Transue refuses to allow the reader of *The Years* the same intelligence and autonomy as the reader of *The Waves*. The specific reading strategies that lead to an appreciation of *The Waves* are not the specific reading strategies that will lead to an appreciation of *The Years*, as the two novels are—and were from the moment Woolf conceived *The Years*—almost exactly opposite in their experimental approach to the idea of the novel as a form and genre.

No-one would ever mistake *The Waves* for a conventional novel, and the position it puts the reader in is that of someone who must discover how to

---

[11] Such critics' responses suggest a subtle class bias. *The Waves* is an overtly experimental novel, thus high art that deserves careful attention; *The Years* seems on the surface to be a more popular form, and indeed became a bestseller when it was published. Critics like Transue seem to fear that an unsophisticated audience will not only be unable to make sense of the novel, but worse: They might come to wrong conclusions. This is entirely at odds with Woolf's own notion of the common reader.

make sense of the text while reading, rather than being able to benefit from knowledge of novelistic conventions. From the first pages, the reader of *The Waves* knows that this is not a novel that follows the traditional conventions of the form. That is one type of experimental writing (the *sui generis* text), but another is the text that unsettles conventions from within. The innovations of *The Years* are embedded within the reader's perception of the book as a novel. It becomes a new kind of "comment on the limitations of the novel in its classic form" for Woolf, and something more than a comment, because readerly experience is central to the effect. The critique of the novel form woven through *The Years* is activated via the expectations the reader brings to it. The text of *The Years* may not be (to use Snaith's term) generically antagonistic, but there is a generic antagonism between the reader and the text. Where *The Waves* stretches toward being an anti-novel in the way it excludes so much of what is conventional within novels generally, *The Years* teases familiar novelistic conventions to then reshape them, making *The Years* a *detournement* of the novel. In a pedagogical sense, *The Waves* requires the reader to learn how to read it from scratch, because from the first pages it is clear that few of our assumptions about how a novel works will be applicable with this text, whereas *The Years* teaches the reader to see the inadequacy of received ideas about how a novel makes meaning and what within a novel is most meaningful. For the critique of patriarchy and family that was so important to Woolf's project in the 1930s, the novel form itself needed to be pulled apart from the inside. She had gathered, she said, "enough powder to blow up St Pauls" (D 4: 77), but for the most effective demolition, she needed to place that powder inside the structure itself.

Despite maintaining the superficial hallmarks of a conventional novel from beginning to end, *The Years* feels less and less conventional with each new page, because as it progresses, conversations become more fragmentary and interrupted (usually it is men interrupting women), memories drift, and communication itself seems, inevitably, to fail. Yet Woolf is not Beckett. Failure and silence are present, but they are not the end point. In a world of fascism, silence can too easily become consent or complicity (normalizing discourses don't mind silence). We must pay attention to the prelude narrator, a voice quite different from any other in the book. Without that narrative voice, it would be more difficult to make sense of the many scattered moments that make up *The Years*. The prelude narrator doesn't do this work for us, but rather, like a good teacher, suggests some possibilities and then lets us try things on our own.[12] The prelude narrator has the freedom to dart from perspective to perspective, fact to fact, moment to moment. As readers, we must free ourselves to do the same. Only with such freedom of movement and such open, flexible perspective will we be able to make meaning from the text that follows each prelude.

The "1880" prelude begins with a description of the season and weather, of country and city. It then starts, slowly, to zoom in: spring becomes April; all the people of London become shop assistants, "ladies in flounced dresses"; "shoppers in the West End"; businessmen; people mailing letters; people standing at the windows of clubs in Piccadilly; "ladies in many-coloured dresses wearing bustles, and … gentlemen in frock coats carrying canes"; the Princess; "servant girls in cap and apron"; "diners-out, trotting over the Bridge in hansom cabs" (3–4). The mass becomes comprehensible as we see how it is made up of individual groups, and how each of those groups is made up of individuals. The narrator then pulls back to describe the moon and the clouds above it all, the world of nature beyond the constructions of human society. The sky unites perception: each person who looks up sees that sky and that moon from their own vantage point. The sky and moon may be indifferent to human life and action, but they are as enmeshed in time as the humans are: "Slowly wheeling, like the rays of a searchlight, the days, the weeks, the years passed one after another across the sky" (4). Despite the floating perception of the prelude narrator, though, there is no unifying perception in the novel. The narration does not do the reader's work; instead, it reminds us to think beyond the immediate perspective in any scene, to imagine the world outside the walls of any one room, to imagine lives lived outside the text.

At the beginning of the novel, Delia and Eleanor stand at a window and watch a cab stop two doors down, and so, too, at the end, Eleanor stands and watches a cab stop two doors down, while Delia admires the loveliness of roses.[13] The moment is circular within the novel's structure, but Woolf's repetition is like jazz, always with some bit of difference, some revision. At the window, Eleanor asks a question to end the long night, a question that was previously asked by Kitty in 1910 as she watched *Siegfried* and by Sara in 1917 when everyone went

---

[12] Taylor notes that Woolf and Freire's approaches are both "problem-posing pedagogies" (2014: 73), and the approach is true of Woolf's novels, as well.

[13] In her "Letter to a Young Poet," Woolf advised: "All you need now is to stand at the window and let your rhythmical sense open and shut, open, and shut, boldly and freely, until one thing melts in another, until the taxis are dancing with the daffodils, until a whole has been made from all these separate fragments" (*E5* 315).

into the cellar for the air raid, and the words are ones Martin stuttered to Sara in 1914 when trying to get her to speak to him, and they remain a question for all of us: "And now?"

A blank space follows, and then only the final sentence: "The sun had risen, and the sky above the houses wore an air of extraordinary beauty, simplicity, and peace." Eleanor's question isn't answered. The gap, that blank space, stands between the individual characters (trapped in their time and circumstances) and the egoless, enraptured moment of the sky's beauty, simplicity, and peace. "We are forced to lay down our weapons as readers," Jane Marcus wrote of Woolf's work. "All our egotism and individuality, the swords and shields of the hated 'I, I, I' must be abandoned outside the doors of her fiction" (1988: 82). If we can imagine a way to bridge the gap, then we have learned what we needed to learn.

Propaganda and pedagogy

Woolf was torn by a yearning to address the social and political issues that concerned her but also to avoid didacticism; in the speech that was an initial impetus for *The Pargiters*, she opposed the profession of *the writer* to that of *the preacher*, saying that the move from writer to preacher is "extremely unpleasant for you, poor imagination" (*E* 5: 644). She had famously condemned Arnold Bennett's novels for their facts at the expense of insight and further criticized novels of the Edwardian era for their social activism. "Woolf's generation," Julia Briggs writes, "had despised the teaching and preaching so characteristic of Victorian literature, suspecting any writing that had manifest designs upon its readers" (2005: 283). As Woolf's comments on Plato show, in her mind, argument does not require manifest (clear and obvious) designs. Indeed, for any argument (whether conveyed via essay or novel) to be artful, Woolf and her contemporaries believed the design must *not* be obvious, for it is obviousness that is didacticism's primary failing, its lack of art.

The critical history of *The Years* demonstrates, however, that Woolf's decisions consistently raise two problems for readers; the first from the moment of the book's publication, the second a result of archival work on *The Pargiters*. Both are problems of context that readers bring to their reading.

First is the problem mentioned previously: the challenge of an apparently traditional novel issued from the pen of a writer renowned for her experimentalism. In a review Woolf liked, Basil de Selincourt said "*The Years* is rather nearer the norm of the novel than *The Waves* was" and proclaimed it "a much easier book to read," while Edwin Muir flat-out declared "after *The Waves* this is a disappointing book" (Majumdar and McLaurin 1997: 371, 388). Though readings of the novel grew more detailed in the following decades, evaluations of its worth and place within Woolf's oeuvre mostly followed the trajectory laid out by the initial press reviews, though esteem for the novel generally was higher at the time of publication than later, with only a few critics such as James Hafley regarding the novel highly and most others agreeing more with Muir.

The second problem is that of what might have been. Since the publication of *The Pargiters* in 1978 and Grace Radin's study in 1981, there has persisted a general sense that Woolf failed to solve the problem of the essay-novel-that-became-a-novel.[14] In his introduction to *The Pargiters*, Mitchell Leaska asserts that "*The Years* as a finished product is a remarkable specimen in fiction where fact and feeling are in deadly conflict" (Woolf 1978: xv) and that "with the disappearance of the explanatory Essays, and with the novel itself so severely cut and edited, we as readers are thrown perhaps too much upon the fertility of our own imaginations to deduce some meaning from the book's seemingly endless ambiguities" (xix). Radin is even more dismissive of the finished volume, writing that "the continual shifts from representational narrative to fragmented speech, from static detached description to dramatic scenes caught *in medias res*, from one center of consciousness to another can easily confuse the reader" (1981: 152). Radin suggests that the incoherence she reads in the book may have been intentional, but she seems more to believe that it was a failure of ability, for "given her experiences during these years, it is questionable whether Woolf could have created the synthesis she had been struggling to achieve," and Radin wonders "whether in fact the novel's stubborn refusal to cohere came from a deep division within herself and within the society she was trying to come to terms with" (158). More recently, Molly Hite has followed in Radin's footsteps, demonstrating great disappointment that Woolf did not continue along the path she set with *The Pargiters*, stating, "this change in form was not 'a good idea'

---

[14] The neglect persists in the scholarship, with *The Years* treated as expendable in a way *Mrs. Dalloway* and *To the Lighthouse* never are. Though some scholars have certainly given excellent attention to *The Years*, it remains possible, for instance, for Jane De Gay in *Virginia Woolf's Novels and the Literary Past* (Edinburgh University Press, 2006) not only to analyze each of the novels except *The Years*, but to never explain this omission—the book's title doesn't appear anywhere in De Gay's text. Similarly, *The Years* makes no appearance in Emily Blair's *Virginia Woolf and the Nineteenth Century Domestic Novel* (SUNY Press, 2007), where it might be expected to be found, given its close relationship to domestic novels (*The Pargiters* is mentioned in passing, and at least Blair makes no pretense of covering all of Woolf's novels—*The Waves* is also absent except for a couple of footnotes).

aesthetically, although the step back into a less experimental structure may have been necessary for Woolf herself because of her own psychological involvement in the materials she had collected" (2017: 166). The focus on the writing process of *The Years* for a long time haunted the published version of the novel and contributed to its marginalization by positioning the finished novel as a failed experiment or de-radicalization of a radical project. A view of the finished novel as a casualty of self-censorship, repression, or even cowardice quickly entered the discourse, and remains today (e.g., Hite) even after the work of Haule (2009), Snaith (2000), and Wood (2013) to show a more complex view of the finished text through re-examinations of Woolf's writing and revision process not based on the presumption of the finished version as a failure.

We do not need to go to the manuscripts to become re-constructors of the novel, however; the finished version itself foregrounds such a position for the reader, which was exactly Leaska's complaint. The novel does, indeed, rely "upon the fertility of our own imaginations to deduce some meaning" from the gaps, ambiguities, and repetitions, but if we read the text's purpose to be, at least partly, the education of imagination, then this is not a failure, but a strategy, and it is a strategy that is aligned with Woolf's previous novels.[15] Radin and Leaska are correct to note that *The Years* is potentially confusing to readers; decades of Woolf scholarship confirm how easy it is for readers to miss the social and political implications of the novel, at least partly because of an expectation that socially and politically committed texts need to be explicit in their commitments (even, to use Woolf's dreaded term, *preachy*) and uncomplicated in their presentation of whatever idea the critic considers acceptable, because what such critics fear most is that the message might be misread. Such a view valorizes the authoritarian rhetoric of propaganda and prefers ersatz ethics to thoughtful inquiry.

Clearly, *The Years* is not propaganda, and its pedagogy has often proved too subtle to resist the overwhelming power of other discourses, but today there is no excuse to ignore the link between the novel's form and Woolf's commitments. In the 1970s, feminist scholarship insisted on the connections between aesthetic

---

[15] In an insightful historical/materialist reading of *The Years*, Linden Peach writes that "In *The Years*, despite its apparent concessions to social realism, Woolf was still working within the parameters of the approach that she first employed in *Jacob's Room* and *Orlando*. Indeed, the novel can be seen in terms of her quarrel with realism in her essay 'Modern Fiction' (1919) and her argument that novels should be less concerned with 'realism' and 'materialism' and more with the inner experience of 'reality'. [...] In *The Years*, her subject continues to be that of *Jacob's Room*, the codified nature of social 'reality' and of the historical *a priori*" (2000: 169). Echoing some of my analysis, Peach also asserts that "Like *Jacob's Room* and *Orlando*, *The Years* revises a traditional genre" (171).

choices and socio-political analysis, making earlier writing about Woolf seem obviously inadequate in its narrow, compartmentalizing view of politics. Jean Guiguet, for instance (one of the best of the early critics), used *A Writer's Diary* to piece together the entwined conception of *The Years* and *Three Guineas*, yet despite all that work did not make much of this connection.[16] Guiguet declares of *Three Guineas*, "whatever may be the faults of the book, [it] entitles one to include Virginia Woolf in the great line of Humanists—and also among 'committed' writers, paradoxical as this epithet may appear when we consider the dominant aspect of her work" (1965: 186). In his separation of the fiction and nonfiction, Guiguet represents a consensus common among even the most attentive readers before the 1970s, seeing in *The Years* only a "kaleidoscope" of images of social situations that left the committed side of Woolf unsatisfied: " ... at the point to which the world had come, with German rearmament, the arrogance of Italian Fascism, the Spanish revolution, these images by themselves, with their impassivity, the remoteness conferred on them by art, provided deliverance to the novelist in her but not the simple human being. For that, something more explicit, more direct, was needed" (191).

The *remoteness* and *impassivity* that Guiguet reads as pushing Woolf toward the more explicit approach of *Three Guineas* are in some ways accurate—*Three Guineas*, for all its polyphony, is written in a more expository mode than a novel—but I take the frequent negative evaluations of *The Years* by readers who ought to be at least vaguely open to its pedagogy as a lesson for us as readers rather than a lesson about the book. To enter into a transactional relationship with a text that produces meaning beyond the pages of the text itself, readers of literature must train their imaginations toward what Gayatri Spivak calls "a flexible epistemology that can, perhaps, keep saving our world" (2014: 23). In "How Should One Read a Book?" Woolf argued that to read a novel "You must be capable not only of great fineness of perception, but of great boldness of imagination if you are going to make use of all that the novelist—the great artist—gives you" (*E* 5: 575). From early on, Woolf, too, saw imagination as a tool for epistemology, as a 1918 entry in her diary shows: "The reason why it is easy to kill another person," she writes, "must be that one's imagination is too

---

[16] Before the rise of feminist scholarship, critics who were sensitive to *The Years* recognized many of the features we still value in its structure (Richter [1970] is probably the best of the early critics on this), but Guiguet is one of the few who bother even to note any socio-political implications. It was the pioneering feminist readers who demonstrated that "committed" was not, as Guiguet claims, a paradoxical epithet for Woolf.

sluggish to conceive what his life means to him—the infinite possibilities of a succession of days which are furled in him, & have already been spent" (*D* 1, 186). An imagination that is *not* sluggish would, then, be one capable of imagining other people's conceptions of their lives, and such knowledge would make killing much more difficult. The training of the mind toward such imagination would be a training against war and toward peace, a training toward community, shared humanity, and, perhaps, saving the world.

Writers such as Rod C. Taylor, Beth Rigel Daugherty, and Natasha Periyan have produced excellent work showing the extent to which Virginia Woolf was engaged with issues of education throughout her life and career, and how that engagement affected the content of her writing. Taylor sees *Three Guineas* as promoting a critical pedagogy similar to that of Paulo Freire, particularly in the book's arguments about learning and knowledge: "At its core, Woolf's pedagogy anticipates Freire's in that both systems inquire into knowledge and how the production of knowledge is constituted, but Woolf's orientation toward knowledge is that of ambivalence toward new understanding—even that which resists oppressive systems—rather than political absolutism on one side or another" (2014: 57–58). This is accurate, but Taylor limits his study of Woolf's critical pedagogy to *what* her writings say rather than *how* they say it, which is equally important, particularly if we are to recognize the way form, for Woolf, becomes not only an extension of content but an extension of ethics. "Though Woolf is highly critical of the educational institutions of her time," Rachel Hollander notes, "she is also deeply invested in questions of pedagogy and ethics" (2007: 55)—questions that find expression both in the ideas she explores and in the textual structures she shapes:

> The issue of education in the text has crucial implications for the question of whether or how the novel might be said to "teach" its readers. And while the charge of didacticism is most often deployed to condemn a work of literature as heavy-handed or formulaic [...] Woolf, like George Eliot before her, demonstrates a wide-ranging and subtle understanding of the many ways the relationship between reader and text is steeped in ethics and pedagogy. (60)

In *Three Guineas,* Woolf builds her argument slowly and carefully through various voices, historical and fictional, creating a collage effect. The reader must pay close attention to the voices Woolf uses, for here as elsewhere she creates a choral structure to undermine the power of a single, authoritative voice—a move even more radical in nonfiction, where the narrator's authority is often taken for granted, than in fiction. (It is rare to find an intentionally unreliable narrator in nonfiction, while they are common in fiction.) The form supports Woolf's political analysis, as Teresa Winterhalter astutely notes: "If, for Woolf, war is the product of assuming the infallibility of one particular viewpoint, then narration inevitably participates in this dynamic of power. By subverting expository tradition, she hopes to perform a significant act of engaged rebellion against linguistic practices that align with totalitarianism" (2003: 239). Such rebellion is not Woolf's alone; to make sense of the text, readers must also themselves rebel against the reading protocols of the expository tradition and find new linguistic practices with which to create meaning.

In addition to having to listen for the various voices woven through the main text of *Three Guineas*, we must also move back and forth between that text and footnotes, which sometimes present information to complicate the statements that are footnoted. Such polyphony promotes active reading and thinking. Passivity, Woolf knows, renders us vulnerable to authoritarians who are more than willing to provide us with meanings so we don't have to think for ourselves. To combat authoritarianism, we cannot sit and let a predetermined message wash over us; we must participate, must think and doubt, must find our own voice among the voices that we meet. Like Coetzee later, she is wary even of her own authority. *Three Guineas* is not propaganda, for "although she hopes for social consensus on the 'simple truth' of pacifism, she does not impose it on her readers through a totalitarian voicing" (Winterhalter 2003: 250).

To better highlight Woolf's unique strategies, we can compare *The Years* and another generational novel written in the 1930s by a writer who was not a Modernist or metamodernist and who did not have any fear of didacticism: *Honourable Estate* by Vera Brittain.

At the beginning of this chapter, I noted that Woolf read Brittain's 1933 memoir of the First World War, *Testament of Youth,* and declared it a good book of the new type, "the hard anguished sort, that the young write; that I could never write" (D 4: 177). Woolf had previously been aware of Brittain, who had praised *A Room of One's Own* in her "Woman's Notebook" column for the *Nation and Athenaeum*, and who attended the January 1931 lecture by Woolf that led to *The Pargiters*. As Woolf's comment about *Testament of Youth* makes clear, the two writers were significantly different from each other, and Woolf, at least, knew it.

During some of the time that Woolf was working on *The Years*, Brittain was working on an ambitious, multi-generational novel of her own. She struggled terribly with the manuscript, partly because of its scope, but also because after *Testament of Youth*'s success, she felt the pressure of being a well-known writer, a writer whose next book would inevitably be highly anticipated and scrutinized. There were other obstacles, too: at the beginning of August 1935, Brittain's father, who had never really recovered from the death of Vera's brother Edward in the First World War, drowned himself in the Thames; and then in September, Brittain's greatest friend and confidante, Winifred Holtby, finally succumbed to Bright's disease. After these catastrophes, writing the novel became drudgery, but she pulled through it, bringing it in some ways in dialogue with Holtby's final novel, *South Riding*.[17]

Victor Gollancz published *Honourable Estate* in November 1936. The response of the public and press was less enthusiastic than it had been for *Testament of Youth*, but not openly hostile (as it would be for some of her later pacifist writings). The consensus seemed to be that the book was rather dull and awkward. *Honourable Estate* included a foreword from Brittain that began with an epigraph from the poet Geoffrey Dearmer (a World War veteran whose brother died at Gallipoli): "Overproduction is due largely to the fact that so many authors have never asked themselves the all-important question: 'Why do I write?' But if all authors had a creative philosophy as well as a creative faculty, critics would be interested in their apologies and explanations, for who can know half so much about a book as its author?" (Brittain [1936] 2000: 1). Brittain was happy to take on this encouragement to explain herself, telling readers that the novel "purports to show how the women's revolution—one of the greatest in all history—united with the struggle for other democratic ideals and the cataclysm of the War to alter the private destinies of individuals" (2).

Brittain anticipated criticism for her didacticism:

> I make no apology for dealing in a novel with social theories and political beliefs, nor for the extent to which these are discussed by some of the characters. I cannot share the outlook of that school of literary criticism which seeks to limit the novelist's "legitimate" topics to personal relationships. Personal relationships have no more significance than the instinctive associations of the sub-human world when those who conduct them are devoid of ideas. If large areas of human experience—political, economic, social, religious—are to be labelled inadmissible as subjects for fiction, then fiction is doomed as an organic art. (3)

---

[17] It is also worth noting that Holtby wrote one of the first books about Woolf, published in the fall of 1932, a book that wrestles with the differences between Woolf's more "poetic" writing and Holtby's own highly prosaic aesthetic.

Honourable Estate begins in 1894 and ends in 1930. Brittain says in her foreword that she has "purposely ended it in the year when the women's movement for equality and the workers' contest for freedom and power had come nearer to the realisation of their ideals in England and elsewhere than at any time since their beginnings in the French Revolution." After 1930, women's rights, workers' rights, and democracy as a governing ideal suffered setbacks. "But the fact that we are now living in a period of reaction makes it the more important to contemplate that which was gained during the four decades which ended in 1930" (3).

No-one who read the novel could possibly have missed its messages, but Brittain's decision to write the foreword suggests her distrust of fiction as a vehicle for her ideas. Certainly, it was a vehicle she was less skilled at maneuvering than nonfiction, and even her generally sympathetic biographers Paul Berry and Mark Bostridge admit that "all too often in *Honourable Estate* the tracing of the course of actual history is accomplished at the expense of the development of the characters who appear much of the time to exist merely as mouthpieces for the novelist's personal philosophies—and rather talkative ones at that" (1995: 346–347). The pontificating (of both the characters and the narrator) dulls a novel that has moments of real emotional power, a raw force common to Brittain's best work.

One way to describe *Honourable Estate* would be as an essayistic novel that aspires to incorporate twentieth-century radical ideals and analysis into the narrative structure of a nineteenth-century realistic novel. We might even say that *Honourable Estate* displays some of the features Woolf was trying to figure out as she worked on *The Pargiters*. It takes no stretch of the imagination to read Brittain's foreword (and some of the more didactic passages of the narrative) as a cousin to the essayistic portions of Woolf's essay-novel. There is no evidence, to my knowledge, that Woolf ever read *Honourable Estate*, and given her feelings about Brittain's writing generally there's no reason to assume she would have had any desire to read it. But there is a good chance Woolf glanced at one or two reviews of the book, and, as she began writing her *Daily Worker* essay and finished final revisions on the proofs of *The Years*, those reviews would have affirmed her fears about the proselytizing novel of granite fact.

Nonetheless, as we have seen, staunchly ideological readers of various sorts have often seemed disappointed that *The Years* does not more closely resemble, for instance, *Honourable Estate* (but with better prose), or perhaps a novel published in the same year: Phyllis Bottome's *The Mortal Storm*, a melodrama about a German family torn apart by Nazism. Bottome had been trained in propaganda during the First World War by John Buchan (writer of *The Thirty-Nine Steps*, among other novels), and she saw *The Mortal Storm* as at least partially a work of propaganda: a book that would offer a logical argument against fascism while also enlisting emotions in the battle through its presentation of sympathetic characters who face hardship and injustice, sometimes with tragic results, but always toward the goal of helping readers feel their way toward the stance Bottome supported.[18] *The Mortal Storm* is one of the few works of the 1930s that, like Woolf's own, saw the centrality of anti-feminism to fascism (and clearly understood the place of anti-Semitism within Nazi ideology), and it is less frequently dull than *Honourable Estate*, but like most politically determined novels, it's not an artful book, not a book offering much of interest now beyond its historical context, and most certainly not a book Woolf could ever have written, even if she had wanted to. Propaganda was anathema to Virginia Woolf's aesthetic.

Aesthetic education, ethical imagination

As we have seen, with *The Years* Woolf discovered a pedagogy different from that of her previous novels: instead of requiring readers to learn a new way of reading for a new form of fiction, she could create a text that invited readers to encounter it as a conventional novel, and then frustrate their ability to understand it as such. Readers would thus need to discover new reading strategies for a novel that seems conventional—a novel that presents specific characters with names, bodies, and manners whose lives intersect in a social system, all represented via straightforward, descriptive prose and dialogue in a fusion that creates situations that feel accurate when read through the lens of a reader's assumptions about human behavior, cause and effect, historical reality, and the systems of the world. (Of course, readers' assumptions differ, but the effect of convention is to control and even mandate such assumptions.) Through an encounter with an apparently-conventional-but-actually-unconventional novel, readers would not only learn the limits of their assumptions, but those assumptions, which so often go unnoticed or unremarked upon, would be made plain to them. The reader

---

[18] For biographical background and full discussion, see Hirsch, "Authorship and Propaganda: Phyllis Bottome and the Making of *The Mortal Storm* (1940)" (2012).

would not be able to remain passive, but would have to use strategies similar to those used with radically innovative texts.

Certainly, for her novels from *Jacob's Room* through *The Waves*, Woolf needed a reader receptive to innovation, but what sort of reader does *The Years* invite? There is no evidence that she thought of *The Years* as a potboiler written to provide nothing more than entertainment; quite the opposite. The turn I see Woolf making from *The Waves* to *The Years* is a turn toward a reader who is not only active, but who is also potentially able to become socially and politically engaged. Woolf had mastered her craft, and could now strike out for new effects. The polyphony of both *The Years* and *Three Guineas* is vital not only to their critique of society, but to their utopian vision of a better, more peaceful future. Their pedagogy is to present readers with some form of polyphonic multiplicity within which flows a yearning for unity, but to leave the unifying to each reader's imaginative work. While Woolf insists that the totalitarian unities of fascism and patriarchy must be resisted and destroyed, she also shows that another type of unity is possible: the unity of paratactic meaning.

In *An Aesthetic Education in the Era of Globalization*, Gayatri Spivak has claimed of Jamaica Kincaid's *Lucy* that what "mainly happens in this novel is, I believe, parataxis" (2012: 354) and we could say the same for *The Years*. On a grammatical/rhetorical level, parataxis simply means the coordination of clauses without conjunctions, but if we extend the word beyond its technical meaning to refer also to the placement of images, objects, and ideas beside each other without overt explanation of the relationship between them, we can see parataxis as one of Woolf's basic strategies in *The Years* (as well as many of her other writings). Once she abandoned the essay-novel form of *The Pargiters*, where the expository prose explaining gaps and disjunctions reduced paratactic meaning, Woolf decided that one of her tasks was "to contract: each scene to be a scene, much dramatised; contrasted" (*D* 4: 261). Her strategy of contraction and contrast creates gaps and juxtapositions requiring readers to supply connections of their own between the chapters and between the scenes within each chapter, between the shifting narrative voices and floating points of view, between the panoply of characters, between history and fiction, between the many repeated words and phrases, between the barrage of sensory images (colors, sounds, smells). Each chapter's prelude is perhaps the most obviously paratactic element, with few of the preludes referencing any of the novel's characters or events and thus immediately requiring readers to speculate on how the prelude connects to the chapter that follows, but parataxis operates at every level in *The Years*. After its prelude, the first chapter begins like a more-or-less conventional family novel, with Colonel Pargiter introduced in his club, talking with "men of his own type" (Woolf 2008: 4) about imperial deeds past, then wandering off to visit his mistress, Mira. Then, just as the Colonel begins to undress Mira with his three-fingered hand, the scene ends and we read a short paragraph in the same mode as the prelude (a brief impression of rain, a street singer, then sunlight) before jumping to the Pargiter children at home in a scene that requires readers to pay attention to a panoply of character names for which we do not yet have associations. The chapter ends with Mrs. Pargiter's funeral, and the next chapter jumps eleven years ahead to 1891, creating the first paratactic relationship between the chapters. Some of what happened between 1880 and 1891 will be referenced in the text, but much will be left for the reader to imagine. Between the scenes within the chapters, there are also gaps, for instance in the 1891 chapter, where Eleanor prepares to give her opinion at a committee meeting but the scene ends with, "She cleared her throat and began" (91), then a space break jumps us to a description of smoke and houses before returning us to Eleanor. It is not until pages later that we learn "she had won her scrap with Judd" (95) at the meeting; later, she will speak of the argument in an exaggerated way that is also not described (98). The absence of a dramatization of Eleanor's argument requires us as readers to imagine it for ourselves, and it focuses our attention not on the content of the debate but on Eleanor's own memory and presentation of it.

In addition to shaping attention and inspiring imagination, parataxis presents us with multiplicity that we must then make the effort of unifying within our imagination. We inescapably feel the need for such effort between the individual chapters, between the prelude sections and what follows, and between the many scenes separated from each other by space breaks (particularly in the "Present Day" chapter), but there is a similar effort necessary when moving between points of view within the same scene. Shifts in point of view are generally signaled by a space break between scenes, but not always, as, for instance, in the moment when Eleanor returns home from the committee meeting. As Colonel Pargiter waits for her, the narrative provides a few paragraphs of the Colonel's thoughts on whether to tell Eleanor about his relationship with Mira, and then, with only a paragraph break, the narrative shifts from the Colonel ("He began to carve the chicken") to Eleanor ("She was very hungry"), a shift smoothed by nothing more than the link of food (98). The chapter then stays with Eleanor's point of view until shifting to a one-paragraph objective scene before returning the narrative to the Colonel's point of view (109), breaking it only for a brief scene with Eugénie's servants (110). The chapters continue in this manner, shifting between perspectives until "1917," where the narrative presents actions and dialogue via Eleanor's point of view alone, and then "1918," the only single-scene chapter, limited to Crosby's point of view. The chapter titled "1918" is followed by the "Present Day" chapter, in which numerous scenes and points of view are juxtaposed and brought together at Delia's party, and the novel ends with one last paratactic leap between the question "And now?" and the rising of the sun over a peaceful morning.

One particularly subtle example of Woolf's paratactic shifts between perspectives occurs in the 1907 chapter, as Sara tries to read her cousin Edward's translation of *Antigone*. She grows tired and hears the world outside: "Everything—the music, the voices—became stretched and generalized. The book fell on the floor. She was asleep" (128). The point of view then moves to a young woman and man outside.[19] They have a brief conversation, then the point of view shifts again: "The moon which was not clear of clouds lay in a bare space as if the light had consumed the heaviness of the clouds and left a perfectly clear pavement, a dancing ground for revelry. For some time the dappled iridescence of the sky remained unbroken. Then there was a puff of wind; and a little cloud crossed the moon" (129). The progression from Sara to an unknown and unnamed couple and then to the moon, sky, and clouds occurs in four paragraphs of fewer than 200 words. The passage moves our imagining first away from a familiar character to strangers and then from strangers to the nonhuman world above. The second part of the movement (from people we don't know to features of the landscape and nature) is similar to many of the prelude sections, but now it is anchored to the people of the main narrative.

In parataxis, Spivak says, "the absence of conjunction is felt as absence, if we read for singularity of language, respecting literature as fiction" (2012: 357). If we read in such a way, seeking out, through a mix of reason and imagination, the absent connections, then the experience of "an overwhelming sense

---

[19] McNees's edition for Harcourt, which I have used for citations through this book, inserts a space break between Sara falling asleep and the shift to outside, creating a greater separation between the points of view. However, this break is not present in either the Oxford World's Classics edition edited by Hermione Lee or the authoritative edition edited by Anna Snaith for the Cambridge Edition of the Works of Virginia Woolf. While many readers would, like McNees, likely read the lack of a space break as an error, the evidence of both this specific scene in the novel and Snaith's meticulous edition suggests that Woolf wanted the point of view changes here to be between paragraphs without added space between them.

of parataxis (and how the relatively more connected passages negotiate it)" allows us to perceive "a formal description, a homology for what the language describes" (355). A lack of conjunction or transition between textual items increases the possibility of the reader becoming confused, and even frustrated, but as we seek paths out of our confusion and frustration, we train ourselves to bridge the gaps. As the paratactic structure continues, revealing the fractal logic in the chaos, we not only continue to practice certain ways of imagining, but we now extend that practice across more and more of the text and simultaneously strengthen previous habits of reading and thinking while also building new habits. Those habits may then be extended beyond this particular novel, thus functioning as a kind of immunization against the ideological force of the conventional novel.

We must come back, though, as always, to imagination. Spivak tells us that "training the imagination" is synonymous with "an aesthetic education." In a foreword to Freire and Donald Macedo's *Literacy: Reading the Word & the World*, Ann Berthoff states that "until the imagination is reclaimed as our human birthright, no liberation will be conceivable" (1987: xvi). Henry Giroux titled his 2013 manifesto for critical pedagogy "When Schools Become Dead Zones of the Imagination." Conventional form can too often become its own dead zone, the literary-aesthetic equivalent of rote learning. But it is not only convention that may suppress imagination; crises also exhaust the imaginative landscape through their life-and-death insistence on immediacy and triage.

A crisis of fictionality

If, as Radin, Transue, Hite, and others would have us believe, *The Years* represents a failure of vision when compared to *The Pargiters*, it seems to me that the failure is in Woolf's stepping back from unsettling the fictionality of the novel. The looming crises of the 1930s impelled her away from fiction and toward a more openly essayistic form, some way to meld imagination with immediacy, vision with reportage, drama with exposition, even exhortation. There were predecessors for the essay-novel form—Robert Musil and Herman Broch, especially—but Woolf could not see her way to making the hybrid form fit her creative desires.[20] Thus, of all the novels I discuss in this book, *The Years* is

---

[20] See Stefano Ercolino's *The Novel-Essay, 1884—1947* (2014) for a fine overview.

the least essayistic, its fictionality unproblematized. Nonetheless, as I have tried to show, its pedagogy invites the reader into an essayistic way of reading the novel, a way of reading that evokes the amputated essay sections of *The Pargiters*.

The Years is not a novel amidst a definite crisis, though it depicts many crises throughout its narrative. Instead, it is a novel in anticipation of crisis, and that anticipation shapes all of its elements. During the time when Woolf wrote *The Pargiters* and then *The Years*, events in Europe became more and more disturbing as fascism gained momentum, and a sense of the future being perilous, uncertain, and dark fills the novel's imagery, particularly as the weight of past years pushes up against the present. Each of the chapters has a specific date until the long final one, which is only "Present Day," an unspecific now. The effect (and affect) is one familiar from Woolf's earlier novels, an effect Paul K. Saint-Amour calls that of the "apprehensive subject." Saint-Amour shows how Woolf's apprehensive subject complicates the standard (Freudian) diagnoses of trauma studies, where "a disaster that cannot be registered in real time and falls into the unconscious has in a sense 'not yet' happened to the subject, making itself known only through encrypted symptoms." When Woolf's fiction depicts shocks and traumas, Saint-Amour maintains, those shocks and traumas may be in the past or they may be anticipated in the future. This is clearest in Woolf's frequent anticipation of a war that would be as destructive or more destructive than the First World War, a war that haunted her and, just as importantly, haunted her entire generation, a generation of soldiers and survivors, making the trauma, haunting, and apprehension communal. Saint-Amour connects the apprehension both to the effect of suspenseful fiction ("Like the reader of sensation fiction, the apprehensive subject is caught in a split or paradoxical relation to the imminent. She is prepared to be taken unawares.") and to an epistemological claim he finds in Woolf's work: "In Woolf's writing, this apprehensive subject, once taken hold of, often recovers and reaches back, arriving at a forceful if belated kind of recognition. We might even say that, for Woolf, anxiety about some imminent blow or shock is the necessary prologue to recognition; that there is no apprehending without apprehension" (2015: 93).

The anxiety and apprehension that lead to recognition (of trauma, but also of oppression and the need for a different world) are depicted within the events of Woolf's fiction but also conveyed via its structure, the choices Woolf makes of what to dramatize and what to leave out. Hers is, as Saint-Amour discusses, narrative fiction that does not rely on suspense for its effects, unlike most popular fiction. *The Years,* for instance, is filled with anticipation, but that anticipation is rarely fulfilled in the moments the narrative dramatizes. Much of the anticipation depends on the reader's own knowledge and awareness, as well. For instance, as Charles Andrews points out, in the 1913 chapter, Martin sits in his room and reads the news of the Balkans.

> Ever so briefly, Martin is aware through newspaper reportage that all is not well in Europe—trouble brews—but turning the page, he avoids further thought and, like many other Britons, supposes that he will be unaffected by the ongoing internecine violence in European hinterlands. Martin's obliviousness to the imminent war captures the tenor of 1914 among the sheltered elite, but it also reverberates with Woolf's growing anxiety through the 1930s about the next war. (2017: 181)

Who is and who is not apprehensive in the novel matters considerably for its meanings, and especially in moments where characters seem anxious for no clear reason, readers must reflect on the sources of apprehension. Such reflection reveals traces of trauma and violence throughout the novel's past. Sarah Cole has shown how violence pervades *The Years* but goes "undernarrated" (2012: 258), its shocks moving through the text "in strange ripples" (259), the violence both "everywhere and nowhere, it impinges and retreats, it is absorbed and enfolded, it resides on the body and then hides itself, it juts out and is re-covered" (260). Yet the reader's attention is rarely drawn to the violence. A reader who does not pause to wonder about the details of injuries, scars, and deformities could, in fact, miss most of the violence entirely. (Even the air raid scene feels anticlimactic if you don't look to where it ripples out across the rest of the novel.)

Just how extreme Woolf's technique proves to be becomes clear when we notice that Cole, who so effectively delineates the way violence works in the novel, seems at times puzzled by how determinedly Woolf has submerged in the background numerous dramatic events that almost any other novelist would have brought to the foreground. But Cole sticks with the text and comes to some valuable insights. Pointing to Peggy's question at the end of *The Years* about how a person can find happiness in a world of misery, Cole writes that the

> question might stand for the text's own: what is the value or truth of focusing on one person, one family even, given the greater panorama of suffering and brutality engulfing the world? It is a question of and for the novel in general, the genre that has done the most to lift the fates of "two people" out of the "millions," insisting, at its very core, that the happiness of one pair does matter. Governed by this spirit of self-annihilation, *The Years* anticipates *Between the Acts* in

suggesting that, with tyranny, brutality, and torture announcing themselves on every corner, the novel is resigning, unable any more to assert its fundamental, defining principles. (256)

The final image of the new morning doesn't necessarily support quite as apocalyptic a reading as Cole offers here, however. Much remains uncertain at the novel's end, much offers cause for anxiety and even dread, but the final sentence, given a paragraph of its own and separated from all else, is: "The sun had risen, and the sky above the houses wore an air of extraordinary beauty, simplicity and peace." *The Years* may annihilate the individualistic ethos of traditional novels—whether this ethos is fundamental and defining is arguable—but its ending is far from hopeless.

In contrast to Cole's dire reading of the novel, Andrews sees *The Years* as bringing the reader toward active pacifism:

In *The Years*, Woolf—ever vigilant to resist propaganda—avoids any strong use of pathos, but the background of the Balkans conflict and a foreground of nonchalant class prejudice place within the reader's grasp the unease that attends our realization that war is coming. Giving readers the agency to compile disparate fragments and to realize the shaping influence of war even when characters themselves do not is a key strategy through which the novel enacts nonviolence. (Andrews 2017: 183)

This seems to me a significant part of the pedagogy within the form of *The Years*. Instead of relying, like Phyllis Bottome and many other propagandists, on appealing primarily to the reader's emotions, Woolf seeks something more complex and subtle, an appeal both to intellect and to imagination, a goal that is essayistic in its desires and aesthetic in its expression.

Woolf's impulse to mix essay and novel, fact and fiction, granite and rainbow was an impulse in preparation for the crisis to come. Throughout the 1930s, Woolf's work struggles both with the novel as a genre and fictionality as a technique. Its pedagogy may be urging readers toward nonviolence and hope, but in its relationship to the novel genre, *The Years* may be read as Cole reads it: as a last moment of novelism, a last attempt at fictionality before the unknowable future brings its chaos. The traces of violence that shaped and scarred so much in past years were now threatening to obliterate the present. What would become of the novelist when the crisis arrived?

3

Into Crisis: "The Tale of Plagues and Carnivals"

For Samuel R. Delany, a sense of crisis provided a spur toward experimental form. In a 1998 interview he said, "Only two of my novels started out […] as experimental per se. The first was *The Tale of Plagues and Carnivals*, which began as a response to the AIDS situation, back in 1983. That is, it grew out of a sense of crisis" (Delany 2013: 222).[1] For writers feeling a sense of crisis, the impulse to adjust their writing toward nonfiction, polemic, and propaganda is easily understandable: crisis is immediate, demanding direct response and direct action. Wrestling with ideas of propaganda and literature in 1941, George Orwell said, "You cannot take a purely aesthetic interest in a disease you are dying from; you cannot feel dispassionately about a man who is about to cut your throat" ([1968] 2000: 126). Crisis creates a sense of immediacy, and it would not be surprising to find a writer turning to nonfiction to address, analyze, and chronicle the crisis. A *Guardian* headline writer summed up the feeling well for a (rather muddled) 2011 column by Zoe Williams, asking: "Should we ditch fiction in times of crisis?"

What does remaining with fiction during crisis allow that dispensing with fiction would not? We saw with Woolf that the move to meld the modes of fiction and nonfiction proved unstable, leading ultimately to her need to write *Three Guineas* to express overtly some of what *The Years* could only imply or gesture toward. In contrast to the breakdown of Woolf's essay-novel, Delany maintains the melding with "The Tale of Plagues and Carnivals." As Woolf was

---

[1] The second work Delany says began as experimental writing is the novella "Atlantis: Model 1924," a work that is not only textually complex but also complex in its use and reconfiguration of biographical and autobiographical material. It is also highly metamodernist. There is much to be studied in the novella, but since it was not written in response to crisis, it is outside the scope of this study.

playing with and critiquing the generational family novel genre, so Delany is, throughout the Return to Nevèrÿon series, playing with and critiquing the sword & sorcery genre (for which Robert Howard's Conan the Barbarian stories are a classic example). As Woolf needed first to incite the reader's expectations of a family saga to set her subversion in motion, so Delany works from readers' expectations about sword & sorcery. Kathleen Spencer said of *Tales of Nevèrÿon*, "the knowledgeable reader is likely to come to this work with an unusually specific set of expectations; and Delany subtly but systematically undermines *every single one* of them" (1985: 64). If someone were unfamiliar with the rest of the series but read the book *Flight from Nevèrÿon* in order, by the time they reached "The Tale of Plagues and Carnivals," they would know they were not reading standard sword & sorcery tales. (As would someone who had read either of the earlier books.) But such readers *would* think that they were reading fiction—and, of course, much of "The Tale of Plagues and Carnivals" is fiction. But much is also not. Navigating between varieties of fiction and nonfiction, as well as varieties of fictionality, becomes one important task for any reader working through this story.

The AIDS crisis pushed Delany to experiment, but the nature of the experiment depended on the assumptions and desires he held about texts and contexts. Those assumptions and desires were fundamentally metamodernist. Though too late to be a Modernist proper, Delany read many of the most famous Modernist texts when he was remarkably young, and as he read more and more, he seems to have been especially drawn toward the queer modernism of Djuna Barnes, W.H. Auden, and others—many of them writers of the later Modernist period, writers of what Mia Spiro has called "'crisis' literature" (2013: 5). Queerness and crisis were linked in the Modernist texts Delany read so fervently, and Modernist forms provided the impetus to push fictional aesthetics beyond traditional conventions. That the reader should have to learn to read the text while reading it, rather than the text being entirely legible via well-worn reading strategies, was a central premise of Modernism, and one that the Modernists of the 1930s made particular use of as their world seemed to be falling apart, because a reader learning to read a poem or novel in a new way might also learn to read the world anew. Crisis, pedagogy, and Modernism were all intimately linked by the 1930s, but the text's ability to offer some sort of resistance to the chaos depended on readers, for "while writing itself can be an act of rebellion when it questions meaning and demands new interpretations of social justice, it is only truly resistant if it is matched with a reader who can be enlightened and transformed by an understanding of the social plots we live by" (Spiro 2013: 246). A text that demands an active reader is more likely to be able to speak beyond its immediate crisis than a didactic text, because within the assumption of an active reader resides an assumption of the reader as someone capable of continuing to think and learn beyond the current situation. Born after the crises of the 1930s had passed (or metamorphosed), Delany was nonetheless able to be a reader who was enlightened and transformed by what he read. As a writer, it was only natural that he should want to aim for the same in his own readers, particularly at a moment of crisis.

The Delany coherence

Samuel Delany's writing career has stretched over more than fifty years, and his interests and interventions have crossed various fields, making any approach to even a segment of his work feel daunting to the uninitiated—what does a mortal reader do when faced with a text that draws from the history of twentieth-century anglophone science fiction; vast swathes of American, British, and European culture (high and low); some of the most intellectually challenging of post-structuralist philosophies; and theoretical mathematics ... to name just a few of the wellsprings for Delany's mature writing. It is no wonder that readers tend to pick and choose among his oeuvre, and consequently that many people see the development of Delany's career as being somehow perplexing. Before continuing on to look at Delany as a metamodernist and at the effect of the early years of the AIDS crisis in New York City on his writing, I need to say a few words about the remarkable consistency of Delany's concerns from his earliest years as a writer to today, and to provide an outline of the development of those concerns through his career.

Within the science fiction genre, where Delany is perhaps best known and most celebrated, his career trajectory baffles many people. A very well-read young critic recently said to me, "One can not say that there is coherence to Delany's career, that there is a through-line," and I immediately disagreed. Delany's is among the most consistent and coherent writing careers that I know, especially given its duration. But understanding the coherence requires reading multiple works from multiple eras and genres, and from some genres that many readers are uncomfortable with: not just science fiction, but also pornography and contemporary philosophy.

We may better understand the coherence of Delany's project by contextualizing some junctures and disjunctures within it. We can periodize, though it is always worth keeping in mind that any periodizing imposes a schema, and any such schema will render some things visible while at the same time making other things invisible. Periodizing needs to be strategic and impermanent. One way of periodizing Delany's work is to focus on his science fiction:

> *1962–1970:* His first novel's publication through his numerous nominations for Hugo and Nebula awards from 1966 through 1970 (winning four Nebulas and one Hugo)[2]

> *1975–1987:* After a period without a new novel, *Dhalgren* is published (officially January 1975, but on shelves at the end of 1974), gaining significant attention and causing much controversy because of its challenging narrative and explicit sex scenes; it will go on to sell over a million copies. After *Dhalgren*, Delany's fiction becomes more narratively and intellectually challenging as it displays the influence of post-structuralist philosophy and literary theory. During this time, he publishes various collections of nonfiction about science fiction, including the original editions of *The Jewel-Hinged Jaw, Starboard Wine,* and *The American Shore*.

> *1987–2018:* After the conclusion of the sword & sorcery fantasy series Return to Nevèrÿon in 1987 (with *The Bridge of Lost Desire*, later retitled *Return to Nevèrÿon*), Delany's work moves away from science fiction and fantasy. He wins science fiction awards for his nonfiction and for his career generally, but his new fiction is either pornographic (*The Mad Man, Phallos*) or not science fictional (*Atlantis: Three Tales, Dark Reflections*). The year 2012 sees publication of his longest novel, *Through the Valley of the Nest of Spiders*, which Delany refers to as science fiction (its second half is set in the future), and which receives some attention as such, but the prevalence, or even preponderance, of pornographic writing in the novel limits its audience. In 2018, the magazine *Fantasy & Science Fiction* publishes Delany's first new science fiction story in decades, "The Hermit of Houston," which goes on to win a *Locus* Award and to be included in *The Best American Science Fiction and Fantasy 2018*, edited by N.K. Jemison.

That periodization is familiar and legible to many readers, and from it we can see some reasons for a critic familiar with science fiction to believe that Delany's career is incoherent: the brilliant, highly awarded young science fiction writer

---

[2] See the Science Fiction Awards Database for details (http://www.sfadb.com/Samuel_R_Delany).

turns into an avant-garde novelist and then seemingly scuttles his own career with ever more abstruse writing and an obsession with pornography. One flaw of this periodization is that it relies on showing only what Delany was able to publish, not what he wrote. (Nor does it show what he read—a chronology of, for instance, Delany's reading of Lévi-Strauss, Foucault, Derrida, Lacan, Kristeva, Barbara Johnson, etc. would be differently revealing.) The first novels Delany wrote were not science fiction, and (as his memoir *The Motion of Light in Water* vividly shows) as a young writer he relied on science fiction because he could write and sell it relatively quickly, helping to pay the bills. This is not to suggest that his turn to science fiction was entirely mercenary; he was an enthusiastic reader of the genre, and discovered by writing it that it could bring together more of his interests than most other modes could. But even as he was becoming one of the most prominent young science fiction writers, he was reading and writing other sorts of things.

With the recent publication of Delany's early journals, we have been able to see that literature, science fiction, pornography, and philosophy have all been of interest to Delany since he was young. Some of the pornographic writing from his teenage years shows a similar style to and common concerns with the pornographic writing in *The Mad Man* and *Through the Valley of the Nest of Spiders*, written decades later. His most disturbing pornographic novel, *Hogg*, was written at the end of the 1960s but could not be published until the 1990s because of its content. As I have written elsewhere, his first published pornography, *Equinox* (first released as *Tides of Lust*), has much in common with his celebrated science fiction of the 1960s (Cheney 2007). With the arrival of structuralist and post-structuralist philosophy to the United States, Delany found new paths for philosophical and linguistic interests already apparent throughout his early fiction. Thus, we can see that if we set aside the idea of Delany as primarily a science fiction writer who abandoned science fiction, a different story reveals itself. It is the story of a black, gay male writer deeply interested in the communities of which he is a member and deeply informed by questions of literature, philosophy, and society.

An alternative periodization demonstrates more coherence while still paying attention to disjunctures: the periodization of Delany within gay male history in the United States, and particularly in his longtime home of New York City. The Stonewall riots in 1969 and the rise of AIDS in New York City in the early 1980s are immensely important moments within Delany's life. "As a gay man in America," he has said, "who was twenty-seven at the time of (to pick an arbitrary date) Stonewall, I spent half my life before it and half my life after it. [...] My topics have changed as both position and view have changed" (Delany 2013: 295–296). All of the science fiction stories and novels for which he won Nebula and Hugo Awards were written before Stonewall in the summer of 1969. The other shift occurs with the AIDS crisis. Addressing readers who wonder why Delany writes so much about sex, Lavelle Porter pointed out:

> Once you address the role of HIV/AIDS in Delany's work then it should be much clearer why Delany's later writing deals with sexual politics in a more direct way. If you've read "The Tale of Plagues and Carnivals," if you've read *1984* and *The Mad Man*, and if you understand that Delany's own mortality was at stake, and that he, like so many other people who survived that awful, scary time, lost so many friends to this illness, and if you saw that the response of most mainstream Americans to the epidemic was "Good! Let the faggots die!" then it should be obvious why a sexually active, politically engaged, gay writer in NYC might turn his attention to sexual matters, and why that writer might believe that the way we think about sex and respectability and morality needs to be challenged. (Cheney et al. 2014)

We could, then, periodize Delany's career as *pre-Stonewall* and *post-Stonewall* (with "Stonewall" both a specific event and a metonym for the start of the gay liberation movement in the 1970s in the United States) and *pre-AIDS* and *post-AIDS*. Before Stonewall, Delany published the science fiction for which he became famous and some of his early pornography, culminating with *Hogg*, which he conceived and began writing before Stonewall, but didn't complete until the early 1970s.[3] After Stonewall, he wrote *Dhalgren*, a book that fuses many of the interests apparent in his early science fiction with the interests apparent in his early porn. (The relationship between *Hogg* and *Dhalgren* deserves more scholarly attention than it has so far received; the two novels benefit from being read together.) The sexual concerns of his work up through *Stars in My Pocket Like Grains of Sand* (published in 1984, but conceived in the 1970s) are those of a pre-AIDS world; from "The Tale of Plagues and Carnivals" onward, Delany writes with intense interest in and concern for the AIDS crisis. In a 1996 interview, Delany said,

---

[3] In the first part of his *Literary Hub* interview with Adam Fitzgerald in 2017, Delany said, "*Hogg* is a pre-Stonewall novel, at least the first draft is pre-Stonewall" (Delany 2017b). The Stonewall riots occurred in late June and early July 1969. In the detailed chronology he offers in "The Making of *Hogg*" (Delany 1999a: 298–310), Delany says that he wrote a first draft in four notebooks between March and July 1969 while living in San Francisco. He first typed it up over a period of six weeks in 1972, then produced another typewritten draft in the fall of 1973. It has the interesting status, then, of being a novel that is both pre- and post-Stonewall.

> In general, what I hope at least part of my work performs—or helps to perform—is a necessary deformation of an older, pre-AIDS discourse, which privileged sexual reticence, into a discourse that foregrounds detailed sexual honesty, imagination, and articulation. AIDS makes such a discursive adjustment imperative. (Today, anything else is murder.) But such a deformation also has other benefits, in terms of the liberation of a range of subjects frequently marginalized under the rubric of "the perverse." (Delany 1999a: 123)

While his early work is certainly imaginative and has moments of significant honesty, from *Hogg* and *Dhalgren* forward, Delany unites his commitment to both honesty and imagination, liberating his range of subjects significantly. While that liberation will necessarily shift when faced with AIDS, the imagination and honesty will remain, making Delany bring all of his interests and influences together in some of the richest and most affecting books of his career.

Metamodernist

A seventeen-year-old Samuel Delany wrote in his journal:

> Great novels: The Faulkner Pentology—(which I consider one book): *Sartoris, Light in August, Absalom, Absalom!, The Sound and the Fury, As I Lay Dying*.
> Proust: *Remembrance of Things Past*.
> Joyce: *Finnegans Wake*. (Don't ask me why—but my God, what a book when it hits you.)
>
> (Delany 2016: 28)

According to his autobiography *The Motion of Light in Water*, Delany and his friend (and future wife) Marilyn Hacker had decided at this point to become writers, and his writing was strongly influenced by both Faulkner and Joyce ([1988] 2004: 96). A few years later, he and Hacker visited with W.H. Auden, and after writing about that encounter, Delany declared in 1988, "Today Auden is certainly the modernist poet whose work I know best," but added, "I don't think influence per se is there." Clear influence may not be there, but allusion certainly *is* there, especially in Delany's early novels ([1988] 2004: 170–171). In a 2017 interview, he said that reading Stewart Gilbert's *Ulysses: A Study* and then *Ulysses* itself was a key moment in his learning to write novels and in the development of his aesthetic (Delany 2017b). Throughout his later career,

Delany would cite Djuna Barnes's *Nightwood* as the novel he has re-read most often and in a July 2012 list of books that "if I hadn't read and reread over the years, I wouldn't be myself," Delany put *Nightwood* in the No. 1 spot on a list that includes works by Auden, Beckett, Faulkner, Fitzgerald, Joyce, Pater, Woolf (Delany 2012b). In addition, he has written at length about Hart Crane, both in nonfiction ("Atlantis Rose … " in *Longer Views*) and fiction ("Atlantis: Model 1924"), and his admiration of the quintessential metamodernist Guy Davenport is substantial—since at least the early 1980s, Delany has repeatedly said that Davenport "is among the most elegant writers at the sentence level to work in American prose" (1999a: 113).[4]

The influences on Delany's novelistic and critical practices are not solely Modernist or metamodernist. Science fiction, of course, has been a significant influence. In a 1986 interview in *Diacritics*, Delany proposed that science fiction exists outside of and in opposition to the modernist discourse of High Art inherited from Wagner (" … Wagner's legacy is that which any modern or postmodern—at the gut level—recognizes as art itself … " [1996: 22]), and he has at numerous times discussed science fiction as a way of reading that prioritizes the object over the subject, while the progress of literary fiction over the last few centuries has been toward prioritizing the subject.[5] Delany uses such a formulation to propose science fiction, broadly speaking, as requiring reading strategies distinct from the reading strategies of literary fiction. He describes a "progress of literary fiction" that is inextricable from Modernist fiction's impulse to prioritize subjectivity over, for instance, descriptions of furniture. (We find this priority explicit in Woolf's essay "Modern Fiction.") Delany's object/subject binary overlaid on a science fiction/literature binary seems to propose that science fiction is the way of reading that best approximates William Carlos Williams's well-known (Modernist) statement of "No ideas but in things."[6] Woolf's *The Years* offers a kind of melding of objects and subjects, the socially

---

[4] In 1983, Delany went so far as to send Davenport what he called (in a May 23 letter to Joanna Russ) "a fan letter." References to Davenport are scattered throughout Delany's essays and interviews, but for a particularly interesting discussion of him, see "The 'Gay Writer'/'Gay Writing' … ?" in *Shorter Views* (1999: 111–114).

[5] For a succinct discussion of this, see pages 146–147 of "Disch II" in *Starboard Wine* (2012); for more complex elaboration, see *The American Shore* (2014).

[6] My presentation of Delany's ideas here should not be taken as complete agreement. The object/subject binary he creates and the science fiction/literature binary he puts beside it both seem to me too reductive to be useful. As for the Modernists, though it is indubitably the case that many Modernist fiction writers sought to increase the priority of the subject, it is also the case that many were fascinated by perceptions beyond the individual subject. For discussion of this, see, among others, Mao's *Solid Objects* and Olson's *Modernism and the Ordinary*.

macroscopic and psychologically microscopic, that, in Delany's object/subject schema, might make it verge on being science fiction.

Throughout his career, and especially since the publication of *Dhalgren* in 1975, Delany has embodied the idea of metamodernism proposed by both Furlani and James & Seshagiri. Born a year after the deaths of Joyce and Woolf, Delany had the proximity to canonical Modernists that Furlani (2007: 150) sees as important to the definition of metamodernism (a proximity both temporal and physical, as Delany's encounter with Auden shows); he has written significant criticism on Wagner, Artaud, and Hart Crane; and it is clear from his interviews and the texts themselves that his novels often self-consciously "extend, reanimate, and repudiate twentieth-century modernist literature" (James and Seshagiri 2014: 89)—sometimes quite explicitly, as with "Atlantis: Model 1923," which he said was written "to see what it felt like to have the experience of writing such a work" as *Ulysses*, *The Waste Land*, and *The Cantos*, three texts he considers to be "for better or worse, our waning century's paradigmatic literary works" (Delany 2013: 225).

Attention to metamodernism is not merely a matter of taxonomy. Such attention helps make visible, as David James later said in describing "modernist futures," "how artistic precedents are regenerated, their initiatives redeployed, and their styles not simply mimed but reanimated for the markedly different characterological, descriptive, or political concerns of the appropriating artist" (James 2012: 31). Furlani, too, emphasizes metamodernism as regeneration: "The metamodernists succeed rather than revive or repudiate a modernism the vitality of whose legacy they understand to depend on renewal rather than veneration" (2007: xliv). Of course, implied in all of this is that we can know and understand a writer's influences. The question of influence inevitably raises problems of the reliability of authors' own statements about their work and the limits of authorial intention.[7] James wrestles with these problems in *Modernist Futures*, arguing that writer's own statements of influence, intention, and ambition "are not simply arbitrary or deceptive but provide another layer for critical evaluation, providing a form of contextualisation that is as legitimate as any cultural or historical one" (2012: 33). For Delany himself as a critic, influence and intention are important

---

[7] If one believes that such intention can even be located, an idea certain types of criticism reject. Certainly, it is the death of criticism to be beholden to authors' stated intentions, but there is plenty of room between being beholden and rejecting discussion of influence altogether. My own feelings are similar to ones William Empson expressed in a response to a "Questionnaire on Criticism" in 1976: "The deep intention may often be a thing the author himself is doubtful about, but this is no reason for forbidding us to recognize the more superficial layers" (2006: 623).

even though, having devoured much post-structural theory, he fully recognizes how problematic and fictional they can be. In "Wagner/Artaud," he declares both that "it is our critical duty to look at art that can still speak to us in, as far as possible, its historical context" and

> If the work is not a manifestation of an intention (is not a representation in signs of a certain psychology), then [...] it can be anything and everything. Not only do all classical standards vanish, but there is no way to distinguish between art and anything else, from found objects and scenes in nature ... to the maunderings of the mad—or of the bourgeois banal. (1996: 42, 30)

In a 2001 interview he asserted that "Above all things, the story, the poem, the text is—and only is—what its words make happen in the reader's mind. And all readers are not the same" (Delany 2009: 100). That is not, though, a puritanical statement of art's autonomy, because *what* the words make happen in any one reader's mind is only half the story, with the other half being *how*. Historical context, ideas of influence, and analyses of intention, however flawed all may be, allow us to account for at least some of the variety of readerly effects a text has produced and may yet produce.

For my purposes, the most important value to situating Delany and Coetzee as metamodernists rather than, for instance, postmodernists is to keep clear their fundamental opposition to propagandistic fiction, since such commitment poses specific challenges during times of social and political crisis. We have already seen how Woolf was torn by just such a commitment during her metamodernist final decade, and while Delany and Coetzee's understanding of language and representation are neither the same as Woolf's nor each other's (though there are significant overlaps, particularly between Delany and Coetzee), nonetheless they share a general sense that propaganda is anathema to art.

Critical fictions

We have seen how at a moment of personal and political crisis Woolf felt drawn to the essay-novel form and then how her attempt to write such a novel led to a particular narrative pedagogy in *The Years*. Like Woolf, Delany has often been drawn to a melding of nonfictional and fictional approaches within his novels even early in his career (e.g., the journal entries that serve as epigraphs in *The Einstein Intersection*, about which Kenneth James, editor of Delany's actual journals, notes: "While the 'Author's Journal' entries describe real incidents, most were apparently written not on the immediate occasion of the events they recount, but shortly afterward and with their role in the novel already in mind" [Delany 2016: 631, note 364–367]). It was in *Trouble on Triton*, though, that fictional nonfiction would take a more central role, one that would be replicated in Delany's work through the 1980s and 1990s.

Completed in July 1974 and published (as *Triton*) in early 1976, *Trouble on Triton* includes the first two pieces of "Some Informal Remarks toward the Modular Calculus": the novel *Trouble on Triton* itself and the second appendix, "Ashima Slade and the Harbin-Y Lectures."[8] The "modular calculus" is also referred to in the Nevèrÿon books; Delany has explained it as "mostly doubletalk" (1999a: 332) and "an algorithm or set of algorithms (a set of fixed operations) that can be applied to any fitting grammar to adjust it into a guiding grammar." The modular calculus, he says, poses the problem "How do we know when we have a model of a situation; and how do we tell what kind of model it is?" The "Informal Remarks" are not the modular calculus itself, but rather "a model of a system" ([1987] 1994: 285, 286, 290), and that model is embodied by both straightforward fiction (*Trouble on Triton*) and faux nonfiction (the appendices).

Other pieces of "Some Informal Remarks toward the Modular Calculus" appear within the Return to Nevèrÿon series, though not all of the series' parts. Delany explains it thus:

> The "Informal Remarks" do not include the first five tales in the Nevèrÿon series. The "Appendix" to the first five tales, however, forms Part Three of the "Informal Remarks." The novel *Neveryóna, or: the Tale of Signs and Cities* is Part Four of the "Informal Remarks." From their position in that book it is undecidable whether or not "Appendix A: The Culhar' Correspondence" or "Appendix B: Acknowledgments" is or is not part of Part Four. The first two tales of volume three are not part of the "Informal Remarks." The third tale in *Flight from Nevèrÿon*, "The Tale of Plagues and Carnivals," constitutes Part Five of the "Informal Remarks." But from their position, it is undecidable whether anything that follows, in volume four (up to and including these notes) is or is not a part. But it would seem that any rich system tends to function through an interchange between what is inside the system and what is outside the system

---

[8] Appendix A is titled "From the *Triton* Journal" and is partly drawn from Delany's essay "Shadows" [*Longer Views* 253–323], which was written concurrently [Peplow & Bravard 46]. "Shadows" is then referred to in Appendix B as the name of a lecture given by Ashima Slade, who was born in the year 2051 [*Trouble on Triton* 301, 297. See also *Longer Views* xxiv–xxvi].

(with what is outside frequently fueling the system proper): and there are always certain elements, such as this appendix, which are undecidable as to whether they are inside or outside—often, though not always, those parts that encourage definition and revision. ([1987] 1994: 291)

Trouble on Triton's "Appendix B: Ashima Slade and the Harbin-Y Lectures," the second of the "Informal Remarks," includes the dedication/subtitle "A Critical Fiction for Carol Jacobs & Henry Sussman," and *critical fiction* is a useful term for much of Delany's overall project. It is a phrase he has used in other contexts, as well, for instance the essay "Wagner/Artaud" is subtitled "A Play of 19th and 20th Century Critical Fictions," where the term does not refer to any formal element so much as it makes an admission to the reader that this essay, like all essays, is a radical selection and arrangement of material, and that ultimately what it is doing is not proposing an argument about some sort of "unprocessed history" (a concept Delany scoffs at in an interview in *Silent Interviews* [1994: 145–146]) so much as it is asking, "What if … ?" (Thus, this critical fiction is a bit like science fiction.) Elsewhere, a "critical fiction" means for Delany an imperfect or even inaccurate concept used strategically, for example: "The division of content from form is a necessary (but only provisional) critical fiction. The reason it is only provisional is because, at a certain point in the discussion, form begins to function as content—and content often functions as a sign for the implied form with which that content is conventionally dealt" (1999a: 259).

If we attach some of the properties of this description to the larger critical fiction of the "Informal Remarks" and the Return to Nevèrÿon series generally, we can see a kind of planned obsolence in them: they are highly provisional and self-consciously incomplete ("*Some* Informal Remarks"), and at a certain point they stop being useful and start blending in with whatever is their supposed opposite. Under such a deconstructive frame, once the critical fiction has done its work of rendering visible what was previously hidden, then it may be dispensed with, or our analysis may shift toward what the critical fiction itself ignores or hides.[9]

---

[9] This is a rather different use of the term *critical fiction* than we might use with Woolf or Coetzee, where in *A Room of One's Own*, *Three Guineas*, and *Elizabeth Costello* techniques mostly associated with fiction-writing are used for argumentative and analytical purposes. There is overlap, though, in works such as *Orlando*, *Flush*, *Elizabeth Costello*, *Slow Man*, *Summertime*, and *Diary of a Bad Year* where the reader's sense of fictionality is teased and frustrated. We might even suggest a lineage between the Marys (Beton, Seton, Carmichael) in *A Room of One's Own*, Delany's fictional academics K. Leslie Steiner and S.L. Kermit, and Coetzee's Elizabeth Costello. But that is a question for another time.

The various "Informal Remarks" show a sustained interest from Delany in bringing forms of nonfiction into fiction—but nonetheless, they remain fiction. The distance between fictionality and nonfictionality is maintained because, as Delany says, the modular calculus is "mostly doubletalk," a kind of fictional nonfiction with certain ancestral lines going at least as far back as DeFoe's *Journal of a Plague Year* and getting perhaps a bit of a spark from science fictional works such as Isaac Asimov's spoof article "The Endochronic Properties of Resublimated Thiotimoline" (1948; see Wilkins 2012). We might be taken in at first, reading the fiction as nonfiction, but there are enough hints within it to raise our skepticism: obviously imaginary history, concepts that dissolve in paradox or incoherence, etc. When the paratexts suggest a fictional text is nonfictional, then readers rely on a network of features within the text to signal its status. If we ignore the fact that the "Informal Remarks" are included within books labeled fiction (and the texts being labeled as appendices may cause us to do that), then we will find plenty of other evidence to make us at least doubt just how nonfictional these writings really are. As we read, we are forced, then, to evaluate the fictional status of the text, and thus the *critical* part of the critical fiction becomes activated. Most, if not all, readers will ultimately recognize that the "Informal Remarks" texts that appear to be nonfiction are, in fact, fictional, and the process of working toward that recognition becomes an important part of the reading experience, an experience that is different from the more immersive experience of reading a conventional narrative. A critical fiction encourages readers to conceive of the text as a thought experiment at least as much as they conceive of it as a story, allowing fictionality itself to become a tool of philosophy, and, in Delany's case, an extension of the speculative *what if?* properties of science fiction.

The first and fourth of the "Informal Remarks" (the novels *Trouble on Triton* and *Neveryóna*) are obviously fiction; the second and third "Informal Remarks" (the appendices) use a nonfictional form for the purposes of fiction. The designation of these disparate texts under a single label pulls them away from their ostensible genres and regenres them as one: no longer novels and appendices, they are united as "Some Informal Remarks toward the Modular Calculus," and so readers who notice this designation begin to seek out similarities between the texts rather than differences. (The differences feel obvious; the similarities, less so.) Genre becomes a lens for interpretation. To regenre a text is to invite a different set of protocols for reading that text.

Grouping novels and appendices together as "Informal Remarks" may affect reading protocols, but it doesn't necessarily cause the reader to reconsider the text's relationship to reality. The appendices are faux-nonfiction, and quickly enough the fauxness becomes obvious to most readers, letting the critical fictions remain unquestionably fictions. That fictionality reaches its limit in the fifth of the "Informal Remarks," however: the novel-length story "The Tale of Plagues and Carnivals," where the obviously fictional and the obviously nonfictional compete for the reader's attention. Here, for the first time, Delany brings fictionality and nonfictionality together in a single text. He does so at a moment of personal and social crisis.

Plagues and carnivals

The first official notice of what would later come to be identified as HIV/AIDS was in June 1981, when the US Centers for Disease Control and Prevention's (CDC) *Morbidity and Mortality Weekly Report* published a notice that "5 young men, all active homosexuals, were treated for biopsy-confirmed *Pneumocystis carinii* pneumonia at 3 different hospitals in Los Angeles, California" (Gottlieb et al. 1981: 250). In the May 11, 1982, issue of the *New York Times*, Lawrence K. Altman reported that a "serious disorder of the immune system that has been known to doctors for less than a year—a disorder that appears to affect primarily male homosexuals—has now afflicted at least 335 people, of whom it has killed 136," and that scientists "call it A.I.D., for acquired immunodeficiency disease, or GRID, for gay-related immunodeficiency" (C1). The CDC first used the term "AIDS" in September 1982, the same month that the first legislation to fund AIDS research was introduced to the US Congress, H.R.7192 (it was referred to the House Committee on Appropriations, which took no action) ("Timeline of HIV/AIDS").

Archival evidence shows Delany likely conceived "The Tale of Plagues and Carnivals" in the fall of 1981 as a response to Bakhtinian ideas, but in the summer of 1983 he started referring to it in letters to friends and colleagues as a story of "AIDS Comes to Kolhari." This places it very early in the history of AIDS literature, as what is generally considered the first "AIDS novel," *Facing It* by Paul Reed, was published by Gay Sunshine Press in 1984 (Nelson 1993: 356). Before 1984, any mentions of the disease within literature were like those of Andrew Holleran's 1983 novel *Nights in Aruba*, where, in conversation, a character says that people "of our sexual demimonde were dying of bizarre cancers" ([1983] 1984: 232) and that this cancer "has everyone so frightened now that they won't just sleep with anyone that moves" (233), but the disease itself remains offstage.

Though it is clear that Delany added an AIDS focus to the story by the summer of 1983, it is harder to pin down the date when he began thinking of adding in the nonfictional elements that would make the story so different from the others in the Return to Nevèrÿon series. I am intrigued by a draft of a letter (addressee unknown) that he wrote in his journals likely between the last week of November and the first week of December 1982 (based on contextual evidence and assuming he wrote the material in order): He describes reading Rilke's novel *The Notebooks of Malte Laurids Brigge* alongside a collection of Rilke's letters, and he notes how much from the letters goes into the novel verbatim. Delany tells his correspondent not to be surprised if paragraphs from letters in which he related stories of his own life appear later in Nevèrÿon tales. The next journal contains significant notes and drafts for "The Tale of Plagues and Carnivals," but nothing yet proving he had settled on the ultimate form for the story. His journals in the spring and summer of 1983 include some musings on autobiographical writing and what such writing of his own might contain—musings that include features later found in "The Tale of Plagues and Carnivals"—but he does not yet seem to have connected his ideas for autobiographical writings to that story. Given the evidence, then, we can say with some confidence that Delany's decision to write the story in the form he did was made sometime between August 1983 and January 1984.

It seems to me a logical assumption that Delany chose the form of the story as a response to the AIDS crisis rather than choosing to fit the AIDS crisis into a form he had already settled on. Yet such a statement is highly speculative, because what is clear from the evidence is that AIDS was but one of the impulses affecting "The Tale of Plagues and Carnivals"—just as important was Delany's growing desire to incorporate autobiography into his writing. The letters and journals at this time show him working through a feeling that his own experiences and point of view were different enough from those of other writers that to write from an explicitly autobiographical standpoint could make a valuable literary and perhaps socio-political contribution. This is the importance of his discovery that Rilke incorporated passages from actual letters into *The Notebooks of Malte Laurids Brigge*: It provided Delany not only with inspiration but also with a certain permission both to write more autobiographically and to transpose writing from such genres as private letters into his public fiction. That transposition would not make significant changes to the words or to the stories told, but would instead envelop the writing within the rhetoric of fictionality, providing it with a different epistemological, hermeneutical, and even ontological relationship to an audience.

Delany's desire to write autobiographically and his sense that the circumstances of his own life would be of interest to readers were not specifically caused by the AIDS crisis (in 1979 he had published his memoir of life as part of a commune, *Heavenly Breakfast*), but given his materialist philosophy and his sense that all personal life is inevitably inflected by political significance, the AIDS crisis would only have increased his perception of his own life experience as being an important body of data. *Experience* for Delany, though, could not be a simple concept. In the essay "Aversion/Perversion/Diversion," written in 1991, he said,

> It is often hard for those of us who are historians of texts and documents to realize that there are many things that are directly important for understanding hard-edged events of history, that have simply never made it into texts or documents—not because of unconscious repression but because a great many people did not want them to be known. And this is particularly true about almost all areas of sex. (1996: 140)

Before experience can be interpreted by history, it must be entered into history, it must be somehow recorded, or else it is invisible. Writing autobiographically for Delany means, in Georgia Johnston's analysis, "translating that invisibility so that the space between discourses allows both discourses, and then exchanging that space of the subject with the reader. The 'I' moves from the individual to the social, through a margin to articulated discourse" (2003: 234). Hence the value Delany sees around the summer of 1983 in beginning an autobiographical project, a project that must not only include a record of his artistic ideas, but also a chronicle of the sexual life of a sexually active gay man in New York City. And not just any sexually active gay man.

As his 1988 memoir *The Motion of Light in Water* shows, and later autobiographical writing expands upon (including his 2017 essay "Ash Wednesday"), Delany throughout his adult life has sought sexual encounters in public spaces such as restrooms and movie theatres, leading him to estimate in a 1993 appendix to *Flight from Nevèrÿon* that up to 1990 he had annually had between 150 and 300 encounters each year in New York City, though by 1993 circumstances had reduced the average to about 50 ([1985] 1994: 366). (This is in addition to sex with his regular partners.) In a September 1984 letter, Delany said, "Every once in a while, the unusualness of my sexual situation vis-à-vis the standard bourgeois world does, I'm afraid, strike me" (2000: 249), and it is in the ways that Delany senses himself as being different from "the standard bourgeois world" (though not necessarily from the standard urban gay male) that his life experiences may be useful material for both art and argument. As a writer, he can be a guide, witness, and interpreter of experiences that sit outside not only the lives of many of his readers, but even outside their imaginations. His impulse to use autobiography is much more than personal or exhibitionistic. The AIDS crisis quickly reveals a significant obstacle for scientific research: the inability of the majority population to imagine, in even the most general way, the experiences of a minority population.

Throughout his writings about AIDS, Delany points to the limitations of research conducted without awareness of how gay urban men live and, most importantly, how they have sex. In "The Gamble," written in 2004, he vividly illustrates this by describing a conversation he had with a heterosexual graduate student in English (Chuck) and an HIV-positive gay porn star and prostitute (B.J.) who had come to one of his readings. B.J. insists he got HIV through oral contact, a method of transmission Delany believed to be under-studied and even unlikely, though the lack of rigorous study of it made any conclusion impossible (I will discuss this topic itself in the next chapter with regard to *The Mad Man*):

> … I said to Chuck: "Oh, you know—I just thought what I really should have asked B.J.: Was he ever in an orgy or orgy-like situation, around the time or in the months before he seroconverted, either on a job or during a film shoot, where someone who had taken a load of cum in his mouth might have licked out his asshole within five, ten, or fifteen minutes. I think that would have to count for getting the virus anally—though he might have been unaware of it, or not even noted it—because no one stuck a dick up his ass. Of course that's something that, if it happened to him, he might not even have remembered it. But I still think, from the kinds of things he was talking about in his general sex life, there's a greater statistical chance that he picked the virus up that way than that he got it through sucking. The problem is, straight people—who, alas, are the ones doing most of the research—don't think of questions like that." (Delany 2005: 162–163)

The explicitness in this conversation is important (and Chuck responds, "Jesus Christ, Chip—I have *never* heard people talk about sex the way you guys were talking about it!") because it shows exactly the sort of knowledge necessary to make the kinds of differentiations that are required for accurate science. Accuracy in such cases is literally a matter of life and death, and shows the necessity for conversations via both of what Delany calls in another essay "street talk" and "straight talk" (1999a: 41–57). Explicit discussion of the varieties of ways people live (and have sex) is more important than simply as scientific data, as Delany said in "The Rhetoric of Sex/The Discourse of Desire" in 1993:

> The material fact that has made it desperately important for people, when writing about sex, to write about what they have done and experienced and seen themselves, is, of course AIDS. This disease [...] is certainly the largest material factor in the transformation of the discourse of desire and that transformation's manifestation in the rhetoric of sex. (Delany 1999a: 34)[10]

It is no surprise, then, that Delany's work becomes much more openly autobiographical from the first years of the AIDS era onward. He had published autobiographical material before (in addition to *Heavenly Breakfast*, mentioned earlier, there are autobiographical passages in "Shadows," an essay completed in 1974 and included in the original edition of his first essay collection, *The Jewel-Hinged Jaw*) but his life becomes much more of an overt topic for his nonfiction from the later 1980s on, beginning with *The Motion of Light in Water*, which is not only an autobiography but also a meditation on memory and textuality. After *Motion*, the late-'80s/early-'90s essays collected in *Longer Views* and *Shorter Views* contain more unabashedly autobiographical content than his earlier essays and demonstrate what Kenneth James has noted as "a conscientious turn toward nonfiction reportage on gay life" (2000: xiii). This turn traces directly back to "The Tale of Plagues and Carnivals," a work that in its form embodies the dialectic tension between fictionality and autobiography, a tension given particular force by the crisis of AIDS.

The AIDS crisis itself, especially in its early days, seemed to prevent writers from fictionalizing, and also from writing novels. "The rapidity with which people died in the epidemic's early years discouraged many from undertaking large-scale projects, such as novels, in favor of more modest literary forms, such as stories, poems, memoirs, and diaries. The challenge for writers working in these forms lay in how to capture a life affected by illness, without simply inscribing it in the stereotypical narrative arc of irreversible decline and death furnished by mainstream accounts of AIDS" (Dean and Ruszczycky 2014: 715). Poetry and short narratives dominated the early days of the epidemic's literary writing, but there was an effect on ideas of language, form, and purpose that went beyond the length of the work. In 1998, Gregory Woods argued

---

[10] This view is similar to a more recent one given in 2015 in the *American Journal of Public Health* by Peter Aggleton and Richard Parker, who write that "Nowhere is the deeply political character of the response to HIV so clear as in the uncritical use of language deployed to talk about the epidemic. More than 25 years ago, Treichler described HIV and AIDS as 'an epidemic of signification.' Yet as time has passed, critical reflection on the problematic use of language has waned. Now more than ever, it is important to ask whether the language and the concepts we use to talk and think about HIV are up to the task" (1554).

that "If the term 'gay literature' is to have any practical significance during the present epidemic, it must be defined in such a manner as to include documents relating to the health of gay men" (367)—documents not only including memoirs and research reports, but also pornography, which became a vehicle of both safer sex education and radical polemic. As Woods notes, the early works of AIDS literature were often not works of fiction: "many of the most effective narratives of the individual's struggle within the AIDS universe have been factual [...] Collections of AIDS-related journalism have made some of the most persuasive contributions to the lasting literature of the epidemic without necessarily proving any more ephemeral than 'creative' writing on the same themes" (367). Also in 1998, Reed Woodhouse, in surveying "A Canon of Gay Fiction 1945–1995" (including Delany's *The Mad Man*), after praising the many poems and memoirs that movingly chronicle the AIDS crisis, wrote, "For whatever reason, the number of AIDS novels, works that cause, as Nabokov said, 'the sudden erection of your small dorsal hairs,' is still tiny" (203).

It is undoubtably true that there were fewer novels focused on the AIDS crisis than there were other types of literature. However, this has sometimes provided an alibi for scholars to ignore what they might benefit from researching more fully. For instance, in Monica B. Pearl's 2013 *AIDS Literature and Gay Identity*, Samuel R. Delany's name never appears, and Pearl confidently justifies her decision to exclude early AIDS fiction because 1988 is

> the year that noted gay novelists published their first works of AIDS literature. Paul Monette's *Borrowed Time* and Edmund White and Adam Mars-Jones's collection of AIDS short stories *The Darker Proof* [neither of them novels] were published in 1988, marking the beginning of a serious and lasting AIDS literature. It was also in 1988 that other previously known gay novelists published their first pieces of AIDS fiction, including Christopher Bram's *In Memory of Angel Clare*, Robert Ferro's *Second Son*, and Ethan Mordden's *Everybody Loves You*. (Pearl 2013: 3)

Pearl's condemnation of earlier AIDS fiction is along the lines of condemnations of, for instance, "committed" novels of the 1930s: "The earliest AIDS fiction, books like Paul Reed's *Facing It*, the first AIDS novel, was desperate and often more invested in instruction than aesthetics" (4). Pearl's idea of literature opposes *aesthetics* and *instruction*, but her ignorance of Delany's work is telling: In 1984, he published a novel-length work of fiction that was invested in both aesthetics and instruction.

From appendix to tale

"The Tale of Plagues and Carnivals" offers clear examples of the pedagogy of form, and to begin our exploration of this pedagogy, we can begin with a change between the first edition and subsequent ones that shifts some of the effect, obscuring (or at least rendering more subtle) one concern of the pedagogy: a concern with the relationship between centers and margins.

The first edition of *Flight from Nevèrÿon* appeared as a Bantam Books paperback original with May 1985 listed as the publication date. This was the only edition to print "The Tale of Plagues and Carnivals" as "III. Appendix A," a liminal label that makes "Tale" both one of the main chapters and the first appendix. Future editions gave "Plagues and Carnivals" the same textual status as "The Tale of Fog and Granite" and "The Mummer's Tale," but moved what in the original edition is an italicized, unlabeled final part to now become "Appendix A: Postscript"—a significant change, given that this part begins, "I beg my readers not to misread fiction as fact" ([1985] 1994: 361), then provides AIDS statistics (updated through 1993 in subsequent editions) and contact information for the Gay Men's Health Crisis. While the postscript is clearly separate from the main text of "The Tale of Plagues and Carnivals" because it does not have the sectional numbering of the rest, the two texts are united within the first edition's "Appendix A," whereas in later editions, "Plagues and Carnivals" is more united with the other tales and the postscript is an item of its own, separated as an ancillary text.

All of the books in the Return to Nevèrÿon series include appendices, though there is some discrepancy between editions (these discrepancies don't, though, shift meanings in the way the differences between the first and subsequent editions of *Flight from Nevèrÿon* do).[11] The relationship of the appendices to the main text is important (as is the relationship of the many epigraphs to the main text). Discussing the faux academic essay placed as an appendix to *Tales of Nevèrÿon*, Kathleen Spencer writes:

> The presence of a supplement to a text—a preface, an appendix, notes, and so on—creates a philosophical dilemma. On the one hand, we have traditionally

---

[11] The largest discrepancy is that the original edition of *Flight from Nevèrÿon* included "The Tale of Plagues and Carnivals" as Appendix A and "Closures and Openings" as Appendix B. The Wesleyan edition includes "Postscript" as Appendix A and "Buffon's Needle" as Appendix B, with a revised version of "Closures and Openings" moved to the appendix of *Return to Nevèrÿon*, a move necessitated by Delany's decision to continue the series after having originally planned "Plagues and Carnivals" to be its end.

assumed that the text itself is primary, and thus is complete and sufficient. However, supplements add something to the text, presumably something important and necessary: that means that the text is not complete after all, since it lacks something which the supplement is required to provide. Thus the supplement is both more and less than the text it supplements. (Spencer 1985: 86)

Spencer discusses the ancillary material in *Trouble on Triton* and *Tales from Nevèrÿon* within a Derridean frame; while Derrida was certainly one of the primary influences on Delany's work from the 1970s forward, the ancillary material can also be seen somewhat more generally within the margin/center context Delany develops most fully in his essays of the 1990s. Analyzing, for instance, the hegemonic discourse of desire, he writes: "What we on the margins have been most able to appropriate of this discourse is the power analysis that so much of the discourse of patriarchy is structured precisely to mystify. In many cases, its demystification is precisely what has allowed us to survive" (1999a: 21). The power/knowledge from the margins is not the power/knowledge from the center.

From Spencer's Derridean analysis, we can see how Delany's aaesthetic-textual choices meld here with what may seem to be more socio-political concerns: The dominant discourse is primary, and for those for whom such discourse is unproblematic, it is complete and sufficient. The marginal discourse, however, makes evident that the central discourse is not exhaustive—and not only is it not exhaustive, it is not sufficient. The marginal exists in excess of the central. The implications for society of such a structure are especially clear in *Times Square Red, Times Square Blue*, where Delany notes that in a democracy it is unacceptable to argue that what is relevant to the marginal is *only* relevant to the marginal:

> People are not excess. It is the same argument that dismisses the needs of blacks, Jews, Hispanics, Asians, women, gays, the homeless, the poor, the worker—and all other margins that, taken together (people like you, people like me), are the country's overwhelming majority: those who, socioeconomically, are simply less powerful. (Delany 1999b: 90)

Here is where the significance of the changes between editions of *Flight from Nevèrÿon* becomes clear. In the original Bantam edition, the argument that the aggregate of the marginal is in fact the majority is physically apparent: the central text ("The Tale of Fog and Granite" and "The Mummer's Tale") takes up about 170 pages, while the appendices ("The Tale of Plagues and Carnivals" and "Closures and Openings") take up about 210 pages. By 1989, when Grafton Books reprinted *Flight from Nevèrÿon* in the UK, what had previously been marginal was now central, and the new appendices only required fifteen pages.[12]

The basic structural differences between the original edition of *Flight from Nevèrÿon* and the later editions have a slight, though meaningful, effect on how readers may experience the text. We can see this effect if we imagine how readers make their way through the book. For a reader who comes to *Flight* after reading the first two Nevèrÿon volumes (and/or *Trouble on Triton*), appendices may *be* fictional but they are not *positioned* as fictional, and so they are read with somewhat different expectations and protocols than straightforward fictional narrative is.

For that reader, turning the last page of "The Mummer's Tale" in the original edition leads to a different set of expectations than turning the last page of "The Mummer's Tale" in subsequent editions. In the original edition, the reader is confronted with a title page that announces the third section/chapter and an appendix before the title (Figure 1), and that reader would then likely assume the appendix is, as all the previous ones are, a text that may or may not be fictional but is nonetheless (unlike the various "Tales") written as if it is nonfiction. With an assumption of a nonfictional mode in mind, the reader then reads the first paragraph of "The Tale of Plagues and Carnivals":

> 1. On—th Street, just beyond Ninth Avenue, the bridge runs across sunken tracks. Really, it's just an extension of the street. (In a car, you might not notice you'd crossed an overpass.) The stone walls are a little higher than my waist. Slouching comfortably, you can lean back against them, an elbow either side, or you can hoist yourself up to sit. (Delany [1985] 1994: 183)

This reader is not likely to assume this paragraph necessarily takes place in Nevèrÿon. Indeed, given the evidence of previous appendices, the best assumption is that the setting is closer to what is considered reality. (The title "The Tale of ... " would be the only element to complicate this assumption, as so far everything titled "The Tale of ... " has been set in Nevèrÿon.) To understand how this matters, we can compare the Bantam edition with later editions.

---

[12] The Wesleyan University Press edition of 1994 continues the Grafton structure, not the Bantam.

III

Appendix A:

THE TALE OF PLAGUES AND CARNIVALS,

or: Some Informal Remarks toward the Modular Calculus, Part Five

> Ours, too, is an age of allegoresis...
> —Allen Mandelbaum
> *Inferno,* Introduction

> "If you believe that," the tutor remarked, "you'd believe anything! No, it wasn't like that at all!..."
> —Joanna Russ
> *Extra(Ordinary) People*

> Does this amount to saying that the master's place remains empty, it is not so much the result of his own passing as that of a growing obliteration of the meaning of his work? To convince ourselves of this we have only to ascertain what is going on in the place he vacated.
> —Jacques Lacan
> *The Function of Language in Psychoanalysis*

Figure 1 Original title page of "The Tale of Plagues and Carnivals," Bantam, 1985.

The Tale of Plagues and Carnivals,

or: Some Informal Remarks toward the Modular Calculus, Part Five

Ours, too, is an age of allegoresis . . .
— Allen Mandelbaum
Inferno, Introduction

'If you believe that,' the tutor remarked, 'you'd believe anything! No, it wasn't like that at all! . . .'
— Joanna Russ
Extra(Ordinary) People

Does this amount to saying that the master's place remains empty, it is not so much the result of his own passing as that of a growing obliteration of the meaning of his work? To convince ourselves of this we have only to ascertain what is going on in the place he vacated.
— Jacques Lacan
The Function of Language in Psychoanalysis

Figure 2 Title page of "The Tale of Plagues and Carnivals," Grafton, 1989.

After the original Bantam edition, "The Tale of Plagues and Carnivals" was no longer an appendix. Its title page now became the same as the title pages of the previous tales (Figure 2). Thus, the reader beginning the story has no reason to believe it is anything other than another Nevèrÿon story. There is nothing in the first few paragraphs that overtly contradicts this assumption; the first suspicion is likely to occur with the last sentence of the fourth paragraph: "Except for this twentieth-century detail, it has the air of a prehistoric structure" (Delany [1985] 1994: 183). (The narrator of previous tales has mentioned differences with the twentieth century, however.) The next paragraph introduces the first-person point of view: "At various times over the last half-dozen years, I've walked across it, now in the day, now at night." (This does not set the story outside of Nevèrÿon, however, like "The Mummer's Tale," which precedes it, is written in first-person.) It is not until the end of the eighth paragraph that the text contains a clear, unambiguous statement that what we have read so far is *not* about Nevèrÿon:

> Give it the pedestrians you get a few blocks over on Eighth Avenue, just above what a musician friend of mine used to call "Forty-Douche" Street: kids selling their black beauties, their Valiums, their loose joints, the prostitutes and hustlers, the working men and women. Then put the market I saw on the Italian trip Ted and I took to L'Aquila at one end, and any East Side business district on the other, and you have a contemporary Bridge of Lost Desire. (Delany [1985] 1994: 183)

When reading any of the post-Bantam editions of *Flight from Nevèrÿon*, we must now revise our assumptions. Instead of the title page (potentially) pulling us out of the fantasy setting before we read the first paragraph, we must do that work ourselves. It's not difficult, but it is briefly jarring, as any experience of assumptions being suddenly proved wrong is jarring. Such a reading experience is a hallmark of a pedagogical structure, and the paragraph's imperative mood not only establishes a narrator–audience relationship but also sets up the narrator as an instructor of the audience.

The first edition of *Flight from Nevèrÿon* emphasizes the margins as the center of the text by labeling the majority of the book as an appendix. Doing so encourages readers to see "The Tale of Plagues and Carnivals" as separate from the other Nevèrÿon tales and to approach it as faux nonfiction rather than fiction. The later editions sacrifice the margins/center subversion for a different effect, setting the reader up to assume fiction and then using that assumption for pedagogical purposes.

The different effects of the different editions end by the eighth paragraph of "The Tale of Plagues and Carnivals," because that is the paragraph that makes it clear that the setting is not Nevèrÿon. Whether the writing is fiction or nonfiction is unclear, but the setting is a world that seems contemporary and realistic, a world people familiar with New York City will likely recognize. But readers of any edition of *Flight from Neveryon* must revise their assumptions again with the second section of the tale, which returns us to Nevèrÿon via mentions of a "kitchen girl" (an archaic term unlikely to appear in a contemporary story about New York City) and Lord Vanar. The section also gives us a third-person point of view, further separating it from the beginning of the story. We might assume at this point that the story will alternate between settings and points of view (which it does), but there is one more feature that we must assimilate into our reading protocols: The section is not numbered simply 2, but rather 2.1. The next section, which discusses Susan Sontag's *Illness as Metaphor* and AIDS, is not numbered 3, but 2.2. (Any assumption that the odd-numbered sections will take place in New York City and the even-numbered sections in Nevèrÿon is quickly dispelled, as the structure is more complex than that.) This hierarchical system of numbering the sections is most similar to Wittgenstein's system in the *Tractatus Logico-Philosophicus*, a system that has led to much argument among philosophers but which in Delany is relatively straightforward. In "The Tale of Plagues and Carnivals," the numbering system both indicates relationships between the parts of the text and also suggests to an informed reader that the text is (or at least wants to appear to be) something other than a work of fiction. Hierarchical numbering is atypical in fiction, but not in mathematics, logic, and philosophy; it suggests a system of propositions that are connected. Though for most of "Plagues and Carnivals," New York and Nevèrÿon remain separate, their connection as part of the system of the text is evident from the moment the reader understands the numbering system of the sections.[13]

A pedagogy of margins

Many of the early sections of "The Tale of Plagues and Carnivals" that are written in a nonfictional mode discuss the limitations of metaphor with regard to illness, and these sections directly answer Susan Sontag's argument that, in Delany's words, "Diseases should not become social metaphors." However,

---

[13] Delany would go on to use the system briefly in "The Tale of Rumor and Desire," completed in February 1987, and throughout *The Motion of Light in Water*, his autobiography completed in August 1987, as well as in the second part of *Times Square Red, Times Square Blue*, " ... Three, Two, One Contact: Times Square Red." It is a system he has associated with the Nevèrÿon stories and with autobiographical writing, but the only text in which it is associated with *both* is "The Tale of Plagues and Carnivals."

Delany understands that metaphors are complicated; they "fight each other. They also adjust one another" ([1985] 1994: 184), so "perhaps the job is to find a *better* metaphor," a metaphor that becomes useful because it "destabilizes short-run strategies, the quick glyphs, the clichés, the easy responses history has sedimented." Such a metaphor, or system of metaphors, would allow "restraint of judgment as well as a certain order of complexity" (187).

In 1996, Delany could reflect on the ways metaphor had worked through the AIDS crisis, saying to interviewer Thomas Long (who proposed that "apocalyptic discourse is America's chief structure for constructing social identity" [Delany 1999a: 131]) that by 1985

> people were beginning to realize that the constraints metaphors such as "plague" and "victim" imposed had much farther-reaching effects than had been heretofore supposed. Susan Sontag's very weak book on AIDS (*AIDS and Its Metaphors*, a follow-up to her extremely strong *Illness as Metaphor*) locates the range of military metaphors as the fall guy in AIDS rhetoric—and totally misses the boat. I know that she never saw my novel. If she had, she might have noticed that the controlling metaphoric structure for AIDS from the very beginning was: "What metaphor shall we use for it?" AIDS has been from the beginning a term-in-search-of-a-metaphor—and, in that sense, both her book and mine fall right into the controlling, dominant metaphoric structure. (Delany 1999a: 137)[14]

Ten years later, in a short piece titled "Art & AIDS" (written for a New School conference panel on "Beyond Lament: AIDS and the Arts"), Delany would express a very different opinion of Sontag's *AIDS and Its Metaphors*, calling it an "extraordinary work" and averring that "To say that it 'holds up' is to pay it a compliment quite shy of its actual import. I do not think a book could be more relevant to us today" (2).[15] What Delany appreciates in Sontag's essay now is its attention to how metaphors control epistemology, ethics, and education. "Passage after passage, I wanted to print out in large letters and post on the walls

---

[14] The plague metaphor has been discussed at length in literature about AIDS, and it is beyond the scope of this study to survey that literature here. Gould cites complaints about the terms *plague* and *epidemic* from as early as 1982 (76 note 34), and Sontag analyzed the term in chapters 5 and 6 of *AIDS and Its Metaphors* (132–156), as did James W. Jones in his 1993 review-essay, "The Plague and Its Texts: AIDS and Recent American Fiction." The metaphor is powerfully persistent and has been given new life by David France, who uses it in the book and (Academy Award-nominated) movie *How to Survive a Plague*.

[15] I am referencing a Microsoft Word document of "Art & AIDS" that Samuel Delany sent me, and use the page numbers here to give a sense of where in the three-page, double-spaced manuscript the passage appears. I have silently corrected only obvious typographic errors. I expect the text will be published in an upcoming collection from Wesleyan University Press.

of all offices dealing with AIDS and AIDS education" (3). What Sontag does not see, however, is that the dominant ideology creates a

> complex metaphoric system in which AIDS is constantly the disease that finally escapes *all* metaphors; it is the disease for which no single metaphor is adequate. It is a phenomenon in which no metaphor is ever taken to extreme, or ever carried totally through, but is rather abandoned midstream and changed to another, so that even a glib reading of Sontag's own analysis, that reads her as saying get rid of the metaphors (or any non-critical attempt to distance oneself from one or another of them), is finally in league with that system. It is precisely because AIDS uses up so many metaphors and abandons them that fuels its stability in the social circuits from which we would try to dislodge it. (3)

Keeping in mind the idea that AIDS is a phenomenon constantly slipping away from metaphors, we might still find it useful for the moment to think of metaphor simply as comparison (an idea Delany himself once proposed [1994: 3]), because doing so allows us then to recognize that the juxtaposition of imaginary and real cities in "The Tale of Plagues and Carnivals" invites readers to think metaphorically—to build for themselves, as they read, a system of metaphor to account for the juxtaposition of the two settings in the text. Though united across a textual field, Kolhari and New York are separate settings produced by separate histories and existing at different levels of fictionality. As such, they are able to produce different systems of metaphors individually; for instance, "plague" in Kolhari does not mean quite the same thing as "plague" in New York 1983. "What metaphor shall we use for it?" is a question that does indeed flow through the text of "Plagues and Carnivals," but because of the two very different settings, any answer to the question, whether from the writer or readers, will not necessarily work in both settings, and certainly will not work in the same way, since the separate histories and different levels of fictionality affect the metaphorical systems. Though, as Delany says, his need to find a metaphor (or metaphors) for AIDS is part of the dominant discourse of his time and place, juxtaposing the fictional world of Kolhari with the less fictional world of New York in 1983 sets up a dialectic that may provide some cracks in the dominant discourse by encouraging the reader to compare what is perceived as real with what can be imagined. Any clearly imaginary world incites readers to think about how that world differs from the reality they perceive themselves to live in—this is one of the important insights of Delany's theories of science fiction, though the process applies in a general sense as much to fantasy, surrealism, or even to descriptions of a real place the reader is unfamiliar with.[16]

Even though, by dispensing with the label of "Appendix" for the longest section of the book, the later editions of *Flight from Nevèrÿon* lose the neat presentation of margins as center, all of the editions maintain a pedagogy that requires attentive readers to consider, cross, and subvert borders.

"The Tale of Plagues and Carnivals" begins by asking the reader to think about Kolhari and New York separately in the text, with the different sections serving as boundaries, but the boundaries become porous as the text continues. First, the New York sections comment on the Kolhari sections: 4.11 begins, "If a mid-twentieth-century orthodox Freudian could return to Kolhari and present Nari with the theory of 'penis envy' […] Nari, a primitive woman in a superstitious time, would probably find the notion intriguing, even plausible" ([1985] 1994: 192). This application of Freud to characters in Kolhari continues in 4.231, 4.31, 4.41, and 4.51, while 4.32 sets the narrator as the writer of the Nevèrÿon stories: "There is something incomplete about Pheron. (Since there *is* no Pheron, since he exists only as words, their sounds and associated meanings, be certain of it: *I* have left it out.) My job is, then, in the course of this experiment, to find this incompleteness, to fill it in, to make him whole" (196). The melding has been quick: 4.11 arrives just under ten pages into "Plagues and Carnivals." The reader thus learns the conventions of this text quickly, and then those conventions are adjusted and adjusted again.

Section 4.5 brings the movement together: Kolhari and New York, fiction and metafiction, tale and autobiography all merge.

> She thought of Lord Vanar and, as an aged woman might at that time, pondered magic, disease, power, and felt …
> An absence? She noted somehow it was hers. No. It's not. It has been inflicted on you by …
> That's me, of course, protesting ineffectually across the ages. But my inability to reach her on that morning, millennia ago, only confronts me with my own failings, incompletions, absences.
> I content myself with noting, then, that she does not much resemble our housekeeper when I was a child, Mrs Bembry. (Delany [1985] 1994: 198)

---

[16] See *Starboard Wine* and *The American Shore* for detailed explorations of this concept. Delany insists on more of a separation between science fiction and other modes than I do, as, for instance, in his discussion of Kafka's "The Metamorphosis" in *Starboard Wine* ([1984] 2012: 135–136). Whatever particular differences in applying the labels *science fiction, fantasy, surrealism*, etc. that Delany and I may have, it seems clear to me that the Return to Nevèrÿon series depends very much on readers wondering about the imagined world and its relationship to our own consensus reality.

Now, fifteen pages into the text, everything that had been set up before as separate has been brought together, separated only by a couple of ellipses. Soon, other sorts of merging occur via narrative shifts in one of the New York sections (5.1):

> "Hey!" Joey said. "How you doin'?"
>
> The man looked up and said, matter-of-factly: "Oh, you're here? I was just gonna kill myself."
>
> "Yeah: How?" Joey squatted down before the mattress to watch.
>
> You gotta understand, Joey told me, I thought he was joking. I was livin' in my clothes and sleeping out, which means I wasn't sleeping much. (Delany [1985] 1994: 201–202)

Between the third and fourth paragraphs there, the narrative shifts from dramatized dialogue to reported speech, the dialogue becoming submerged in the first-person account not of Joey but of the narrator. Toward the end of the story (and section), the reader must be alert to who is telling which story:

> There was no breath, no heartbeat, no nothing. So I left him there with the needle still hangin' off his arm.
>
> But he'd just decided it was time to go.
>
> In the almost three years I've known him, I've seen Joey dragging through the retarded slough of pain that is his biweekly bout of heroine deprivation sickness. (Delany [1985] 1994: 202)

The first paragraph is Joey speaking, but without quotation marks, his "I" now assimilated into the narration. The third paragraph reveals its "I" to be not Joey, but the standard narrator (a textual Samuel Delany), though we only learn this after reading "I've" twice without getting an indication of the shift until Joey's name appears. The second paragraph is ambiguous: grammatically, the antecedent to "he'd" ought to be the same as the antecedent to "his" and "him" in the previous paragraph, since no new noun has been provided; however, the "but" at the beginning of the sentence and the context of the next paragraph suggest that the "he" is more likely to be Joey. The reader must choose: one or the other ... or both.

From here, the text's dialogism expands: some sections set in Kolhari are narrated by The Master (the addressee of "The Mummer's Tale," giving us a different view of him); various writers are quoted (Baudelaire via Walter Benjamin, Jeremy Campbell's *Grammatical Man*, and, at some length, Artaud on plague); Imperial criers shout out through Kolhari that the plague is not an emergency; the (elsewhere stylistically conventional) Kolhari sections are disrupted by section 6, a fragmented, lower-case, unpunctuated representation of Pheron in fever; and the Delany-narrator provides substantial statements from his friend Peter, a volunteer at the Gay Men's Health Crisis.

By the end of "The Tale of Plagues and Carnivals," the text has merged all of its modes, images, ideas, and settings. The final section, number 13, is one of three that have no subsections (the others are 1 and 10; 10 is a metafictional discussion between K. Leslie Steiner and S. L. Kermit of whether the text we have been reading is accurate and effective). In section 13, fantasy and reality collide, as Noyeed, one of the main characters in the Nevèrÿon tales, appears as a homeless man on the banks of the Hudson River, and the first-person narrator of the New York sections, who we've previously associated with Samuel R. Delany, has a conversation with him. The man struggles to speak English ("the accent recalled something Middle Eastern" [354]), telling the narrator that he flew a dragon, but his words are hard to understand, so the narrator says, "Tell me in your own language. Go on. I'll understand" (355), and then an italicized monologue begins, its vocabulary and syntax (and described landscape) familiar to us from previous tales. After the monologue, we read the final few paragraphs:

> "Tell me," I said at last, "since you've only been here a little while, how do you find our strange and terrible land? Have you heard that we have plagues of our own?"
>
> Curious, he looked at me across the fire, turned to the river, glanced at the city about us, then looked at me again.
>
> And I would have sworn, on that chill spring night, he no longer understood me. (Delany [1985] 1994: 360)

Section 13 returns us to the bridge of section 1, but unlike when reading that beginning, the reader is now well practiced in negotiating the movement between New York and Nevèrÿon and between various modes of fiction and nonfiction. Communication between real and imaginary worlds occurs, but any pretense of an omnidirectional communication breaks off in the final sentence. We are left to wonder what we ourselves have understood. As with Woolf's *The Years*, the text provides readers with a collage of scenes, images, characters, and ideas that are pieces within an overall system that readers must unify for themselves.

Delany makes explicit the reader's role in section 11.41[17], where he writes about the limits of narrative fiction to propose what he calls "the *radically successful metaphor*"—limits that show that the radical potential of the text itself exists in "letting the fragments argue with one another, letting each display its own obsolescence, suggesting (not stating) where still another retains the possibility of vivid, radical development." Realizing such potential, though, is "the job of the radical reader" because writers, "whatever their politics, only provide raw material—documents, if you will" (348). The end of section 9.7 had previously declared, "the Nevèrÿon series is a document" (280) and sections 8.5 and 8.55 both raise the question of art as a document of its times ("How can one make a recognizable pattern that *isn't* a document of its times?" [249]), so here we have not only "The Tale of Plagues and Carnivals" but the whole of the Return to Nevèrÿon series set before us as raw material for whatever radical thinking we can make from it.

In section 11.41, Delany-the-narrator discusses the inevitable incompleteness of his portrait of the character Pheron in Nevèrÿon, an incompleteness partly resulting from Delany's own lack of experience with AIDS support groups, but no narrative portrait can possibly be complete without extended imagining by the reader: "One could make Pheron far more 'whole' by thinking in fictional terms precisely where he was among all these possibilities that night with his particular support group, what precisely had happened, and how. Go on, then, *mon semblable,—mon frère!*" (349). With an allusion to both Baudelaire and T.S. Eliot in the final phrase, Delany here exhorts readers to make the characteristically Modernist move of completing the portrait to our own satisfaction via the exertion of our own knowledge, experience, and intellect. We, the readers, are openly encouraged to become activists of imagination. Imagination is vital to any process of learning. Kutz and Roskelly see imagination as the vehicle that allows us to move between fantasy and reality, knowledge and ignorance, experience and fantasy: "the imagination names the active mind, and the mind's activity is a process of making sense of the world through discovery of

---

[17] In every edition after the Bantam paperback, 11.41 is a second, repeated 11.4, but it seems to me this is likely an error. Delany agrees, telling me in an email of September 13, 2017, that he does not remember making the change and doesn't think he would have done so, but perhaps for a moment, when correcting the text for the Grafton edition (which provided the plates for the Wesleyan edition), made the change "to indicate that the first [section] should really not be in the book at all." Given the various and important ambiguities within "The Tale of Plagues and Carnivals," any definite judgment about whether there should be two 11.4s or an 11.4 and 11.41 seems to me worth keeping suspended, though here I will refer to 11.41 for the sake of clarity.

connections and formulation of concepts. The imagination therefore forges the essential link between the outer and inner world, between object and perceiver" (221). That essential link explains the textual dance between the two worlds of Nevèrÿon and early 1980s New York City. The textual dance between the fictional and nonfictional modes teaches the reader how to use imagination to discover knowledge, even if the knowledge discovered is more about the limits of what can be known than about anything else.

Nevèrÿon is clearly imaginary, while the diaristic form of the New York material creates an impression of nonfictionality. The reader who wants the fantasy story must either skip the New York material or figure out a reading strategy to unify it with the Nevèrÿon material; the reader who prefers the diaristic/journalistic mode of the New York material must do the same. The sections are not entirely separate, however, and as the novel continues, they overlap more and more. One pedagogy of the text, then, is to frustrate readers' genre expectations and to provide the readers who continue reading with some tools to turn frustration into understanding. The possibilities of that understanding become clear when we consider Delany's postscript:

> I beg my readers not to misread fiction as fact. *The Tale of Plagues and Carnivals* is, of course, a work of imagination; and to the extent it is a document, largely what it documents is *misinformation, rumor,* and *wholly untested guesses* at play through a limited social section of New York City during 1982 and 1983, mostly before the 23 April 1984 announcement of the discovery of a virus (human t-cell lymphotropic virus [HTLV-3]) as the overwhelmingly probable cause of AIDS. (Delany [1985] 1994: 361)

Again and again throughout "Plagues and Carnivals," the reader must negotiate various levels of fictionality, particularly in the sections that seem to be nonfictional, not only because the fictional and nonfictional modes seem sometimes to weave into (and through) each other, but because by the end of the text the fictional and nonfictional have merged: The figure we have come to associate with Samuel R. Delany has a conversation on Riverside Drive with a figure who seems to be Noyeed from Nevèrÿon. The next sentence after "And I would have sworn, on that chill spring night, he no longer understood me" is the first of the Postscript: "I beg my readers not to misread fiction as fact."

If Delany had simply wanted readers not to misread fiction as fact, he would have given them a work of fact. Instead, he requires readers to learn how to separate fiction and fact from the text, to understand how fiction and fact work together, and to acknowledge when fiction and fact cannot be separated. Though as a writer Delany is more fond than most of italicizing words, the words he italicizes in the first paragraph of the Postscript deserve their emphasis, because the text provides us not with lots of fact to separate from fiction, but rather lots of "*misinformation, rumor,* and *wholly untested guesses.*" The Postscript does the didactic, factual work; it is the text before the Postscript that provides the pedagogy helping readers to understand why the epistemological skills the text requires are necessary and important. Before we can make good use of the information in the Postscript, we must practice ways of thinking about not only that information, but also about the contexts affecting its status and transmission as information.

4

Improper Arts: *The Mad Man*

The feelings excited by improper art are kinetic, desire or loathing. Desire urges us to possess, to go to something; loathing urges us to abandon, to go from something. The arts which excite them, pornographical or didactic, are therefore improper arts. The esthetic emotion (I used the general term) is therefore static. The mind is arrested and raised above desire and loathing.
—James Joyce, *Portrait of the Artist as a Young Man*

In the third update to his "Tales of Plagues and Carnivals" postscript, written in July 1988 (for the Grafton edition of *Flight from Nevèrÿon* in the UK), Delany addressed the effect of AIDS on his own life: "In spring of '84 I could write that personally I knew no one with the disease. Today it is the single largest slayer among my friends and acquaintances" ([1985] 1994: 364). As the crisis deepened, as knowledge of the disease's etiology and vectors developed, as AIDS came to be seen not as a local problem but an international health emergency, as political activism grew more and more sophisticated in its quest to increase public awareness and influence medical and political institutions, Delany's writing strategies shifted.

Whenever asked, Delany denied being an AIDS activist, saying, for instance, in a 1996 interview, "Outside of writing and writing-related activities (lecturing to and talking with various groups, usually in colleges around the country), I've done very little. I am not a member of any organization" (1999: 125). Jeffrey Tucker has written that "in his numerous works of fiction and nonfiction essays that address AIDS [...] Delany effects his own brand of AIDS activism" (2004: 233), which, whether we agree with the idea of writing-as-activism or not, does identify an impulse within many of Delany's writings from 1983 through the 1990s, and helps explain some of the shifts in his writing career during that time: an impulse to address (and perhaps shape) the discourse of AIDS in a way that would not reify homophobic and heteronormative assumptions.

In 1987, Paula Treichler wrote that the "homophobic meanings associated with AIDS continue to be layered into existing discourse" because the "text constructed around the gay male body—the epidemic of signification so evident in the conceptions cited above and elsewhere in this essay—is driven in part by the need for constant flight from sites of potential identity and thus the successive construction of new oppositions that will barricade self from not-self" (285). Those barricades were in need of storming: "The question is how to disrupt and renegotiate the powerful cultural narratives surrounding AIDS. Homophobia is inscribed within other discourses at a high level, and it is at a high level that they must be interrupted and challenged" (285–286). In many ways, Delany's work had sought at least since *Equinox*, *Hogg*, and *Dhalgren* to interrupt and challenge homophobic discourses, but from "The Tale of Plagues and Carnivals" onward, it would add an energetic, radical intervention into the "powerful cultural narratives surrounding AIDS" that Treichler identifies.

The writer in crisis

After *Return to Nevèrÿon* (originally released as *The Bridge of Lost Desire*) in 1987, Delany published no new science fiction or fantasy until his 2012 novel *Through the Valley of the Nest of Spiders*, which in its first half or so is set in something like the recent past and present, then extends into the future.[1] From 1987 to 2012, his fiction tended toward the recent past and present (*The Mad Man*, *Dark Reflections*) or historical topics (*Atlantis: Three Tales*, *Phallos*). In a 2014 roundtable discussion of Delany occasioned by his being named a Grand Master by the Science Fiction Writers of America, critic Michael Dirda efficiently summed up common feelings about Delany, particularly within the science fiction community:

> Given that Delany was so wonderful when a young writer, what happened? Why have his later books proven to be so problematic? Have we, as readers,

---

[1] *They Fly at Çiron*, published in 1993, included some new material, but it was an expansion of material written in the 1960s. It has most recently been reprinted as part of the 2015 omnibus collection *A, B, C: Three Short Novels*, where Delany writes in the introduction: "Although *They Fly at Çiron* was, in fact, the third of the three [novels] here to be published [...], while I think of it as my second novel, actually it was my nineteenth published" (xiv).

simply not been able to keep up with him? Or did his prodigious intellectuality gradually inhibit anything resembling conventional storytelling? His career—prodigy, master, academic, grand old man—isn't all that unusual, except that he and most of science fiction diverged and have never, it would seem, really come back together again. (Zinos-Amaro 2014)

As an account of what many (especially heterosexual) science fiction fans feel about Delany's career, Dirda's is an accurate representation. The various participants in the roundtable discussion define Delany's "early work" in two different ways: for some readers, it means "pre-*Dhalgren*," for others it means "pre-*Stars in My Pocket Like Grains of Sand*." As I discussed in the previous chapter, such definitions hide the major social influences of the gay liberation movement and the AIDS crisis on Delany's development as a writer. Delany began drafting *Stars in My Pocket Like Grains of Sand* in the late 1970s and had a substantially completed draft by the spring of 1983, when he began sending it to friends. Bantam originally scheduled it for May 1984 publication, but postponed it to December.[2] Though the novel was finished while Delany's awareness of AIDS was increasing, it was a novel conceived and mostly written before AIDS had become a crisis for him. That, along with the end of a long-term relationship, contributed to his inability to write the announced sequel, *The Splendor and Misery of Bodies, of Cities*, as he discussed in a 2009 interview:

> I was in a major relationship at that time, that kind of fueled the first volume, *Stars in My Pocket Like Grains of Sand*. And that relationship broke up, and that was the beginning of the Eighties, at the same time the AIDS situation came in. A lot of it, as the diptych was originally planned out, was a celebration of a lot of the stuff I saw at the time in the gay world. Sort of in allegorical form, a lot of that was being celebrated. There was a lot of the gay situation that made me rethink some of that, not in any kind of simplistic way, but in a fairly complicated way. So between the personal breakup, which was an eight-year relationship that came to an end, and the changes in the world situation, there were other things that sort of grabbed my interest more. (Anders 2009)

[2] The first notes toward what would eventually become *Stars in My Pocket Like Grains of Sand*, at least that I've been able to identify, appear in Delany's journals in late 1974/early 1975. The first piece of what is now recognizable as the opening page of the novel appears in a journal of 1977. Work continues in that journal alongside draft material of *Neverýona*. Between October and December 1982, Delany was making notes on what work remained for *Stars* while also beginning to draft small pieces of its sequel, *The Splendor and Misery of Bodies, of Cities*, and in a letter of February 18, 1983, to Robert Bravard he says he had lunch with his Bantam editor who has scheduled *Stars* for May 1984 release (and also announces that he has just returned from a doctor's appointment in which he was told he does not have any signs of AIDS). In May 1983, he sent a copy of the manuscript of *Stars* to Bravard.

In some ways, this statement downplays the crisis in Delany's life at that time. As readers of *1984: Selected Letters* would be aware, *Splendor and Misery* was essential to any hope Delany had of escaping the perilous financial situation he was in at the time, and which haunted his life for at least the next decade. He was unable to get very far in writing the book, however, and between *The Bridge of Lost Desire* (*Return to Nevèrÿon*) in 1987 and *The Mad Man* in 1994, no new Delany novels appeared, a gap almost as long as that between *Nova* and *Dhalgren* (though unlike earlier, in the later gap, Delany wrote a significant body of nonfiction). As with the earlier gap, the novel that resulted was significantly different from what Delany had published before.

Though concerned with sexual practices, "The Tale of Plagues and Carnivals" is not pornographic.[3] Though pornographic, Delany's earlier novels *Equinox* (aka *The Tides of Lust*) and *Hogg* were written more than a decade before the AIDS crisis. *The Mad Man* is, then, his first post-AIDS pornography, and Delany employs pornography to explore crucial questions about AIDS and urban gay male culture. In addition, at this time Delany began full-time work teaching at the University of Massachusetts, Amherst; this experience, along with the beginning of his relationship with Dennis Rickett (chronicled in the 1999 graphic narrative *Bread and Wine*), would provide some of the seeds for *The Mad Man*, a book of which Delany said "the most important genre—or subgenre—it takes to itself is the 'academic novel'. [...] Exploding, or just messing with, the expectations of the academic novel is where it does its most subversive work" (1999a: 312).

The Mad Man is a long novel (about 500 pages in its print editions) telling the story of a quest by its narrator, John Marr, to find out what happened to the up-and-coming philosopher Timothy Hasler, stabbed to death when he was twenty-nine in 1973 in a gay bar. Marr is a graduate student in philosophy, a black man and a gay man; Hasler was gay and Korean American. Marr finds some solutions to the mysteries, but he also discovers a lot about himself and how his own sexual desires overlap with Hasler's. Marr ends up in a relationship with a homeless white man known as Leaky (another homeless man Marr has sex with goes by the name Piece of Shit), and the novel includes many long, detailed scenes of sexual activity, much of it involving urine and feces. Marr narrates

---

[3] Delany insists that his pornography be seen as pornography (particularly because his theory of reading requires a clarity of genres): "*The Mad Man* is a serious work of pornography. I suppose I ought to be flattered by some readers' confusing it with realism. But, finally, it is a pornographic work. [...] Those who say it is not a pornographic work (and that I am being disingenuous by saying that it is) are, however well-intentioned, just wrong" (1999a: 133–134).

the story from the period when Delany was writing it ("It's now 1994, going on '95" [Delany [1994] 2015: Kindle loc. 9699 of 11147; hereafter K9699, etc.]), and the events cover the period from Marr's entrance to graduate school in the late 1970s up to the early 1990s. Though the subject matter in summary seems perhaps bleak and disturbing, that is not at all the tone of the book. Ray Davis calls *The Mad Man* "the cheeriest of Delany's novels" up to that time (1996: 128), and Davis's claim seems to me true (though a later novel, published after Davis's essay, *Through the Valley of the Nest of Spiders*, is, if anything, even cheerier—and even dirtier). *The Mad Man* is in numerous ways a truly subversive novel, and its tone is part of the subversion.

One element of the subversive work of *The Mad Man* is to infuse the academic novel genre with other genres: porn, crime fiction, social realism, philosophy. Such generic mixing serves a specific purpose for Delany: to invite (and incite) certain ways of reading, for, as he has said, "no genre (or its language) is necessarily subversive—or even challenging—by itself. The challenge—the subversion—is always in the way a specific text is read by a specific reader. That's why readers—and articulated readings, in the form of criticism—are so important" (1999a: 311). Reading conventions elicit and control readers' expectations for a text, and those expectations affect how that text is interpreted and evaluated, as we have seen in the cases of Woolf's *The Years* and Delany's "The Tale of Plagues and Carnivals." What *The Mad Man* gives us is a more complex field of genres than any of Delany's previous novels, requiring readers to learn to switch or blend reading conventions nimbly if they are to grasp an overall meaning for the novel. That one of the primary genres Delany invokes in *The Mad Man* is not just *pornography* but *urophilic and coprophilic pornography* adds another level to the challenge, because such pornography is, for many readers, repellent, even nauseating, a feeling that may be an obstacle to the careful practice of shifting reading conventions. This, too, though, is something that readers can learn from if they work through it: As Reed Woodhouse writes, "*The Mad Man* constantly forces the reader to reexamine the whole question of sexual desire: how it should be expressed, whether it should be restrained, and if so, by what means" (1998: 213). Call it the Pedagogy of the Repulsed.

Art and sex can both be pedagogical. In *Cruising Utopia*, José Esteban Muñoz discusses how in *The Motion of Light in Water* Delany juxtaposes his at-first-disappointed experience of Allan Kaprow's *Eighteen Happenings in Six Parts* (an experience of art that he first approached with the wrong expectations, then, through experiencing and reflecting on it, learned new ways of perceiving the work and developed a richer set of expectations for future encounters) with his early experiences of public sex, first among a mass of men seeking quick sex on the Hudson piers and then at the St. Mark's Baths. Muñoz reads all three (*Eighteen Happenings*, the piers, the Baths) as avant-garde performances, with Delany's representation of his visit to the piers as a discovery of "a care of the self that encompassed a vast care for others" (2009: 51), and then his first visit to the bathhouse as an apex of aesthetic, sexual, and utopian possibilities:

> His moment of seeing the whole of public sex is a utopian break in the narrative—it is a deviation from the text's dominant mode of narration. Public sex culture revealed the existence of a queer world, and Kaprow's happening explained the ways in which such utopian visions were continuously distorted. [...] Kaprow's performance and the piers were adjacent happenings that presented only shades of the whole; the blue light of the bathhouse offered a glimpse of utopia. (52)

Muñoz's focus is utopia, so though he notes the hermeneutical development described in *Motion*, he does not emphasize the insight Delany's wrestling with the meaning of Kaprow's happening causes:

> Mine was the disappointment of that late romantic sensibility we call modernism presented with the postmodern condition. And the work I saw was far more interesting, strenuous, and aesthetically energetic than the riot of sound, color, and light centered about actorly subjects in control of an endless profusion of fragmentary meanings that I'd been looking forward to. Also it was far more important: as a representation and analysis of the situation of the subject in history, I don't think Kaprow's work could have been improved on. And, in that sense, *Eighteen Happenings in Six Parts* was about as characteristic a work as one might choose in which to experience the clash that begins our reading of the hugely arbitrary postmodern. (Delany [1988] 2004: 208)

What Delany describes here is (among other things) the development of his aesthetic knowledge beyond what he had learned from the Modernism that had to that point shaped his understanding of the value and possibilities of art. This development required him not only to encounter a work of avant-garde performance, but to be productively frustrated by it: "I'd expected a unified theatrical audience before some temporally bounded theatrical whole. But it was precisely in this subversion of expectations about the 'proper' aesthetic employment of time, space, presence, absence, wholeness, and fragmentation, as well as the general locatability of 'what happens,' that made Kaprow's work signify," though he did not immediately have access to the performance's systems of signification because they were alien to him ([1988] 2004: 206–207). As such, he was forced to start from what he knew and expected, and then to confront the failure of the systems of meaning (conventions, expectations, protocols, assumptions) that he applied: "Figuring it out for myself, I began by reviewing my expectations" (205).

Though he does not analyze his first encounters of the piers and the bathhouse as fully as his experience of Kaprow's work, Delany tells the stories in detail across the chapters of *The Motion of Light in Water*, showing how his curiosity and desire move him from bewilderment and hesitation to full participation in and enjoyment of what the sites had to offer. He began an assumption that the piers might be "kind of scary" (216) and on first encountering the bathhouses he felt "a kind of heart-thudding astonishment, very close to fear" (292), but he did not stop there; he entered the experiences and learned what they could teach. His expanded knowledge and experience then helped him understand the worlds he entered, and how they related to the wider world, more fully, much as his reflections on Kaprow's happening allowed him to expand his sense of art and history:

> Institutions such as subway johns or the trucks, while they accommodated sex, cut it, visibly, up into tiny portions. It was like *Eighteen Happenings in Six Parts*. No one ever got to see its whole. These institutions cut it up and made it invisible—certainly much less visible—to the bourgeois world that claimed the phenomenon deviant and dangerous. But, by the same token, they cut it up and thus made any apprehension of its totality all but impossible to us who pursued it. And any suggestion of that totality, even in such a form as Saturday night at the baths, was frightening to those of us who'd had no suggestion of it before—no matter how sophisticated our literary encounters with Petronius and Gide, no matter what understandings we had reached with our wives. (Delany [1988] 2004: 293)

Totalities may be impossible to know, and lack of an adequate hermeneutical frame (the knowledge and experience that shape expectations) may make some encounters both frustrating and frightening, but more can be known, even if the total can't be exhausted, and hermeneutical frames can be reconfigured and expanded. Experiences in life allow this, but so do experiences of reading. Moments of crisis make the distance between life and reading feel too great, and so the writer in crisis feels an imperative to seek out new ways of writing that reduce the distance, that provoke new ways not only of reading, but also, perhaps, of living.

Pornotopia

A disclaimer prefacing *The Mad Man* provides readers with a lens through which to view the novel:

> *The Mad Man* is a work of fiction—and fairly imaginative fiction at that. No character, major or minor, is intended to represent any actual person, living or dead. (Correspondences are not only coincidental but preposterous.) Nor are any of its scenes laid anywhere representing actual establishments or institutions. Certain parks, commercial sites, churches, and city landmarks, mentioned as locations of minor off- or on-stage actions, do exist (or have existed). But these mentions are only to lend verisimilitude to what the reader is expected to take wholly as a pornotopic fantasy: a set of people, incidents, places, and relations among them that have never happened and could never happen for any number of surely self-evident reasons. (Delany [1994] 2015: K30-35)

Pornotopic has a specific meaning for Delany: "'Pornotopia' is not the 'good sexual place.' [...] It's simply the 'sexual place'—the place where all can become (apocalyptically) sexual. 'Pornotopia' is the place where pornography occurs—and that, I'm afraid, is the world of *The Mad Man*" (1999a: 133). Pornography as a genre is concerned with arousal, but as Roger Bellin pointed out in a review of Delany's later *Through the Valley of the Nest of Spiders*, the effect of Delany's pornographic writings is for many, if not most, readers *libidinal estrangement*: "all the characters' pleasures, all their 'glittering extremities,' are decidedly not shared by their reader, and the sheer quantity of verbiage devoted to bare descriptions of who drank or ate what, while who else put his penis where, might strain the limits of anyone's patience." Delany himself made a similar point in the essay "The Scorpion Garden", meant as a preface to *Hogg*, where he writes that though "the majority of the goings-on inside [the novel] depict sex between males, I would be astounded if even a plurality of male homosexuals found these goings-on particularly to their tastes" (1989: 13–14). In an accompanying essay, "'The Scorpion Garden' Revisited: A Note on the Anti-Pornography of Samuel R. Delany," published under the non de plume of K. Leslie Steiner (whose "scholarship" appears in the Nevèrÿon books as well), *Hogg* is said to bypass eroticism because of its novelistic richness—the "sheer quantity of verbiage" Bellin noted—so that even if "a particular act described happened to be Your Thing, he is always telling you *too* much about it for you to lapse into the fantasy state necessary for excitement" (18). The overabundance of detail,

Delany-as-Steiner argues, moves the reader toward a more analytical position with regard to the text, because the reader has encountered an incompatability of genre expectations, since even the best pornography tends toward a thinness of traditional novelistic detail.

Whether a reader is estranged by the acts depicted (libidinal estrangement) or by the thickness of the novelism (genre estrangement), the result is more or less the same: We become distanced from the narrative, pulled from the immersion in its imaginative world, and likely to wonder, "Why am I reading this?" That may be a useful question for readers to ask if they are to analyze the text, but it is not useful for keeping them reading. If we are to continue, something else must urge us forward. A text that is solely pornographic and does not arouse a particular reader is useless to that reader (though it may be useful to a different reader). Part of the importance of the other genres *The Mad Man* invokes is that they make reading itself a valuable activity even if the pornographic elements are not arousing to individual readers. If we are aroused, then all the better, but if we are not, then the other generic elements pull us along, and by continuing to read we continue to consider the content and purpose of the pornographic material.

In many ways, the pedogogic power of *The Mad Man* is increased for the reader who does *not* respond with arousal to the pornography, and it is a pedagogic power somewhat different from that of Delany's pornographic writing before this novel. There is a new groundedness in familiar reality with *The Mad Man*. Where *Equinox* is a wild fantasy and *Hogg* a tale of relentless sadistic horror, *The Mad Man* begins from a point of more familiarity to many of its readers, given that it is set in contemporary New York and the world of academia, a world at least vaguely familiar if not from a reader's personal experience then perhaps from representations in media and the culture generally. For the sort of readers *The Mad Man* was first marketed to (mostly gay men, mostly urban, mostly American), the characters are likely more immediately familiar from life than those of *Equinox* or *Hogg*. The familiarity is an important effect, because it lures readers into assuming a certain congruence between the characters' desires and their own. The extent and variety of the desires and acts in the novel then pose a challenge wherein the familiar and arousing get mixed with the unfamiliar and unarousing, even disgusting. Such readers must then confront the fact of not being aroused by what does, in fact, arouse other people, including the (familiar, sympathetic) characters in the novel.

Even the reader who skips through the many, many pages of pornographic writing in *The Mad Man* must wonder why there are so very many pages of such material. The question answers itself if you find that material arousing, but if not, then you must imagine people for whom this material is more arousing than tedious, and because such people are characters in the novel, you must test your ideas against the representations of those characters. The reader has now entered into the pedagogy. For instance, if a reader thinks that coprophilia is more than "not my thing" but also disgusting and therefore immoral, then that reader will, if they continue reading the novel, have to come to some reconciliation with a representation of characters who get much pleasure and little harm from coprophilia. The pornography is pornography, but it is also in service to the novel's other goals, both philosophical and social. Even if the porn in *The Mad Man* is not your porn, you can gain much from reading it because of the intellectual structure that frames and shapes the pornographic material.

In *Times Square Red, Times Square Blue* (which is in many ways to *The Mad Man* what Woolf's *Three Guineas* is to *The Years*), Delany states a credo: "given the mode of capitalism under which we live, life is at its most rewarding, productive, and pleasant when large numbers of people understand, appreciate, and seek out interclass contact and communication conducted in a mode of good will" (1999b: 112). Much of *The Mad Man* serves to illustrate this idea, and in doing so shows not only a social vision notably different from that of mainstream American society at the time of the novel's publication (and now, for that matter), but also a perspective on the AIDS crisis that is both a consequence and extension of that vision.

The effect is, in some ways, as didactic as an essay, even if *The Mad Man* rarely breaks into overtly essayistic discourse. The didacticism may be an inescapable effect of the novel's genre as pornography. In "The Scorpion Garden" Delany declared, "Pornography is didactic. That is one of its intrinsic qualities—a quality that has more to do with the time of *at*tention we pay to it than the *in*tention of the writer" (1989: 2). It's not a claim that he supports with much clarity in the essay, but that is partly because the essay was written in 1973, before a maturation of his critical insight, and much of his writing about *Hogg* seems to me to show a certain defensiveness and confusion, given how repulsive the book is, and yet, as he says, "it is the most rigorous and honest fictional exploration I can render of what crawls and wriggles and grubs among the roots of my own scorpion garden" (1989: 14). By the time he wrote *The Mad Man*, Delany had had time to work out his ideas about sex and fiction more fully, and the AIDS crisis made a didactic mode of sex-focused fiction especially relevant: Because of bad information, people were dying.

Steven Shaviro provides a useful entry to *The Mad Man*'s relationship to AIDS discourse:

> *The Mad Man* is a novel quite cognizant of, and continually haunted by, death: in the form of Hasler's death which is the starting-point of the narrative, and the homeless man's death which is its conclusion, and more generally in the ever-present reality of AIDS in the world of its narrator. But this death is in no way intrinsic to or carried by the sexual acts that the narrative describes; rather, death *always comes from outside* (to use or abuse a phrase from Deleuze). Death arrives in *The Mad Man*, and the book thereby takes on a fully tragic dimension. But although death is inevitable, for we are all mortal, and it is more of a danger for gay men than for many other groups of people (because of the sort of society we live in), nonetheless death is also *inessential*. It is not a constituent and motor of sexual desire. One cannot imagine a greater contrast to the transgressive—Kantian or Hegelian—logics of Sade, Bataille, and so many others. (Shaviro 2006)

As Shaviro says, this separation of sex from the narrative of death is not a utopian association of sex with redemption either. Rather, it is not so much sex acts that matter, but the kinds of community and mutuality they promote. "Sexuality," Shaviro says, "for Delany is a kind of communism, where anonymous relations with multiple others coexist with the exclusivity and special passion of (romantic?) love for one particular other person." That a novel like this contains tragedies but is not shaped around a tragic arc is one key to its intervention. "The most shocking thing about this book," Woodhouse writes, "is not its presentation of extreme sexual acts [...] but its assumption that even they can be occasions of friendship or love." Furthermore, if the characters were presented "as desperate, compulsive people, most readers would be perfectly content with them. But this is precisely the sort of smug judgment Delany will not permit. He and his hero are heartwarmingly aboveboard in their pursuit of pleasure— John in his life, Delany in his deliriously dirty text" (1998: 213). This makes it a profoundly anti-heteronormative text, as well, because it works against the tragic discourse of AIDS narratives that made those narratives amenable to mainstream discourse. AIDS confirmed, for many otherwise very different audiences, a narrative of queer life as tragic and diseased. Deborah B. Gould's *Moving Politics: Emotion and ACT UP's Fight Against AIDS* offers a particularly thorough examination of this dynamic:

> Dominant understandings of AIDS tended to blame gay men and gay male sexual practices for the spread of the virus. The media and politicians, not only those from the religious right, consistently made distinctions between "innocent AIDS victims"—children, hemophiliacs, and other ostensibly straight, middle-class people—and queers, junkies, and prostitutes, the lowlifes of society who were "guilty" not only of bringing AIDS on themselves, but of spreading the plague to the innocent. Dominant discourses sanctioned repressive and punitive measures—including quarantine—to deal with the epidemic. As well, there were frequent assertions by the media, politicians, and bureaucrats that the scientific-medical establishment was doing all it could to fight the epidemic. There was no public acknowledgement of the role that homophobia, racism, and sexism were playing in the government's and other institutions' handling of the crisis. (Gould 2009: 236)

Gould shows in great detail that the dominant discourse(s) of AIDS proved to be both a blessing and curse for activists, creating new avenues for sympathy while also reifying prejudices about sexual practices.[4] This discourse was not at all limited to conservatives or heterosexuals. Gould provides numerous examples of a phenomenon well described by Carol Patton as early as 1986:

> Even gay liberation ideology was equivocal: if an initial goal was the assertion of "gay is good," then perhaps the solution to AIDS was to consider the years of promiscuity and exploration to be the community's "adolescence," which now (though admittedly tragically) should "mature" into "responsible," directed, even monogamous sexual expression. (Patton 1986: 107–108)

Gould writes, "The sort of distancing that created a good gays/bad gays dichotomy corroborated homophobic stereotypes and fostered heteronormativity, even among lesbians and gay men. This reproduction of heteronormativity, in turn, (re)generated gay shame and further encouraged politics that demonstrated lesbian and gay 'normalcy' and 'respectability'" (2009: 85). It is exactly this temptation toward distancing that *The Mad Man* engages within its pedagogy—a

---

[4] This discourse continues, and has adapted to developments in HIV/AIDS knowledge, treatment, and communication since. In 2002's *Globalizing AIDS*, Patton writes: "The continuing reinforcement of the idea that African cases were different—first sociosexually and later virally—influenced mainstream North Americans' conviction that it was virtually impossible for 'ordinary people' (now encompassing straight, native-born, white, and probably middle-class folks) to contract HIV during 'ordinary intercourse.' This latter activity probably meant 'missionary-position sex,' but it was rarely clear what activities were proper to the 'ordinary' person and whether, for example, individuals who engaged in 'nonordinary' sex were thereby somehow liable to transmit HIV even when they engaged in 'ordinary intercourse.' Just as there was confusion over whether male-male intercourse was a risk practice or the defining activity of a risk group, there was confusion over who needed to consider safe sex, and those who were encouraged to see themselves as 'ordinary' or as members of the 'heterosexual community' were discouraged from thinking much about it" (xiv).

pedagogy aimed not only at undoing the temptation to create a "good gays/bad gays dichotomy" wherein the reader is on the side of the "good gays" against the "bad gays," but to provide the reader with habits of mind that will make the dichotomy's destructive nature apparent.

Jeffrey Allen Tucker writes that in *The Mad Man*, "Delany seems to be committed to not only validating sex and a range of specific gay sexual practices, but also rethinking the parameters of 'sex' itself, which in a sexually spread epidemic is a matter of immense importance" (2004: 264–265). Pornography and AIDS education both require specificity about sexual practices (though of course pornography is not necessarily AIDS education any more than AIDS education is necessarily pornographic): *vague pornography* verges on the oxymoronic, and vague AIDS education is at best inaccurate, at worst murderous. All of the questions raised in the postscripts to "The Tale of Plagues and Carnivals" (and, later, "The Gamble") are dramatized within *The Mad Man*, which includes as an appendix the Kingsley et al. study "Risk Factors for Seroconversion to Human Immunodeficiency Virus among Male Homosexuals: Results from the Multicenter AIDS Cohort Study." AIDS becomes part of the sexual equations of *The Mad Man* because the syndrome is fatal and because the exact mechanisms of its fatality are unknown. As Tucker shows (2004: 268–275), *The Mad Man* stands in opposition to a general idea that frequent sexual contact and the exchange of bodily fluids are high-risk factors for HIV transmission; rather, Delany both argues and dramatizes that it is very specific acts (particularly anal intercourse) that have the highest risk, while other common acts (such as oral intercourse) likely (but not certainly) have little-to-no risk.[5]

---

[5] It is not my purpose in this study to argue whether Delany is correct about this; I expect he is right about the risks generally, but I am not an AIDS scientist, and my most thorough knowledge of the science dates back to the mid-1990s when I trained as an AIDS educator. (Coincidentally, the same time I first read *The Mad Man*.) The advice of most HIV/AIDS-prevention organizations to use a condom with any male partner whose status is unknown remains sound, it seems to me, given that oral practices do appear to have some small chance of transmitting HIV, but we are unlikely to know with any certainty for a long time, if ever. The scientific literature of the last fifteen or twenty years typically (and responsibly) points out the practical limits of researching specific sexual practices, and also notes areas of more and less certainty. That more research is necessary is undoubtable, but there is enough of a body of research now for some meta-analyses to have provided useful information. For more recent studies and discussion, see Tucker, *Sense of Wonder* 273–274, as well as Wood, Lianna F., et al. "The Oral Mucosa Immune Environment and Oral Transmission of HIV/SIV" (*Immunological Reviews*, vol. 254, no. 1, July 2013, pp. 34–53); Patel, Pragna, et al. "Estimating Per-Act HIV Transmission Risk: A Systematic Review" (*AIDS*, vol. 28, no. 10, June 2014, pp. 1509–1519); and Rice, Cara E., et al. "Beyond Anal Sex: Sexual Practices of Men Who Have Sex with Men and Associations with HIV and Other Sexually Transmitted Infections" (*The Journal of Sexual Medicine*, vol. 13, no. 3, March 2016, pp. 374–382). For a discussion of the legacy of the Multicenter AIDS Cohort Study, see Engels, Eric A., et al. "Invited Commentary: A Landmark Study Launched in a Public Health Maelstrom" (*American Journal of Epidemiology*, vol. 185, no. 11, June 2017, pp. 1157–1160).

The Mad Man juxtaposes the pre-AIDS-era experiences of Timothy Hasler with the experiences of John Marr, the novel's narrator, a philosophy graduate student investigating both Hasler's work and his mysterious death. Marr ends up being able to understand Hasler's world, and to solve his murder (which was only a mystery to people outside Hasler's social-sexual circle), because his own desires are similar to Hasler's, and so his experiences end up repeating Hasler's own. These repetitions are pleasurable and tragic for Marr, but Delany is careful to show separate etiologies for the pleasure and tragedy. Both Hasler and Marr have numerous sexual contacts and literally bathe in bodily fluids, yet the first sentences of the novel are: "I do not have AIDS. I am surprised that I don't. I have had sex with men weekly, sometimes daily—without condoms—since my teens, though true, it's been overwhelmingly … no, more accurately it's been—since 1980—all oral, not anal" (Delany [1994] 2015: K88-90).⁶ It is not disease, sexual promiscuity, or bodily fluids that killed Hasler or kills Marr's friend Joey, but rather the combination of an encounter with someone violently mentally ill along with misunderstandings of economic relations and community etiquette. The world of The Pit bar is not lacking in danger, but this is more a fact than a moral judgment; the same is true of an interstate highway: certain rules and traditions, both spoken and unspoken, limit the danger. A bartender explains to Marr that "the thing that makes this whole place possible is a belief that sex—the kind of sex that gets sold here—is scarce. Because it's scarce, it's valuable. And because it's valuable, it goes for good prices" (K6835-6836). As a known hustler bar, and one where the hustlers can make better money than elsewhere, The Pit is not a place where people openly offering sex for free is received kindly by men trying to sell sex. When someone sympathetic to or reliant upon The Pit's economy is violently inclined, a person openly offering free (or cheap) sex is in real danger. Hasler and Marr knew this, but Mad Man Mike and Crazy Joey did not, and so Mike and Joey ended up being attacked, with Hasler dying because he put himself between Mike and the murderer, Dave Franitz, and Marr unable to repeat Hasler's self-sacrifice so as to save Joey. As Marr quickly figures out, and as Christian Ravela elucidates, The Pit's "logic of scarcity harshly contradicts the premises that undergird value" in Marr's encounters with Joey, Mike, Leaky,

---

⁶ Delany has here given Marr basically his own sexual history, as can be seen from the evidence of *The Motion of Light in Water*, *1984: Selected Letters*, and numerous interviews and essays. See "The Gamble" for the clearest intersections with Marr.

Tony, etc., especially the orgiastic "turning out" at Marr's apartment. "Indeed, it is precisely this conflict between opposing systems of value that prompts the murder of both Hasler and Crazy Joey. In lieu of scarcity, an overabundance of sex structures value in Marr's turning out. [...] Thus, the endless possibilities of different kinds of sexual activity become impossible to structure according to value" (2016: 101).

These systems of economic value are also systems of epistemological value. *Who knows what* becomes a matter of life and death in the presence of violent personalities or fatal diseases. It is inaccurate, though, to suggest that *The Mad Man* proposes that the systems of The Pit are equal to the systems Marr explores with the homeless men. The Pit has had to establish protocols for dealing with the results of violence that would threaten the bar's ability to continue to operate; for instance, they move injured bodies to a nearby parking lot. (Readers familiar with the history, or who have read *Times Square Red, Times Square Blue*, will know that places such as The Pit were ultimately closed by city regulations designed to lessen the spread of AIDS.) For all its systems and etiquette, The Pit is a dangerous place—though whether and to what extent it is more dangerous than other, more socially acceptable, institutions is unclear. The kind of communalism Marr discovers and participates in during Wet Nights at the Mine Shaft and then with homeless men is presented far more positively than the hustling at The Pit, and is also given many more pages in the novel, allowing readers to learn what structures the systems of these encounters and to see various iterations of behavior. Only after these many positive encounters, including the epochal "turning in" scene, are we reminded that this is not a utopian vision: After the turning in and Joey's murder, Mad Mike rapes John.[7] *The Mad Man* does not end there, however, nor does John suddenly recognize the error of his ways and renounce the "mad" life he's lived in favor of monogamy or celibacy. John's relationship with Leaky becomes deeper and more permanent, and together they visit Leaky's family in Maryland, an experience that shows John not only how pleasure and danger exist outside his own world of experience but also how and why, as he says, "Though I love him, Leaky and I disagree about the way the systems of the world work as much as two people possibly can" (K9716-9717).

---

[7] The complexities and implications of the word "rape" (which John insists on) are well explored by Darieck Scott (2010), who also provides the most thorough reading of the use of racialized language within the novel.

Through such complexities, *The Mad Man* renders any "good gay/bad gay" dichotomy nonsensical, and undermines any desire on the reader's part to understand the novel via a culturally dominant, salvationist discourse. If *The Mad Man* is transgressive, it is not so in a way that substitutes one set of predetermined boundaries for another. Rather, it is a novel in which "transgression is more than the crossing of a boundary and is, rather, the subject's exploration of the elasticity of boundaries" (Wachter-Grene 2015: 340), with the reader invited into the exploration. The novel's richest character portraits are of the very "queers, junkies, and prostitutes, the lowlifes of society" that Gould sees the dominant discourse branding "'guilty' not only of bringing AIDS on themselves, but of spreading the plague to the innocent" (2009: 236), and so any assumptions derived from the dominant discourse that the reader brings to the text must be revised or else the text will be unreadable.

That the dominant discourse is raced is also important to *The Mad Man*. Tucker points out that "Delany has forged a representation of black gay life that interrogates anxieties about black gay masculinity and race consciousness" (2004: 252), which is true, but it is also important to point out that Timothy Hasler, the object of John Marr's quest, is Korean American. While discussing *Dhalgren* and urban unrest, Tucker acknowledges the Los Angeles riots and how they "highlighted conflicts within and between different racial and ethnic communities, black antagonism toward Korean-owned and operated businesses in particular" (86), but it seems to me at least worth noting that this novel written shortly after the LA riots is shaped around an African American man's efforts to uncover how and why a Korean American man died. Delany could have chosen to give Hasler any other heritage he wanted; that he did not suggests we ought to bring in the utopian communism that Shaviro identified in the book's sexual politics, a politics that might offer some glimpse of a response to Rodney King's famous question, "Can we all get along?"

Tucker does discuss how Hasler helped his student Peter Darmushklowsky to accept his erotic attachment to Asian women (an attachment that Hasler then wrote into science fiction stories) and makes an insightful connection: "It can be said that Darmushklowsky suffered from a belief in sexual scarcity, which, within the logic of the novel, is a myth that informs the sale of sex at 'hardcore hustling bar[s]' like The Pit, where Hasler was stabbed" (2004: 262) and which is anathema not only to characters such as Leaky, but also to characters such as Pheron in "The Tale of Plagues and Carnivals," both of whom think it is silly to pay for what is easy to find if you know where to look and aren't especially particular.

Darmushklowsky didn't gain happiness by following Hasler's practices—he ended up happily, heterosexually married, without any apparent promiscuity or water sports—but rather found happiness by learning a philosophy of sex and social relations from him, telling Marr:

> I think that I'm a reasonable and happy man today, and that I'm married to Sue—and very happily, I might add—basically because of ideas about what we were allowed to do in this world that I'd never realized before and that Tim first introduced me to. And I think I'm still married to Sue, if you know what I mean, because of ways that he suggested that a person act with another person that he cares about, that he loves, that he wants to stay with him. (Delany [1994] 2015: K4057–4060).

The complexity of *The Mad Man*'s pedagogy becomes clear in the scenes with Darmushklowsky, particularly the conversation between him, Sue, and Marr, because that conversation depicts a straight white man, a gay black man, and a straight Japanese woman coming to agreement about ways of being in the world, even as their individual practices of being in the world are quite different. Peter and Sue Darmushklowsky are vital to the novel's plot because they provide key information about Timothy Hasler; they are vital to its pedagogy because they allow us a way to think about what it means to be outside the practices the novel depicts without condemning those practices. Indeed, a philosophy that can guide those practices may prove nourishing even for lifestyles utterly different from those of the philosophers.

The ways that *The Mad Man* explodes the common racial groupings within porn is also important, as Darieck Scott has shown well. While a reader unfamiliar with hardcore pornography might be most surprised by the prevalence of urine and feces, Scott writes that it is the fluidity of racial groupings within the novel that is less common to pornographic genres:

> The bulk of North American gay male pornography, written or visual, does not feature characters of identifiable African descent at all, though of course there is a significant market niche of porn videos centered on African American, Puerto Rican, Cuban, and Brazilian actors. Gay male pornography centrally featuring African American men and other men of color might be said to constitute a slice roughly equal to or only slightly greater than that of BDSM of the work produced. Depictions, let alone explorations that rise to the level of the thematic, of interracial or cross-racial sexual play in the general category of gay male porn, BDSM and non-BDSM, occupy a still smaller portion of the market—though in this relatively small group, black-white interracial pairings may well be in the

> majority. The three groupings (men of color, interracial, BDSM) are generally separate: there are some African American, Latino, or Asian men who appear with white men in BDSM porn fiction or video, but vanishingly few, and all-black or all-Latino porn will sometimes feature the paraphernalia or, less frequently, the explicit evocations of BDSM practice; but these depictions or themes are marginal to arguably already marginal spheres of porn. The proportions and numbers of the depictions of men of color or interracial sex decline significantly in the case of written porn—though my impression is that BDSM erotic fiction seems to hold a fairly large segment of the written porn market. (Scott 2010: 211)

Scott's analysis is useful both for expanding our understanding of the various assumptions Delany's text challenges and also for adding to our understanding of *The Mad Man*'s pedagogy for certain audiences. A porn-familiar gay male reader attracted to the book because of the porn will be challenged in his assumptions about who should be represented within such a story. We are thus returned to the question of the usefulness of porn that is not *your* porn. What makes it not yours? Repulsion is one thing, but if you are a reader for whom the bodily fluids and specific sexual activities are not necessarily turn-offs, then *The Mad Man* asks you to interrogate your assumptions about other features—including about racial categories and the ways they mix. Delany doesn't offer a clear answer to whatever questions the novel raises for you about your own racial-erotic imaginary, but he provides frequent provocations to question, to dig deeper into any reader's assumptions about not only what is arousing and not, but what is acceptable and not. Those questions, most valuably, also require readers who find a particular erotic attachment or behavior unacceptable to acknowledge that judgment, and by acknowledging, to open themselves to analyzing it.

In addition, *The Mad Man* (and most of Delany's writing) poses real challenges to contemporary Queer Studies, particularly what Kadji Amin identifies as "the recent, though incomplete, emergence of the ideal of homosexuality as erotic symmetry." Amin argues:

> It may be that today, power to discipline sexuality and categorize sexual types as normal or deviant operates less through the ideal of heteronormativity than through that of erotic egalitarianism. Insofar as erotic egalitarianism is now the ideal, if not the reality, of heterosexual and homosexual relationships alike, those couples that too ostentatiously broadcast their structuration by age, race, and class polarities appear far more aberrant, suspicious, and threatening than do comparatively innocuous age-, race-, and class-"appropriate" homosexual couplings. (Amin 2017: 38)

Delany's pornography has always shown sex between people of different ages, races, and classes.⁸ In a late 1980s interview, Delany said, "The easier it is to name, survey, and pathologize the eroticization of any particular set of class relations, then the more dangerous that set of relations—and their eroticization—is to patriarchal status quo phallocentric society. What makes certain such relationships dangerous is that they represent lines of communication, fields of interest, and exchanges of power" (1994: 136–137). *The Mad Man* assiduously avoids the salvationist discourse common both to mainstream rhetoric around AIDS and to liberal gay and lesbian politics generally. "Transgression, sexual dissidence, and the role of the pariah," Delany has said, "[…] must be removed from salvationist discourse if they are to be anything more than a return to orthodoxy" (1999a: 136). To move away from orthodoxy—and from the particular orthodoxy of "good gay/bad gay"—Delany invites the reader to analyze discourses of power.

The systems of the world

Darieck Scott asserts that *The Mad Man* does not attempt to escape the discourse of oppressor/oppressed, but rather to complicate and redeploy it, for "insofar as an identification with the oppressor is part of what is operating, such identifications seem, within the realm that Delany has created, a universal condition, in that, in a sense, everyone has an oppressor both external and internalized. Delany suggests that this is an inescapable aspect of existing in a social world: we are always in some way objects of interpellation in claiming

---

⁸ Of *Hogg*, Ray Davis wrote: "one could say that *Hogg* is the (otherwise imaginary) porn which '80s anti-porn crusaders attacked: made up of violence against women and sexual abuse of children, with a dash of racism, all rolled in a thick coat of filth" (1996: 172). *Hogg* is an angry, often intentionally nasty book; most recently, *Through the Valley of the Nest of Spiders* is a kind of anti-*Hogg*: its pages overflowing with plentiful, polymorphous sex between people of different races, classes, and ages, but now in a utopian frame: "all the sex here serves as a kind of community outreach, reaffirmation of friendship, and shared recreation" (Bellin 2012), turning the sex into what Keguro Macharia calls "a form of pleasant sociality" (2014b). Macharia identifies *Through the Valley* as a "post-transgressive" novel "because it seems relatively uninterested in whether or not its bourgeois readers and critics will 'conquer' their disgust. And, also, I think, because it is so invested in 'fun' and 'affection.' Whereas the 'transgressive' novel is invested in a big 'fuck you' to the world, *Through the Valley of the Nest of Spiders* is interested in what a livable world might be" (2014a). *The Mad Man* gestures toward—yearns for—the utopian vision of *Through the Valley*, but in even a pornotopic fantasy of early '90s New York City, such a vision is impossible to sustain in the manner the rural, post-Millennium *Through the Valley* does. (As Delany shows how and why The Dump was created and sustained, the rural location is a key feature.)

subjectivity or agency" (2010: 255). Alternatively, we might say that Delany suggests that the oppressor/oppressed binary is part of the discourse of power, and since both the social world and desire are shaped by discourse, they are highly susceptible to whatever discourse of power infuses the particular site of interpellation. It's not so much that the binary is itself inescapable in social life, but that social life is shaped by discourses of power, and so any anti-oppressive politics must account for how such discourses work, which may not necessarily be in the form of such a binary (a topic more fully explored in *Trouble on Triton* and the Return to Nevèrÿon series).

Scott demonstrates that the racialized language filling *The Mad Man* (and all of Delany's pornographic writings) does not lose its oppressive power in a context of mutual pleasure and consent; instead, it depends on that power for its ability to arouse desire (other, less powerful and offensive words, simply would not do). As much as anything else in the novel, the effect of wielding the power these words possess depends on the system(s) shaping the encounter and the discourse(s) controlling how the words mean. For instance, the words' power is used and contained differently within the frame of John and Leaky's relationship than it is in other relationships. As Scott shows, these systems and effects are clear in the novel's events and character relationships, but there is also the relationship of the words to the reader:

> Fantasy's connection to perversion and perversion's connection to the foundational instinct for freedom in both life and death instincts, blackness's connection to perversion and its nature as psychical (and thus political) rather than material reality—these connecting bridges and overlapping territories seem to correspond with the blueprint of Delany's project in this pornographic novel: which is to run the labyrinth-tracing thread between blackness, perversion, and (the will to, the imagination of) freedom, all through the arena of abjection, as abjection participates in and informs each, wherein we can discern blackness-as/through-abjection and blackness-as-power. (Scott 2010: 252)

Blackness, perversion, freedom, abjection, and power are shown within *The Mad Man* to be fuzzy concepts: John's blackness, for instance, has a different meaning for Leaky than it does for John's advisor Irving Mossman, since they come from significantly different backgrounds and exist in utterly different worlds. That, perhaps, is the least surprising complexity among the concepts, however, because it is a complexity familiar in countless stories; what is less common is Delany's similar exploration of the valences of perversion and abjection, showing that the perverse and the abject are products of discourse and what Hasler calls "the systems of the world" as much as blackness, and as such all may interweave in ever more complex ways.

That complexity (or what Delany in his early novella *Empire Star* called *multiplexity*) is what the pedagogy of *The Mad Man* helps readers learn to see. Readers may bring numerous assumptions to the novel (beyond whatever assumptions they have about its genre)—assumptions not only about the transmission of AIDS or about safer sex practices, but more generally about sexuality, race, desire, language, homeless men, dirt, feces, urine, and semen. While no reader will necessarily arrive to the book with assumptions counter to all of what it explores, it is hard to imagine anyone (other than Delany himself) who would not arrive with some sort of assumption that the novel would then challenge. All such assumptions are pushed toward a recognition of complexity like that John develops regarding The Pit, noting that each visit adds new observations about how it works, its inclusions and exceptions, so that your description of the customers on your third visit is different from your fourth, and you must confront the fact that "the pattern you first intuited is only a reduction—or taming—of a vast number of exceptions to itself that, at any moment, make up the customer configuration" ([1994] 2015: K6680-6681). The same is clearly true not only for the systems affecting the customers at the Pit, but for all the discourses, etiquettes, and systems affecting every character and relationship in *The Mad Man*.

The use of racial language for erotic effect provides another example of Delany's complex approach to these systems. Because a frequent—even indispensable—element of the erotic fantasy in *The Mad Man* is not just racialized desire or imagery, but racialized language, freedom is imagined via a discourse that in nearly any other context would be wounding, offensive, even cause for violence. Scott asserts that the racialized language of the novel is more than simply erotic: its "eroticism has political meaning" (2010: 229). That political meaning may be read in a variety of ways, but I see it as tied to an idea of the utopian potential within erotic attachment, a meaning that suggests lust (more than desire) may be powerful enough to reconfigure the systems of the world. The language of racist and oppressive discourse possesses some sort of erotic charge already, and the discourse's history is saturated with sexual oppression and violence; the racist language in *The Mad Man* draws from this charge and history, as the words would not have the arousing power they have without it. However, the text suggests that so long as the language remains part of a libidinal economy that is also infused with the "communistic" values that Shaviro identifies in Delany's approach to sexuality, then the negative charge of the words may serve pleasurable—even liberating—ends for everyone involved. There are limits, though, because the world itself has not been reconfigured by a similar erotics, and outside the space of sexual encounter, the words once again exist within the discourse that shapes the larger society. Scott identifies moments in the novel that demonstrate "the ease with which such apparently agreed-upon, lust-producing uses of insults that we see at its greatest clarity with John and Tony can slip toward less fully consensual, nonsexual uses" (232). Without their negative charge, they would lose their erotic power, and so the words are not reclaimed, they are not made positive, they retain all their danger because they do not exist separate from discourse, and the discourse outside of pornotopia is one in which they do damage. It is only within the pornotopic discourse that their negative charge may have positive effect. In Delany's pornotopia, racist language is a Derridean *pharmakon*.

While many of the ideas about abjection, perversion, freedom, power, and discourse are all apparent to some extent or another in "The Tale of Plagues and Carnivals," the genre of pornography allows Delany a way to explore them differently than the genre of sword & sorcery, both because of the sexual explicitness that is de rigeur in porn and also because of the different reading conventions of the two genres. *The Mad Man* pushes against the generic conventions of pornography as much as "The Tale of Plagues and Carnivals" does of sword & sorcery, but while it is in its own way as essayistic as "Plagues and Carnivals," it does not position any of its text as Delany's own autobiography, and the "Disclaimer" warns the reader away from reading the novel as social realism, even as it draws from social realities. The presence of pornography serves to distance and distort the other material much as the presence of fantasy distances and distorts the journalistic material in "Plagues and Carnivals"; in the latter, though, this distance and distortion were regulated by the general separation of the modes via the section numbers as well as via a more explicitly metafictional approach.

The Mad Man has some metafictional moments, though, for instance when Marr refers to a character important to the early parts of the book: "I never saw my Piece of Shit again, which—this early in a book—makes a pretty unsatisfactory conclusion for a character in a novel. But then, 'unsatisfactory conclusions' is what AIDS seems to be about" ([1994] 2015: K3781-3783). Since *The Mad Man* could be described as the autobiography of John Marr, it is odd to see him refer to Piece of Shit as a character *in a novel*. This breaks the conceit of the fictional autobiography. At the moment when the reader's attention is directed toward the book as a book *and* as a work of fiction, "what AIDS seems to be about" comes in as a topic. It is as if here, relatively early in the text (page 174 of 502 in the 2002 Voyant paperback), the crisis that cracked open the fiction of "The Tale of Plagues and Carnivals" threatens to crack the fiction of *The Mad Man*. Marr notes a historical (and epistemological) cleft between the world before AIDS and after: "it was becoming clear that soon the lives—at least the sexual lives—of those who had lived in an age that was, no, not more innocent than ours, yet by the same token was as different from ours in its outlines and articulations as sexual ages could be, would be all but incomprehensible to those coming after" (K3796-3798). The rift between the fiction and the reality is quickly healed with the arrival of a letter from Darmushklowsky, who was, among other things, a model for a fictional character Timothy Hasler included in some of the science fiction stories he wrote and published in graduate school. Thus, a (fictional) letter from a (fictional) character who, within the fiction, was transposed into a character in (the fictional) Hasler's own fiction serves within the text of *The Mad Man* as the impetus to move away from an acknowledgment of nonfictionality and return to the distance of fictionality. Much later, in a humorous aside, Marr's narration recognizes the book it is part of as containing copious descriptions of penises, and so to some extent positions itself within pornography: "in a book like this you just can't say someone's was the biggest cock you've ever seen. Because in a book like this, calling something the biggest cock you've ever seen doesn't mean anything. It's been said too many times ... " (K8110-8112). The difference between this instance of the narration's acknowledgment of itself and the earlier one is that here there is no mention of the book as a novel. It is simply *a book like this*. By that late point in the novel, though, the reader will have come to some sort of decision, however tentative, of what *a book like this means*, because by this point—almost exactly three-quarters of the way through—the reader will have settled on some reading protocols.

The Mad Man positions itself as an autobiography written by a man seeking biographical information about another man. Though its characters and story are fictional, its mode is that of nonfiction, and it draws considerably from

Samuel Delany's own life and repurposes material that is included in his letters and essays.[9] The closing of distance between fictionality and nonfictionality through the positioning of Marr not only as a first-person narrator but as a character writing an autobiography allows Delany different rhetorical effects than would be available in a narrative where the first-person narrator made no acknowledgment of the book in the reader's hand, while the fiction of Marr-as-autobiographer rather than Delany-as-autobiographer allows fiction's freedom of invention. Though he invents and shapes the characters and situations, Delany still maintains fidelity to details of social reality from his own experience. He does exactly what he discovered Rilke did with *The Notebooks of Malte Laurids Brigge*, incorporating material, events, and even verbatim passages from his own letters into his novel (e.g., in *1984: Selected Letters* [2000] the letter of November 28, 1984, to Robert Bravard, particularly pp. 317–326, which is incorporated into Marr's immensely long letter to Sam Mossman[10]). What the frame of fiction provides is access to reading conventions different from those of actual autobiography or memoir: *The Mad Man* is able to draw on the protocols of pornography, the detective story, the academic novel, etc. while still employing the essayistic, didactic, and even polemic modes more expected of nonfiction.

Such an approach may also allow something like the object-priority that Delany has repeatedly said is one of the attractions of science fiction for him. One of his clearest explanations of this idea is in the "Author's Introduction" to *Starboard Wine*, where he says that science fiction is a writing category ("the complex of reading protocols, the discourse") that encourages "a clear view of the figure/ground antagonism in all narrative matters" via indirection "by the continual (and, from specific SF text to specific SF text, the continually varied) ground/ground antagonism science fiction provides, where one ground is the fictive ground of the story and the other is the ground of the reader's given world."

---

[9] In "The Thomas L. Long Interview," Delany explained his perception of the autobiographical elements: "As far as my own experiences, suffice it to say that, without reproducing any of them photographically (the closest I come to that is the 'Sleepwalkers' letter), *The Mad Man* covers a great enough range of them so that a reader who bears in mind that it is written by a fifty-and fifty-one-year-old man about a twenty- to thirty-five-year-old man, and thence allows for the necessary novelistic exaggeration and foregrounding, would probably not be too far off in most of his or her assumptions about my own sex life" (1999a: 132).

[10] In the 2002 Voyant Publishing paperback of *The Mad Man*, Marr's letter runs from page 98 to page 162 (about 30,000 words). It's possible that readers find that the length of the letter, like a particularly pornographic penis, strains credibility. But in *1984*, Delany's September 1, 1984, letter Camilla Decarnin is thirty-five pages long (nearly 20,000 words), and the November 28 letter to Bravard is about twenty-three pages (roughly 13,000 words). Delany's archives contain a number of novella-length letters. His practice was to write these over weeks and sometimes months, send them to the original addressee, then copy or cannibalize them in letters to other close correspondents.

In contrast, the writing category of literature ("of which I take contemporary bourgeois fiction (mundane fiction) to be, today, the representative example," and which is distinct from paraliteratures such as science fiction, pornography, comics, etc.) puts priority on the subject rather than object. Literature "encourages the reading of an extentional relation between figure and ground, between fictive subject (invented character or narrative voice) and fictive object (the fictive or biographical decor, the setting, the landscape, the institutions whose representations evoke the fictive or biographical world)." A title such as Susan Sontag's *I, Et Cetera* "announces literature's commitment to the subject and literature's equal commitment to the subordination of the ground, rendering ground an expression of subject, of personality, of sensibility" ([1984] 2012: xv). These distinctions are descriptive, not evaluative, but Delany's writing career stands as a testament to his own preference (as a writer, if not reader) for exploring the relationship between "the fictive ground of the story and [...] the ground of the reader's given world." Such exploration is most fully provided, in his theory of fiction and discourse, by paraliteratures rather than literature.

Here we see another reason *The Mad Man* needs to draw from the conventions of paraliterature, particularly pornography: in Delany's view, those conventions will de-emphasize subjectivity and encourage readers to speculate on how and why their world (and all that is its case) differs from the world within the novel. By positioning the text as both fiction and paraliterature (pornography, detective story), the force of subjectivity inherent to autobiography and memoir is diminished. *The Mad Man* may then remain a fictional autobiography in form, but its paraliterary status provides it with a rhetorical and epistemological breadth otherwise unavailable.

Having explored the limits of fiction in "The Tale of Plagues and Carnivals," Delany pulled back from those limits when returning to fiction with *The Mad Man*, finding the fictional autobiography to be particularly effective for his goals when deployed via paraliterary categories. The clearly nonfictional preface and Appendix that frame the narrative set limiting terms for the fiction, however. The Disclaimer that is a preface insists that the narrative is not only fiction but "fairly imaginative fiction at that" and lays out some of what Delany sees the text excluding: "It is specifically a book about various sexual acts whose status as vectors of HIV contagion we have no hard-edged knowledge of because the monitored studies that would give statistical portraits of the relation between such acts and seroconversion (from HIV- to HIV+) have not been done." Furthermore, it "is not a book about the homeless of New York—or, indeed, of the country. No book could be that all-but-omits scenes of winter and does not deal with—indeed, focus on—the criminally inadequate attempts by the municipality to feed, clothe, and shelter these men, women, and children. Such a novel would have to be substantially darker than this one—which, I suspect, will be found quite dark enough" ([1994] 2015: K30-50).

The Appendix addresses the polemical point about sexual acts and HIV vectors, reprinting the 1987 *Lancet* study by Kingsley et al. (a study that is also referenced within the text: At the beginning of Part 3, Sam Mossman sends it to John Marr some years after he sent her his long letter[11]). *The Mad Man* ends by appropriating the authority of academic discourse and one of the world's leading scientific journals, placing the reader about as far outside fictionality (and subjectivity) as is possible. The Disclaimer and Appendix not only situate the fiction, but highlight—indeed, insist upon—what is absent from the fiction that is present in the world of the reader, and even more so what is unknowable in both the world of the fiction and the world of the reader. Over the course of the book, attentive, engaged readers will have learned both that there are limits to fiction and that sometimes the limits of fiction are also the limits of reality.

Recognizing such shared limits allows a utopian impulse to bloom: as Muñoz writes, referencing Adorno, "Our criticism should [...] be infused with a utopian function that is attuned to the 'anticipatory illumination' of art and culture. Such illumination cuts through fragmenting darkness and allows us to see the politically enabling whole. Such illumination will provide us with access to a world that should be, that could be, and that will be" (2009: 64). The pornotopia of *The Mad Man* is not utopia, but its rhetorical achievement and pedagogical effect are to give intellectual and emotional force to speculations about the systems of the world as it is and also about all that those systems cannot encompass or allow. These speculations then carry their emotional and intellectual force into the question that inevitably follows, the question common both to Modernists and to critical pedagogy—the question of what the new systems we desire might need. If we think about those needs, and if we allow ourselves to develop our speculations, then we imagine the tools, environments,

---

[11] "Not too long ago, a kid here almost got in trouble for distributing an article that I'm enclosing with this letter. Probably you've seen it: 'Risk Factors For Seroconversion to Human Immunodeficiency Virus Among Male Homosexuals: Results from the Multicenter AIDS Cohort Study' by Kingsley, Kaslow, Rinaldo, et alia, from *The Lancet* for Saturday, February 14, 1987. Although the medical stuff in your '84 letter is really out of Cloud-Cuckoo Land, my friend, the article (from a study completed three years later) may suggest some of the reasons why you're still HIV negative—assuming you still are" (Delany [1994] 2015: K4598-4602). See also note 5 above.

behaviors, and conditions that could help new systems of the world come into being. Once we have imagined these things, we (as individuals and as members of groups) may then better understand what we can do to bring the systems we desire into existence. And, just as importantly, we may better understand what we can do to weaken the systems that restrict and oppress us, or at least to lessen their effect in the world. An imagination trained toward such speculation is an imagination prepared to survive crisis.

5

Away from Crisis: *Elizabeth Costello, Diary of a Bad Year, Summertime*

In *Summertime*, Sophie, a colleague and occasional mistress of the fictional (and deceased) John Coetzee, tells the interviewing biographer that John was not political, which causes the biographer to ask if she means "apolitical." "No," she says, "not apolitical, I would rather say anti-political. He thought that politics brought out the worst in people. It brought out the worst in people and also brought to the surface the worst types in society. […] You want me to say what lay behind Coetzee's politics? You can best get that from his books" (Coetzee 2012: 456). This is a provocative statement for Coetzee to write for one character to say about a character who shares his name, because it teases the question of commitment and politics that was so often raised about his work during the apartheid years, when critics such as Nadine Gordimer complained that his books were not sufficiently committed to political reality. Yet, it is important to look closely at Sophie's statement: She does not say you can discern the politics in the books, but that *what lay behind* the politics is in the books. This suggests a common originating/inspiring force between politics and art, a force that impels both politics and aesthetics. "He looked forward to the day when politics and the state would wither away. I would call that Utopian." He was anti-national, she thought, and also fatalistic: "He accepted that the liberation struggle was just. The struggle was just, but the new South Africa toward which it strove was not Utopian enough for him." What would be utopian enough for him? "The closing down of mines. The ploughing under of vineyards. The disbanding of the armed forces. The abolition of the automobile. Universal vegetarianism. Poetry in the streets. That sort of thing" (457).

Sophie bristles against the attempt of the biographer, Mr. Vincent, to fit John into a clear ideological camp: "Hostile, sympathetic—as a biographer you above all ought to be wary of putting people in neat little boxes with labels on them" (457). The conversation continues in a variety of directions, many of them offering different inflections on ideas from earlier in the book, and then the interviewer says, "So, all in all, you see Coetzee as a conservative, an anti-radical," to which Sophie replies, "A cultural conservative, yes, as many of the modernists were culture conservatives—I mean the modernist writers from Europe who were his models" (465).

Too much truth for art to hold

Though there is disagreement among critics about whether J.M. Coetzee's work is best classified as a type of modernism or, instead, as a type of postmodernism, there is no disagreement that British and European Modernists have provided some of his most important influences and references. He wrote a master's thesis about Ford Madox Ford and a doctoral dissertation about Samuel Beckett's novel *Watt*; Franz Kafka is a touchstone; his nonfiction frequently discusses Modernist writers. Coetzee's interests are not confined to Modernism (Cervantes, Defoe, and Dostoyevsky are as important to his writing as Beckett and Kafka), but the form and purpose of his work would be utterly different without Modernism, which much of the critical writing on Coetzee has acknowledged. Derek Attridge opens *J.M. Coetzee and the Ethics of Reading* with a chapter on "Modernist Form and the Ethics of Otherness," and argues that Coetzee "does not merely employ but extends and revitalizes modernist practices" (2004: 6), thus creating a "modernism after modernism" (5). David James picks up this categorization in *Modernist Futures*, writing of "Coetzee's reprise of modernist aesthetics" (2012: 99). With Urmila Seshagiri, James proposed what seems to me to be the least ill-fitting designation for Coetzee, the term I have used for all three of the writers in this study: *metamodernist*, which James and Seshagiri propose as a label for writers who "extend, reanimate, and repudiate twentieth-century modernist literature" (2014: 89).

The desire to extend, reanimate, and repudiate Modernism may have been Coetzee's regardless of his country of origin, but it is clear from *Dusklands* through *Disgrace* that his analysis of power and his need to press against the limits of language and representation stemmed from his experience as a white South

African—indeed, a white South African who initially tried, and failed, to escape South Africa.[1] Modernism offered means and examples by which Coetzee could avoid didacticism but still challenge fiction as a form, and in doing so explore how such challenge might inspire a critical practice for reading the world. The inescapability of his context as a South African writer during the apartheid years created a tension within Coetzee's writing between his desire to write from a position of more freedom and his recognition of historical situatedness. But during the apartheid years, Coetzee's approach could be unacceptably complicated in the eyes of anyone seeking clear, forceful statements. Writers wanted—needed—to believe their words might change the world. Coetzee was not so sure. "On the question of the social effectiveness of literature," he wrote in 1984, "I have one comment: that it is in the interest of the community of writers (among whom I number journalists) to believe in the efficacy of products of fantasy as instruments of action; and that it is not in the interests of those who actually wield power to disabuse anyone of this notion" (Ai et al. 1984: 11).

In his 1987 Jerusalem Prize speech, Coetzee identified one of the main concepts that his novels through *Disgrace* explore:

> In a society of masters and slaves, no one is free. […] The masters, in South Africa, form a closed hereditary caste. Everyone born with a white skin is born into the caste. Since there is no way of escaping the skin you are born with […] you cannot resign from the caste. You can imagine resigning, you can perform a symbolic resignation, but, short of shaking the dust of the country off your feet, there is no way of actually *doing* it.

The socio-political system of South Africa thus leads to "a banal kind of evil which has no conscience, no imagination, and probably no dreams, which eats well and sleeps well and is at peace with itself" (Coetzee 1992: 96). The inability of the South African writer even to pretend to separate politics and literature becomes the subject of Coetzee's speech, which he concludes by saying: "We have art, said Nietzsche, so that we shall not die of truth. In South Africa there is now [1987] too much truth for art to hold, truth by the bucketful, truth that overwhelms and swamps every act of the imagination" (99). (Woolf would have understood what Coetzee meant, as the conclusion of her August 1940 letter to Benedict Nicolson showed: soldiers interrupting writing, air raid sirens, machine guns in villages, a world at war.)

---

[1] For the fullest available account of Coetzee's years in Buffalo, New York (1968–1971), and the events leading to his return to South Africa, see Kannemeyer (2012) chapter 7 (pp. 166–204).

It wasn't until that caste system of South Africa was (legally, if not socially) abolished that Coetzee was able to shake at least some of the dust off his feet by moving to Australia in 2002. His reasons for moving were many, as J.C. Kannemeyer has most fully demonstrated, but inevitably the international press read the move through the lens of the coruscating portrait of South Africa in *Disgrace* or the controversies the novel faced in Coetzee's home country on its release (Kannemeyer 2012: 526–532). In December 1999, Coetzee wrote to David Malouf about his desire to apply to immigrate to Australia, noting that he was retiring from his academic career and saying that South Africa is a country "in a deeply interesting phase of its historical evolution. But it is not a good place to grow old in. Ever since I first visited Australia in 1991 I have felt a tug toward the country and its landscape" (qtd. in Kannemeyer 2012: 536). Kannemeyer interpreted Coetzee's decision not as a move *away* from South Africa but rather as move *to* Australia.

It is difficult to forget, though, the many times Coetzee implied, and sometimes outright stated, that whites in South Africa have no legitimate claim to the land. As early as 1986, Stephen Watson could write in *Research in African Literatures* that the key to understanding Coetzee's work is to recognize that he "is not only a colonizer who is an intellectual, but a colonizer who does not want to be a colonizer" (377). María J. López develops her entire book *Acts of Visitation* around what she sees as Coetzee's core metanarrative of the Europeans' illegitimacy in South Africa, and she finds it expressed outright in *Youth*, where the Coetzee figure is motivated by "his feeling that he is an illegitimate visitor both in South Africa (owing to his European ancestry) and in England (owing to his immigrant status)" (2011: 220). This idea was taken up by Coetzee's neighbor Mariana Swart in an email Kannemeyer quotes at length:

> I ask myself: What are you doing in Adelaide, Australia? I just don't get it. I don't understand why you have left. [...] You should be settling down somewhere in the Karoo, and preparing yourself to write your last 2 or 3 (or whatever) books. Or is it maybe that you truly believe that whites have no place in Africa, and that you morally felt obliged to leave? (Kannemeyer 2012: 542, bracketed ellipses in original)[2]

As I discuss below, the sentiment was also imputed to Coetzee by one of his own characters in *Summertime*.

---

[2] For an exploration of the connections between South African and Australian colonialism in Coetzee's later work, see Elleke Boehmer (2011), "J.M. Coetzee's Australian Realism."

Whatever Coetzee's reasons for moving to Australia, the change in his location correlates with a change in his novels, particularly in their relationship to fictionality. From *Dusklands* (more a collection of two novellas than a novel per se) through *Disgrace*, most of the novels at least draw their impetus from the situation of South Africa.[3] It is possible to read the post-*Disgrace* novels as abandoning the sort of postcolonialist concerns that many readers have seen in Coetzee's work up to that point, but most of the concerns that Coetzee's early work explores—particularly of authorship and authority—carry through to his later work, and that later work is shadowed by the violence and oppression of colonial states and cultures, even if colonial violence is no longer foregrounded. David Attwell paraphrases Coetzee's own feeling that "it is the experience of his particular generation of settler-colonials to live out the end of Empire and decolonization," a decolonization that "is a form of profound disembedding" (Attwell 2011: 10).

The disembedding Attwell identifies finds form in the unsettling of the texts' fictionality. Such unsettling is one of the primary features of the texts that leads (usually hostile) critics to say the books are not novels, not fiction, too didactic or allegorical. Those criticisms may derive from various causes, particularly the dominance of scene-based fiction in the United States and United Kingdom from roughly the early nineteenth century onward, a dominance that conditioned readers of both popular and literary novels to expect and desire mimetic physical description, psychologically familiar character development, and conversational dialogue that adds up to a reality effect (even in highly fantastical novels, such books require determined tools of verisimilitude to aid the reader in suspending disbelief).

Gayatri Spivak has speculated that the changes in Coetzee's novels after *Disgrace* might result from the ways *Disgrace* was read in South Africa; specifically, she sees *Summertime* as "a rewriting of *Disgrace*, making the persona of the located South African who wants to claim South Africa as also his country a different one. [...] Here, the author-function is put aside, but not let go as in *Disgrace*, in favor of an older technique of unreliable narrator, that bad readers

---

[3] Aside from *Waiting for the Barbarians* (1980), *Foe* (1986), and *The Master of Petersburg* (1994), all of Coetzee's novels through *Disgrace* (1999) are set in South Africa, and *Waiting for the Barbarians* got much of its inspiration from the murder of Steve Biko and from other tortures inflicted by the South African police and military (Attwell 2015: 93–95). Furthermore, it seems unlikely that Coetzee would have written *Foe* had he not been a citizen of a settler colony. (*The Master of Petersburg* is an anomaly, but the anomaly is easily explained by Coetzee's long fascination with Dostoyevsky and especially by the fact that it was the novel Coetzee wrote after the death of his son.)

cannot notice. Here, the author-function is present, and everyone is in character" (2014: 125). Regardless of whether this was Coetzee's own goal, the development Spivak outlines is clearly present: again and again, *Disgrace* has proved easy to read for less complex meanings than an analyst like Spivak interprets it to offer. Numerous readers continue to find in *Disgrace* meanings that make Coetzee seem like a grumpy old white man with racist tendencies, or, more recently, make the book seem to have "aged poorly politically" (LaPointe 2018). These are readers for whom the book's pedagogy, however it might be described, has turned out to be ineffective.

As students sometimes discover that a class they loathed was ultimately beneficial to them, so, too, do we sometimes discover that a book we thought had no effect on us has, indeed, held more of a grip than we expected. And there are some (rare) works of art where the pedagogy may be said to be self-annihilating: some of Michael Haneke's films are clear examples of this, particularly *Funny Games* (1997, remade in English in 2007), which critic Robin Wood called "one of the most disturbing films I have ever seen" and observed that it was "no surprise, really, that it is probably the most widely hated film in modern cinema, critics reacting to it with such an intense resentment of what it does to them that it becomes a tribute to the film's power" (2018: 404).[4] Thus, because of delayed effect or because of a negative reaction being the point of the pedagogy, rejection is not in and of itself an indication that a pedagogy has failed with a particular student or reader. However, effective pedagogies require some collaboration between teacher and student, writer and reader. "The opaque or allegorical approach can be very effective," Delany once wrote, "but it requires an educated set of responses" (Ai et al. 1984: 13).[5] A rejection of the collaborative work any text requires likely means a rejection of the pedagogy. We should not be surprised, then, to see a writer like Coetzee, who has experienced such rejection at a significant level—for instance, both Nadine Gordimer and the ANC objecting to *Disgrace* (Kannemeyer 2012: 528–532)—seeking new forms for new pedagogies.

---

[4] Because *Funny Games* makes no attempt to hide its pedagogy—it is a highly didactic film—many people who had negative reactions to it were fully able to recognize what it was trying to do and to reject the lesson. Some negative reviewers of the 2007 remake, such as Tricia Olszewski for *Washington City Paper* (2008), even quoted Haneke's statement about viewers of the original film, "Anyone who leaves the cinema doesn't need the film, and anyone who stays does." The rejections of Coetzee's recent work seem to be of a somewhat different category, in that the pedagogy often gets missed because readers have too much difficulty overcoming their idea of what a book-length work of prose ought to do.

[5] Coincidentally, but appropriately, this sentence appears only one page away from Coetzee's statement about the social effectiveness of literature in *Fiction International*'s "Forum" on writing and politics.

Coetzee's later books foreground problems of reading and interpretation not only for the characters, but for the reader as well, and they do so by making fiction's elements, and often fictionality itself, into an overt problem, one that readers must find a way to solve if they are to make sense of the text. In a letter to Paul Auster, Coetzee said, "I get impatient with fiction that doesn't try something that hasn't been tried before, preferably with the medium itself" (Auster 2013: 165). That impatience shows itself in the development of his writing.

Coetzee's novels up through *Disgrace* offer many ambiguities and avenues for interpretation, and many possible ways for readers to reject them, but their forms and pedagogies remain legible within assumptions of fiction in a way that the post-*Disgrace* works do not. The question of fictionality was not absent before *Elizabeth Costello*; it was prominent in discussions of *The Master of Petersburg*, given how much Coetzee fictionalized Dostoyevsky's life, and certainly present in discussions of *Foe*. But the questions of fictionality in those novels only rarely develop into questions of genre and form. After *Disgrace*, readers and critics struggle more often with the question not only of why Coetzee fictionalizes what he does (or doesn't), but also *whether a particular text is a novel in any sense at all*. That question is not simply taxonomic: it contains assumptions about the value of novels generally, about what the novel as a form should and should not do, and about what a book-length work of fiction even is. A reader's assumptions about what a novel is also affect works that, in fact, the writer or publisher may not call novels; for many readers, a book-length work of prose with at least some clear elements of fictionality is a novel, regardless of what the label on the book says.

After *Disgrace*, only *Slow Man*, *The Childhood of Jesus*, and *The Schooldays of Jesus* are labeled on their covers as novels. *Elizabeth Costello*, *Diary of a Bad Year*, and *Summertime* are not called novels by the publishers or Coetzee. The first two are labeled as "fiction," the third as "Scenes from Provincial Life" or "fiction/memoir" (depending on the edition). Yet to many reviewers (and common readers), any book that is substantially fictional must be a novel, and novels must do certain things. What can one do, then, with a collection of fictional lectures, parables, and allegories (*Elizabeth Costello*); a book of essays with fictional narratives set beneath them on the same pages (*Diary of a Bad Year*); or a book that mixes various accounts of the life of an author similar to, but obviously not the same as, the actual author of the book (*Summertime*)?

Reviewing *Elizabeth Costello* for *The Guardian*, Hermione Lee (2003) said that the book is "more like a collection of propositions about belief, writing and humanity than a novel"; Ron Charles (2005) at *The Washington Post* said that in comparison to *Elizabeth Costello*, "Initially, *Slow Man* looks more like a novel," but the book left him wondering "why one of the world's most celebrated writers would abandon the dramatic structure and implicit truth-telling of novels in favor of hectoring his characters and lecturing at his readers"; in *The Independent*, Justin Cartwright (2007) said *Diary of a Bad Year* is "a wonderful book of essays, a subtle and touching near love story, and an autobiography" and never labeled it a novel, using the word only once, to describe the protagonist, whom he reads as a stand-in for Coetzee himself, as a writer who "has lost his appetite for constructing novels"; and in a *Guardian* review of *The Schooldays of Jesus*, Elizabeth Lowry (2016) said, "In his fidelity to ideas, to telling rather than showing, to instructing rather than seducing us, he does not actually write fiction any more." The assumptions are clear, and from these critics' complaints we can construct a template for what a novel is: A novel is not a collection of propositions, it is a text with a dramatic structure that tells truths implicitly rather than through explicit address (hectoring of characters, lecturing of readers), it is not a collection of essays or autobiography, it does not have a fidelity to ideas, it shows rather than tells, it seduces rather than instructs.

In this narrow conception of the novel's possibilities we see the ultimate effect of setting the novel form up in absolute opposition to propaganda. If, as Delany says, propaganda is "the ultimate aesthetic no-no" ([1984] 2012: 141), then fear of propaganda has led many readers and critics toward so narrow an understanding of what novels can be that those readers and critics are oblivious to aesthetic choices that stage propaganda, didacticism, and essayism to make those modes themselves objects of analysis and, indeed, drama within a book-length work of fiction. Recognizing this narrowing tendency in readers seems to have led Coetzee toward trying a variety of pedagogies to regain some of the lost possibilities of the novel form. In 1997, Coetzee told interviewer Joanna Scott: "A novel is ultimately nothing but a prose fiction of a certain length. It has no formal requirements to satisfy; to that extent, the question of whether X or Y is a novel can't be very interesting" (Coetzee 1997: 87). Coetzee may be right that the question of whether a particular text is a novel or not lacks interest, but a more complex question of how fictionality is summoned and deployed within the text and its contexts is one that remains central to our ability to analyze Coetzee's later works.

Both journalistic reviewers and academic critics, whether receptive or hostile, have connected Coetzee's move to Australia with his move away from narrative novelism: In the Australian newspaper *The Age*, Peter Craven (2007), reviewing *Diary of a Bad Year*, wrote that "In 2002 Coetzee came to live in Australia, in sandstoned Adelaide, and has become a citizen of this country. In the process (or at any rate along with it) he has divested himself of much of the narrative and dramatic resource of the novels that made him famous." After social crisis, Coetzee pushes his texts toward greater crises of fictionality, as if he has found a certain safety—one unavailable in the midst of social crisis—that will allow him to experiment with reducing the rhetorical distance that constitutes fiction. If there is now presumably no longer too much truth for art to hold, then art is more free to put truth into play, making the crisis not one of society but of fictionality itself. To put fictionality into crisis requires more than a metafictional conceit or frame. Any crisis of fictionality may be metafictional in a general sense (such crisis inevitably drawing attention to itself), but Coetzee's post-crisis fictionality-in-crisis is not simply metafictional. Though the post-*Disgrace* books up until *The Childhood of Jesus* are, indeed, metafictional, that property alone does not distinguish them from Coetzee's earlier novels, for he has long been called (rightly or wrongly) a writer of metafiction.[6] The texts now are not only self-conscious of their genre; much like Delany's "Tale of Plagues and Carnivals," they seek to make the determination of genre into a problem for the reader, then use that problem for pedagogical purposes. Such problematization both makes readers reflect on what the text's genre(s) might be (and why), and also invites readers to consider what they expect and desire from genre(s) more generally. In a limited sense, then, these books' pedagogies have been successful even with the most negative reviewers, but in a more general sense they have not, because while those negative reviewers recognized the books as challenges to their assumptions about novels and fiction, they clung to their assumptions and rejected the texts rather than trying to work with them.

If we consider in particular *Elizabeth Costello* and *Diary of a Bad Year* alongside the third of Coetzee's quasi-memoirs, *Summertime*, we can see the texts push against the limits of fiction from two different directions. They do so by weaponizing the reader's expectations. Keeping in mind Richard Walsh's assertion (discussed in the Introduction) that the difference between fiction

---

[6] Reviewing *Foe* in *The Nation*, George Packer said, "This kind of metafiction is not new to Coetzee: *Dusklands* blurs the distinctions between author and character, and between history and fiction; in *In the Heart of the Country* much of Magda's agony is directed toward language itself" (1987: 404). In 1993, Attwell began the introduction to his *J.M. Coetzee: South Africa and the Politics of Writing* by stating "J.M. Coetzee's first six novels constitute a form of postmodern metafiction that declines the cult of the merely relativist and artful" (1).

and nonfiction depends on the kind of interpretive response invited by the text's presentation as one or the other, we can see how a writer like Coetzee can turn readers' expectations into a rhetorical tool. What *Elizabeth Costello*, *Summertime*, and especially *Diary of a Bad Year* all do is place the question of fictionality at the forefront of any reader's thinking about the text.

The reader enters *Elizabeth Costello* and *Diary of a Bad Year* with the assumption that they are works of fiction (they are both labeled as such on their front covers in the US editions), while the reader may enter *Summertime* expecting something at least basically nonfictional.[7] Regardless of whether readers enter expecting fiction or nonfiction, they end up at the same place with all three texts: somewhere in between. These books require us to suspend our expectation that fiction and nonfiction may be easily separated, and if we are to have a reading experience with any hope of satisfaction then we must find a way to be comfortable with how unsettled the texts are. Nonetheless, it is a different experience to have nonfiction reveal its fictionality than to have fiction function in a nonfictional mode, because where the reader enters determines what is (at least initially) questioned. The first lesson of these texts' pedagogies is that their form and genre are unstable, but in *Elizabeth Costello*, for instance, it is not the genre of the essay that is destabilized but the genre of the novel, while in *Summertime* it is the genres of memoir and biography that get destabilized as reading begins.

With the end of apartheid, and then with his move to Australia, Coetzee was able to realize the goal he had spoken of to David Attwell in 1991 when discussing his Jerusalem Prize speech, the goal of being able to be closer to writers like Cervantes and Milan Kundera, whose "deep social and historical responsibility" could be expressed through "the penetration with which, in their different ways and to their different degrees, they reflect on the nature and crisis of fiction, or fictionalizing, in their respective ages" (Coetzee 1991: 67). To be

---

[7] More readers may begin *Summertime* expecting fiction than might begin *Elizabeth Costello* or *Diary of a Bad Year* expecting something other than fiction, particularly in the United States, where the hardcover edition of *Summertime* included the label "fiction" (in the UK, the book was not categorized by genre, but instead given the subtitle common to *Boyhood* and *Youth*: "Scenes from Pronvincial Life." The collected edition *Scenes from Provincial Life* is labeled as "Fiction/Memoir" in small print on the back of the US paperback, perhaps the most accurate label for these texts). But *Summertime*'s predecessors, *Boyhood* and *Youth*, were both marketed and read as at least mostly nonfictional memoirs, and I remember my own reaction on first encountering *Summertime* being some combination of frustration, puzzlement, and amusement as my desires for a memoir of Coetzee's adulthood were smashed. That initial reaction is visible in my 2009 *Quarterly Conversation* essay on Coetzee's memoirs, "Intentional Schizophrenia," an essay that also fits with much of my analysis here of Coetzee's use of genre expectations for particular purposes.

able to address the crisis of fiction and fictionalizing without feeling socially and historically irresponsible, Coetzee needed first to escape the system that made him a colonizer and to leave the country where "truth [...] overwhelms and swamps every act of the imagination." Before he could feel comfortable moving the crisis of fictionality to the forefront of his writing, Coetzee had to get through the social crisis that was life in the apartheid state.

From social crisis to the crisis of fictionality

The first six chapters (or "lessons") of *Elizabeth Costello* began as lectures Coetzee delivered between 1996 and 2002, a period that corresponds to the final years of Nelson Mandela's tenure as South Africa's first democratically elected president through the first few years of Thabo Mbeki's presidency. In the situations of their original presentations, these texts had a similar initial effect as the one I am ascribing to *Summertime*: the audiences expected nonfictional lectures and instead found themselves listening to J.M. Coetzee read about a fictional woman, Elizabeth Costello, giving lectures and having conversations. This situation was highlighted when two of the lectures were published as *The Lives of Animals* in 1999; *Publisher's Weekly* began their review by saying, "The audience of the 1997–98 Tanner Lectures at Princeton probably expected South African novelist Coetzee to deliver a pair of formal essays similar to those on censorship he presented in *Giving Offence*. Instead, he gave his listeners fiction[...]" ("Fiction Book Review" 1999: 193). The reader of *The Lives of Animals* can't help but wonder how much of the clearly fictional narrative is to be taken as expressing Coetzee's own opinions—is Elizabeth Costello, as some reviewers wondered or suspected, just his mouthpiece, a disingenuous tool he uses to distance himself from having to take responsibility for controversial opinions? In his own response at the Tanner Lectures and reprinted in the book, Peter Singer wrote a dialogue between a representation of himself and his daughter in which the Peter Singer character says, "It's a marvelous device, really. Costello can blithely criticize the use of reason, or the need to have any clear principles or proscriptions, without Coetzee really committing himself to these claims" (Coetzee 1999: 91). Singer's own dialogue shows that the dialogue form does not have to allow the radical unsettling that Coetzee's does: Singer's dialogue is a conversation without much tension in which the reader has no reason to believe that anything the Singer character says is not what flesh-and-blood Peter Singer would write in an essay (and, indeed, has). Singer's text offers no crisis of genre or fictionality: it's a light philosophical dialogue that does nothing except what we expect a light philosophical dialogue to do; its fictionality sits at exactly the rhetorical distance we would expect if we'd ever read even just a Wikipedia page about Plato.

There is, though, a clear crisis of fictionality in *The Lives of Animals* and in the other story-as-lecture situations Coetzee created. It is a crisis instigated by the presence of fictionality within the situation and paratexts, a presence announced by the third-person point of view, the present tense, and the lack of a commenting and authoritative narrator. These features are not exclusive to fiction—they are common in many narrative essays and works of journalism, though essays usually include some sort of commenting narrator and journalism is rarely in the present tense—and, indeed, they are features of *Boyhood* and *Youth*, both of which are at least as much memoirs as they are novels. In the situation of public lectures, however, and on pages of what is supposed to be a collection of lectures (with footnotes!), these features stand out and draw attention to themselves.

Whether we believe we are hearing/reading fiction or some sort of narrative nonfiction, the point of view, tense, and lack of unifying, authoritative commentary invites us to reflect on what the presence of fiction in nonfiction achieves, and what narrative may be able to accomplish that more straightforward and polemical essaying cannot. When these texts became part of *Elizabeth Costello*, the event of the Tanner lectures was not emphasized, the footnotes were removed, the texts were no longer surrounded by other writers' critical essays in response, and the book was packaged as fiction, making readers' expectations different from what they were for either the lecture events or the book *The Lives of Animals*. The crisis of fictionality became reversed. Instead of a text that frustrates the desire for a straightforward lecture or essay, Coetzee now offered a text that frustrates the desire for a straightforward work of fiction. The additional chapters beyond those from *The Lives of Animals* complicated the reader's understanding of the character of Elizabeth Costello, creating, in Dominic Head's words, "a more pronounced inconsistency in the central character [that] suits the development of Coetzee's concerns" (2009: 109). The development of his concerns was toward new explorations of fictionality and what Jane Poyner, following Coetzee's lead, calls "the pact of genre." She states that "*Lives, Elizabeth Costello* and *Diary* ask, what is the cost of truth to the genres of the public lecture and opinion piece? Or, what are the necessary conditions for truth to be spoken?" (Poyner 2009: 171).

It is important to note that though the questions Poyner reads the texts as raising may be valid ones, their priority via the individual texts is quite different. *Lives of Animals* indeed places questions of truth and public writing (and public thinking) at the forefront, but *Elizabeth Costello* begins to subsume and complicate them toward other concerns, and *Diary of a Bad Year* highlights the desire and intention to share opinions publicly, but does so with no depiction whatsoever of the presentation and reception of opinions beyond the novel's three characters. In showing the process of creating, expressing, and distributing opinions, *Diary of a Bad Year* precedes *Elizabeth Costello*, and *Summertime* serves as a kind of coda. *Diary* dramatizes the desire to be and/or to encounter a public intellectual; *Elizabeth Costello* often dramatizes the public intellectual on public stages, allowing an exploration of the consequent implications and problems; in *Summertime*, we see the ripples of a public life after that life has ended. It seems to me that the movement Poyner describes shows not that *The Lives of Animals* is a text in congruence with Coetzee's later concerns, but rather is, like *Boyhood* and *Disgrace*, a last reckoning with the situation of the writer who lives amidst social crisis, while *Elizabeth Costello*, *Youth*, *Diary of a Bad Year*, and *Summertime* all seek to help the writer and reader think about life in some sort of *after*.[8]

If we consider *Elizabeth Costello*, *Diary of a Bad Year*, and *Summertime* as together exploring a crisis of fictionality via a pedagogy that makes the crisis one for the reader (in a way that separates those texts' strategies from the concerns and pedagogies of *Boyhood*, *The Lives of Animals*, and *Disgrace*), then we must pay some attention to how each book concludes, because it is at the moment of conclusion that the text leaves readers on their own to sally forth into the world beyond the text, putting whatever lessons they have learned into practice.

Summertime ends with an "undated fragment" written by the now-deceased John Coetzee, a fragment written in the style of *Boyhood* and *Youth*, that begins

---

[8] *Youth* is in many ways the text caught most powerfully in between the *now* of social crisis and whatever lies beyond it: its topic is a first escape from the scene of crisis. Though it doesn't reach beyond Coetzee's time in England, and thus does not describe the events leading to Coetzee's return to South Africa, *Youth* nonetheless conveys a strong sense that the exile the Coetzee figure in the book finds is dismal and unsatisfying, and it ends with the character's reflection on what he assumes will be the death of his fellow computer programmer, Gunapathy, who eats terribly ("despite his MSc in computer science he doesn't know about vitamins and minerals and amino acids"), while he himself is "locked into an attenuating endgame, playing himself, with each move, further into a corner and into defeat." The book ends with a vision of the two exiles dead: "When they have fetched Ganapathy they might as well come and fetch him too" (Coetzee 2012: 284). The word *fetch* twice in the final sentence links the idea of death with the idea of return, for though the image the text sets up in the sentence before it is one of police and medics taking a corpse out of a flat on a stretcher, *to fetch* does not simply mean "to bring out" but "to bring back."

with a return to the Karoo of *Boyhood*, then ends with John facing what he perceives as a choice: Whether to take care of his ailing father or to abandon him:

> It used to be that he, John, had too little employment. Now that is about to change. Now he will have as much employment as he can handle, as much and more. He is going to have to abandon some of his personal projects and be a nurse. Alternatively, if he will not be a nurse, he must announce to his father: *I cannot face the prospect of ministering to you day and night. I am going to abandon you. Goodbye.* One or the other: there is no third way. (Coetzee 2012: 484)

This was not, in fact, a choice Coetzee himself faced. As his actual biographer points out, "This is part of the fiction that *Summertime* interweaves with fact, because [Coetzee's parents] died in the 1980s, while in the 1970s John was married with children. Jack [Coetzee's father] did not at any stage live with John's family" (Kannemeyer 2012: 440). *Summertime* ends with a fiction, and it ends with a stark choice between losing yourself in caring for someone who is ailing and preserving something of yourself by abandoning a parent, a person who, whatever you may feel about them, is intimately part of your creation, development, and life.

Elizabeth Costello ends with the beguiling "Postscript" that is the letter from "Elizabeth, Lady Chandos, to Francis Bacon," the final paragraph of which ends as a plea to "you, who are known above all men to select your words and set them in place and build your judgements as a mason builds a wall with bricks," a description of Bacon that in some ways fits with reviewers' and critics' descriptions of Coetzee's prose. "Drowning," Lady Chandos says, "we write out of our separate fates. Save us" (Coetzee 2004: 230). This plea to a writer and public intellectual to *save us* rhymes with the obligation that John in *Summertime* seems to feel from his father, but it comes from the other direction: this is not Francis Bacon considering whether to devote his life to himself or to someone else, but rather someone else pleading for consideration, sympathy, and help. The crises the characters face are quite different—in *Summertime*, it is a crisis of body and age, utterly concrete and familiar; in *Elizabeth Costello*, it is a crisis of language and philosophy, abstract and difficult to understand—but the texts similarly end by opening space to imagine the value, duties, and limitations of caring; such opening is consistent with the transition in Coetzee's work that María J. López identifies as beginning with *Age of Iron*, a transition that begins a consistent concern with ideas of caring, charity, and *caritas* (López 2011: 276).

The final paragraph of *Elizabeth Costello* is not quite the end of the book, because there is the signature ("Your obedient servant/Elizabeth C.") and a date: "This 11 September, AD 1603" (Coetzee 2004: 230). The date 11 September is among the most infamous of modern times, but even before the terrorist attack of 2001 it was a tragic date in contemporary history, being the day when Salvador Allende died in Chile's 1973 coup d'etat, a coup supported by the CIA, and which led to the murderous dictatorship of Augusto Pinochet. (Isabel Allende, Salvador Allende's first cousin once removed, would go on to be an internationally best-selling novelist.) The year 1603 was the year of another Elizabeth's death, Queen Elizabeth I (who signed official documents *Elizabeth R.*, as does the current Queen Elizabeth). If we accept these dates as meaningful and not random, we might say that *Elizabeth Costello* ends with a plea for help in a crisis of language and then with allusions to death: mass, highly political death, and then the personal death of a highly public person, a monarch with a successor in title and name alive (and elderly) when *Elizabeth Costello* was written and published.[9]

Diary of a Bad Year continues to develop ideas of caring and responsibility up to its last pages, but its conclusion makes a new move in Coetzee's novels: instead of ending only with the death or abjection of the protagonist, in *Diary of a Bad Year*, the protagonist is supplanted. Because of its tripartite structure, the novel's final page concludes three sections. The top, JC's "Second Diary" ends with a paragraph about Tolstoy and Dostoyevsky as writers who clearly set "with such indisputable certainty the standards toward which any serious novelist must toil" and who, through their models, allow a writer to become "a better artist: and by better I do not mean more skillful but ethically better. They annihilate one's impurer pretensions; they clear one's eyesight; they fortify one's arm." (Ever the formalist, Coetzee ends the first of his three sections with a sentence of three parts. The final sentence of the third section will also end with a trio.) The second section is Anya's letter to JC, though presented to us via his own diary, which is what the center section has been up to page 191, when Anya's letter began. "I know you get a lot of fan mail from admirers which you chuck away," Anya writes, "but I am hoping this got through to you."

---

[9] The "Strong Opinions" section of *Diary of a Bad Year* is also dated: "12 September 2005–31 May 2006." Not only is September 12 one day after September 11, but it was also the day of Steve Biko's death in 1977, a day we know from Kannemeyer and Attwell was important to Coetzee. May 31 is less obvious to most US readers than anything related to September 11, but it was the date of the end of the Second Boer War in 1902, the date of the creation of the Union of South Africa in 1910, and the date the Union of South Africa became the Republic of South Africa in 1961.

(*Got through to you*, of course, is an ambiguous phrase. Might Anya's letter get through to him like Dostoyevsky and Tolstoy, might it help annihilate some of JC's impurer pretensions, clear his eyesight, and fortify his arm? That question is up to the reader to answer. Has the letter gotten through to us?) Anya not only signs her name, but adds a parenthesis: "(admirer too)." The third section is Anya's own diary, one JC does not read. If this final page is read from top to bottom, Anya's diary is the last and the end of the book. It is a paragraph in which she imagines his death, and she imagines herself doing exactly what John in *Summertime* considered a burdensome obligation, one he considered fleeing from: Anya will "hold his hand tight and give him a kiss on the brow, a proper kiss, just to remind him of what he is leaving behind. Good night, Señor C, I will whisper in his ear: sweet dreams, and flights of angels, and all the rest" (Coetzee 2008: 227).

This final page of *Diary of a Bad Year* moves us from the public and literary-historical into the private, personal, and intimate. It also moves the book from the voice of the old white male author to the voice of the younger Latina, the woman who writes (her own diary and letters, at least) but who is not a public figure. (With an allusion, it also subsumes another white male patriarch: Shakespeare, via Anya's offhand reference to Horatio's words at Hamlet's death.) Anya's voice doesn't exist solely in its own diary; it infiltrates the other sections, too. In his diary, JC tells us about the effect of Anya's questions and comments on the essays he is writing. In a diegetical sense, in some ways the top section texts are also touched by Anya, as she is their typist. Then, for the last thirty-six pages of the book, Anya's own writing takes over the middle section.

In all of these books' endings, we have a diminishment of a white male figure of at least some public stature (John in *Summertime*, who is a diminishment of J.M. Coetzee and a character who ends in a sad, even pitiful dilemma; Francis Bacon in *Elizabeth Costello*, who, the dates after the signature suggest, can provide no help to Elizabeth C.; and JC, whose voice is displaced even in his own diary). The diminishment of the prominent white male and the suggestion of his uselessness link these endings to that of *Disgrace*. Only *Diary of a Bad Year* has an ending that could be read as hopeful, but these three books' conclusions are nonetheless different from what came before and also united with each other. The difference that unites these texts and separates them from *Disgrace* (as well as *The Lives of Animals*) is that each of these three works somehow unsettles assumptions of fiction and nonfiction (as *Disgrace* does not) while resolving that crisis by returning the reader to fiction at the end (as *The Lives of Animals* does not). As much as the text of *Elizabeth Costello* keeps pushing away from fictionality, the final lesson is the most openly and explicitly fictional, while the "Postscript" breaks from the narrative to offer a fictional epistle (to a nonfictional person) that stages a call for help against the metaphorical and allegorical properties of language and storytelling. Anya, a fictional character, writes the last words of *Diary of a Bad Year*. The situation of John and his father at the end of *Summertime* is completely imaginary. For all the differences in the ways that they push toward the limits of fiction, then, each book ends up, in its own way and to different degrees, back at fiction and as fiction.

In an interview conducted by Jane Poyner, Coetzee said, "It is hard for fiction to be good fiction while it is in the service of something else" (Coetzee 2006: 21). The question from Poyner that led to the response was, "Does fiction have an important part to play in maintaining a critical opposition?" (part of a longer question about the role of the writer in relation to the post-apartheid African National Congress), and so Coetzee's "something else" in this instance means a specific political position. However, fiction's inherent—definitive—distance from fact makes it, in a broad sense, always in service to *something else*. (Wolfgang Iser's triad, discussed in the Introduction, makes this particularly clear, with fiction's form being what allows a transgression of the border between *the real* and *the imaginary*.) While Samuel Delany maintains that science fiction requires the reader to compare the world of the story to the world as the reader knows it, this is the situation of all fiction, and perhaps the situation of any text that requires the reader to exercise imagination, because imagination begins from personal experience and knowledge. The reader of a novel set in a familiar place will compare the writer's description to the reader's experience; the reader of a novel set in a place unfamiliar to that reader will be likely to compare what is unfamiliar to something familiar. The rhetorical mode of fiction always makes metaphor possible, because readers may at any moment compare their experience of the text with their experience of the world, not only in the veridical way of nonfiction and familiar realism ("Does this account of the world match my experience of the world?"), but, with fiction, in a way that could broadly be called allegorical ("What within this imaginary description of a world compares with or stands for something real in the world itself?"). In that sense, fiction is always in danger of being read allegorically, and the possibility and desire for allegory are a possibility and desire that Coetzee often teases from his readers, always to some extent frustrating and complicating it via destabilized meaning and paradox.[10]

As we've seen, social crisis increases the desire among writers and readers to narrow the rhetorical distance that constitutes fiction. Such a desire often finds expression not only via outright didacticism but also through a limiting of the potential allegorical meanings of the fictional text, rendering proper and acceptable only readings that find a one-to-one symbolic relationship between the figures in the text and the figures of the world outside the text. (That desire is vividly demonstrated by Nadine Gordimer in her famous review of *Life and Times of Michael K* for the *New York Review of Books* in 1984.) Dominic Head reads the ending of the last lesson in *Elizabeth Costello*, "At the Gate," as dramatizing the paradox that "the writer cannot escape the imposition of metaphorical levels on his or her expression, and this may produce a nightmarish sense of being misunderstood (as in Costello's parodically Kafkaesque experience 'at the gate'). In this sense, the frustration of Costello is a way for Coetzee to explore and express the limits of fiction and of the writer's authority" (Head 2009: 115).

The death of the authority: *Diary of a Bad Year*

Given the obscurities and ambiguities common to Modernist works, it seems safe to propose that Modernist aesthetics valorize texts that are destabilized and texts that destabilize. Even if, for instance, a given novel is not as difficult to parse as *Finnegans Wake*, in scorning the most familiar established conventions of narrative the given novel will still force readers who normally rely on such conventions to reflect on how to make sense of what they read. Sense begins from familiarity, and as familiarity diminishes, the reader must experiment with new strategies to bring sense to the text. (Or give up on sense altogether.) Thus questions of interpretation become unavoidable when reading works that violate conventions and protocols, making the reading process, if not necessarily unstable, at least destabilized.

---

[10] The question of Coetzee and allegory is one of the most fraught in Coetzee studies, particularly since Derek Attridge's *J.M. Coetzee and the Ethics of Reading* (2004), where the second chapter is titled "Against Allegory." Dominic Head's "A Belief in Frogs: J.M. Coetzee's Enduring Faith in Fiction" (2009) is a thoughtful counter to Attridge's view. See also "Coetzee and Late Style: Exile within the Form" by Julian Murphet (2011) and "Allegories of the Bioethical: Reading J.M. Coetzee's *Diary of a Bad Year*" by Stuart J. Murray (2014).

Destabilization is a familiar experience for readers of Coetzee, but though his oeuvre is filled with destabilizing texts, *Diary of a Bad Year* is clearly the most destabilized. The first page presents four paragraphs from an essay ("On the Origins of the State"), then a horizontal line and one paragraph of first-person narrative, that of an aging writer we will mostly know as JC. With the sixth chapter, the page breaks into three sections, adding the first-person narrative of Anya, JC's neighbor (and, ultimately, assistant) beneath his own. The pages continue in this tripartite, trivocal form. Until the middle of the tenth chapter, each section is syntactically complete, but on page 42, Anya's section ends mid-sentence, forcing the reader into a choice: whether to continue reading Anya's narrative on the bottom of the next page or to move to the top and continue with the essay "On National Shame." The form requires the reader to be active, to make choices, to negotiate changing points of view and changing rhetorics.

By placing text that seems unambiguously essayistic above text presented as characters' diaries, the book sets the rhetorics of fiction and nonfiction beside each other, and in doing so, undercuts any block of text's straightforward existence as rhetoric. The essay cannot remain only an essay, the fiction only a fiction. This is important not only because it is further evidence of Coetzee pressing against the limits of fiction, but also because one of the central concerns of *Diary of a Bad Year* is the value and effect of polemic and public speech. If the Modernist aesthetic is to abjure polemic in fiction, there is no reason that a Modernist essay should not be able to speak directly and forcefully to socio-political concerns (or anything else), and many aesthetics, Modernist or not, consider nonfiction a more efficient mode with which to directly address (and potentially affect) public life. Certainly, as we've seen, Woolf didn't shy away from polemic in her nonfiction. But *Diary of a Bad Year* is set up in such a way that the reader must question the usefulness and ethics of polemic even in nonfiction, and hence must cast a skeptical eye on both the impulse to intervene directly in public and the effect of such interventions.

Much writing on *Diary of a Bad Year*, particularly the reviews on publication, raises the question of whether JC's "Strong Opinions" are John Coetzee's own opinions. It seems to me that Coetzee clearly wants to tempt us toward such a question, but also that he trusts readers of fiction to be skilled enough not to see characters as a writer's mouthpiece. When the book was published, many reviewers failed this test. Even as skilled a reader as Peter Brooks couldn't keep himself from reading what is ascribed to JC as being the unfiltered ideas of J.M. Coetzee: he begins an essay on "The Ethics of Reading" (2008) for

The Chronicle of Higher Education by discussing "Coetzee's fictional persona," but by the end describes one of the "Strong Opinions" essays as "Coetzee's bitter condemnation of our [that is, teachers of literature] role in the world," without once noting that the essayistic passages only take up part of the pages and thus are not given to readers as straightforward, unmediated excursions. While equating a character and an author is usually a sign of a simplistic, even naïve, interpretation, Coetzee knows the trap he is setting. He could have made the character of JC distinctly different from himself—not only given him a different age (as he does), but given him initials that don't fit his own, a background that would not have any echo of his, and a writerly history that does not include the names of books Coetzee himself wrote. Instead, Coetzee chose to make some alignment with JC, a South African writer who has moved to Australia, and among whose works are a book on censorship (one that sounds awfully like Coetzee's *Giving Offense*) and a novel titled *Waiting for the Barbarians*. Part of the project of *Diary of a Bad Year*, then, is to seduce us toward aligning JC and J.M. Coetzee and perceiving the "Strong Opinions" as those of Coetzee himself. But to stop there is to stop at the beginning of the lesson.

Jan Wilm points to Coetzee's frequent "technique of increasing the ambiguous force of a text," a technique that "is directly geared at the reader, but it is also geared at making the reader reflect on reading" (2016: 123). For a reader who stops and reflects on the desire to equate Coetzee and JC, new understandings become possible. One might wonder, for instance, why it matters and how it changes the text to assume that the opinions are those of the in-the-flesh writer J.M. Coetzee rather than a character imagined by that in-the-flesh writer. That question leads the reader toward a choice of rhetorics. To read the "Strong Opinions" and the later "Soft Opinions" (as Anya dubs them [193]) as the opinions of J.M. Coetzee is to read them via the rhetoric of nonfiction; to read them as the opinions of a fictional character is to read them via the rhetoric of fiction. The question that naturally follows is: What difference does such a change of rhetorics make?

Much of Coetzee's earlier work shows that the effect of rhetorical differences depends on how the reader makes sense of the rhetoric and the differences. *Diary of a Bad Year* goes beyond this basic insight, however, to provide—indeed, to make unavoidable—a level of readerly freedom of choice previously unavailable in Coetzee's texts, no matter how much those texts otherwise place questions of interpretation at the forefront of the reading experience or otherwise unsettle writer-to-reader communication. Peter McDonald's experience of reading the novel is likely a common one: "To read *Diary* for the first time is, if my own experience is anything to go by, to feel torn between the conventional novelistic desire to read for the plot, as it were, chasing forward to see how things unfold for either JC or Anya, and the traditional essayistic impulse to reflect on JC's provocative opinions" (2010: 494).

What such a reading experience achieves is both to dramatize certain ideas and concepts within the text itself and to place the reader into a position of having to choose between different possibilities. The range of possibilities opened by the material that comprises *Diary of a Bad Year* nudges the reader toward a field of ethical choices and an awareness of the possibility of ersatz ethics that Jonathan Lear identifies (2010: 69). Like familiar literary forms, ersatz ethics allow conventional thinking, and allow the reader/thinker to avoid examining the status quo structures that make conventions possible. Such conventions provide alibis, they let us think of ourselves as holding upstanding, progressive thoughts when in fact we are filling a template, reciting the lines for the role of ethical thinker without, in fact, doing any meaningful ethical thinking at all.

To combat such ersatz thinking, Coetzee could have used a technique he used previously, one common to many novels: presenting a character that readers must assess for themselves. JC could, in other words, have been another version of David Lurie in *Disgrace*, and readers could have decided to what extent they found his beliefs and actions to be ethical. Or, in another approach, a satirist would have created situations in JC's life that showed him capable of writing liberal-minded essays while behaving in his own life in ways more congruent with what he denounces than what he praises, thus highlighting the hypocrisy, for instance, of a complacent liberal class. (Coetzee's fiction has always been more complex than this.) Though at first *Diary of a Bad Year* may seem to approach satire, it uses a fundamentally different technique. As Lear notes, Coetzee faced a challenge if he wanted to explore ethical thinking: the challenge of his own authority. "The aim of the style," Lear says, "is not for Coetzee to show off—to demonstrate that he, unlike the melancholy, infirm, single-voiced JC, can do postmodern hip. Rather, it is an attempt to defeat the reader's desire to defer to the 'moral authority,' the 'novelist' J. M. Coetzee" (71). In one way or another, all of Coetzee's fiction is anti-authoritarian in this sense; it's one of the reasons many readers find his work vexing. However, in whatever ways Coetzee's previous novels undermined the singular authority of the text, *Diary of a Bad Year* is the first to place the authority of Coetzee's own byline into question (*Summertime* will do this as well, differently).

As we have seen, some readers were tempted to read Elizabeth Costello's opinions as J.M. Coetzee's own; nonetheless, Elizabeth Costello was undeniably a character without any direct equivalence to Coetzee himself. The same cannot be said of JC. The nonequivalence of Costello and Coetzee allows the reader a way out if they want one: If, for whatever reason, I do not want to think that J.M. Coetzee believes what Elizabeth Costello believes, I have plenty of ways to preserve Coetzee as an authority preferable to Costello. Because writers choose the textual structure and content of their books, and those books are given a byline as a sign of the shaping authority, no novel whose author is known can completely disavow the novelist's authority, but, as Lear demonstrates at length, *Diary of a Bad Year* does whatever it can to frustrate the reader who seeks an author-function to communicate an ethical meaning or message. In addition, the book puts the very idea of writer-as-authority at the heart of its concerns with one of the starkest differences between JC and Coetzee himself, which Ana Falcato identifies: "As tempting as it may be for readers to conflate JC and John Coetzee, there is something that sets the two apart unmistakably. JC is willing to publish his strong opinions on contemporary social issues precisely as they stand: parched theoretical fruits from a stage of life of decreasing vitality. John Coetzee is not willing to do so" (2017: 257).

Here, then, we have one way that Coetzee approaches the problem of didacticism and Modernist aesthetics of artistic autonomy: He wraps didactic material within a novelistic context that doesn't simply complicate the content of that didactic material or submit it to critique (as in *Elizabeth Costello*), but that makes both the idea and form of didacticism central to the novel's concerns. The differences between the two diaries are important, too, as it is the soft opinions of the Second Diary that seem most effective to readers, critics, and the characters themselves. The soft opinions are more personal and idiosyncratic, less hieratic, less aimed at some abstract, dispassionate realm of universal laws.[11] The influence and growing prominence of Anya through the Second Diary seem quite fitting from a common feminist standpoint regarding how opinion is valued—what Woolf in *A Room of One's Own* critiqued as "masculine values" that inevitably affect what is seen as authoritative and what is not (Woolf [1929] 2015: 72–73). Even the terminology is familiar to feminist

---

[11] Considering Coetzee's criticisms of Nabokov, discussed later, this may suggest one reason why he chose Nabokov's own title of *Strong Opinions* for JC's writings.

analysis: for instance, the traditional association of men with *strong* and the withering phallic associations of *soft* opinions. Though *Diary* includes just such a gender critique within its implications, its destabilizing of authority is more general rather than specifically feminist, because the book does not offer the reader any ultimate judgment on the various voices and opinions. Anya may be the most sympathetic character and Alan the least, but such sympathies don't lead to a rubric that would help us evaluate the opinions that fill the top sections of the pages. Unlike *Elizabeth Costello*, most of what is discussed in the essays is not discussed by the characters directly, so the opinions are simply there on the page, our perception of them affected, certainly, by how we feel about JC (and, depending on how we perceive the fiction's distance, how we feel about J.M. Coetzee), but the essays take up such a large part of the book that it is difficult to separate how we feel about JC from how we feel about the essays, because much of our perception of JC is a perception of his voice and opinions atop all of the pages. There are a few pages without diary sections, but none without JC's essays, and so every reader must contend with the dominating authority that the opinions attempt to exert. However, everything about the book (texts and paratexts) serves to confirm an insight Fred Moten stated in an interview: "the authority that we tend to want to invest in authorship is always-already broken and disrupted and incomplete."

Diary of a Bad Year stages a crisis of authority that is also an opportunity for pedagogy, one Barbara Johnson identified in *A World of Difference* as "the depersonalization of deconstruction and the repersonalization of feminism" (1989: 44). This is not to say that JC's opinions are models of deconstructive reading; they are not, and for all of his post-structuralist moves, Coetzee himself has never shown a commitment to deconstruction in the way that, for instance, Samuel Delany has. What we see with *Diary of a Bad Year* is an impulse toward deconstruction, an impulse that serves as one tool within the book's pedagogy, as the utopian impulse in *The Years* served Woolf's pedagogy there.

The writings and, to a greater extent, the figure of Paul de Man offer one way to reconcile some of the difficulties *Diary of a Bad Year* offers. From citations of de Man in "Confession and Double Thought" (in *Doubling the Point*), we know that Coetzee was familiar with *Allegories of Reading*, and in de Man's formulation of deconstruction we find ideas that become (at least partly) literalized by the structure of *Diary of a Bad Year*. For instance, after a discussion of a passage from Proust, de Man writes:

> The reading is not "our" reading, since it uses only the linguistic elements provided by the text itself; the distinction between author and reader is one of the false distinctions that the reading makes evident. The deconstruction is not something we have added to the text but it constituted the text in the first place. A literary text simultaneously asserts and denies the authority of its own rhetorical mode, and by reading the text as we did we were only trying to come closer to being as rigorous a reader as the author had to be in order to write the sentence in the first place. Poetic writing is the most advanced and refined mode of deconstruction; it may differ from critical or discursive writing in the economy of its articulation, but not in kind. (de Man 1979: 17)[12]

Johnson includes part of this quotation in an essay on "Teaching Deconstructively," where she positions deconstructive reading as a technique to help students move toward an active mode of reading: deconstructive interpretation "enables students to respond to what is there before them on the page, it can teach them how to work out the logic of a reading on their own rather than passively deferring to the authority of superior learning" (2014: 348). Where in *A World of Difference* Johnson positions deconstruction (or at least its general public perception) as impersonal and thus the converse of personal-is-political feminism, in "Teaching Deconstructively" (first published in 1985) she sets deconstruction in opposition to "humanism," so that "deconstruction is a reading strategy that carefully follows both the meanings and the suspensions and displacements of meaning in a text, while humanism is a strategy to stop reading when the text stops saying what it ought to have said" (2014: 347). That strategy to stop reading when the text doesn't say what, in the reader's assumption, it ought to have said brings us back to propaganda: in Johnson's formulation, humanism desires texts to be Spivak's Narcissus "waiting to see his own powerful image in the eyes of the other," perhaps even to be texts that function primarily as propaganda, while deconstruction allows texts to escape Narcissus and to be something other than propaganda.

Johnson concludes her essay with a deconstruction of the binary she has proposed, claiming that

> no matter how rigorously a deconstructor might follow the letter of the text, the text will end up showing the reading process as a resistance to the letter. The deconstructor thus comes face to face with her own humanism. This is small comfort, of course, since the text has shown humanism to consist in the blindness

---

[12] The chapter this passage appears in was first published as "Semiology and Rhetoric" in *Diacritics* (vol. 3, no. 3, 1973, pp. 27–33), which Coetzee cites in his essay on passives in *Doubling the Point* (1992: 152, 408).

of self-projection. But then, in the final analysis, it is perhaps precisely as an apprenticeship in the repeated and inescapable oscillation between humanism and deconstruction that literature works its most rigorous and inexhaustible seductions. (Johnson 2014: 355–356)

Such an oscillation is at the heart of Coetzee's project in *Diary of a Bad Year* and, in many ways, throughout his other books. In an interview in 2000, Coetzee said of *Waiting for the Barbarians*, "Sometimes the people who believe in and act in terms of humane values get used, and perhaps they ought to be a little more aware." Writing fiction, he says, is for him a way to explore ideas of humane values and to raise questions for the reader not only of how to be "a little more aware," but also of what such values can achieve.

> I'm writing these books to pose the question of what good humane values are. And to pose that question without having the answer signalled from the beginning—namely, that humane values are everything or humane values are nothing. We cannot only believe in humane values quite sincerely; we must also act in terms of humane values. The question is, is that going to be enough? (Coetzee 2016: 228).

Humane values are not enough, rationality and argument are not enough, abstracted ideas are not enough. Is there an "enough"? Coetzee has no answer to that question—or, at least, no positive answer; one might easily imagine him answering, "No"—but it is the posing of the question that is necessary, even if it is unanswerable, because posing the question and stretching for answers may be a productive activity to help us make our ethics more actual, less ersatz.

Like the Magistrate in *Waiting for the Barbarians*, JC is "a man of humane values." Those values are expressed through his essays, which in their form as *Strong Opinions* are impersonal and seeking a kind of universal value that the lower parts of the pages undercut not through argument, which is a minor part of the diary entries, but through a presentation of context. Presenting a context for the essays creates a new (and more feminist) way of deconstructing a text, a way of requiring the reader to see the text, as de Man says, simultaneously asserting and denying "the authority of its own rhetorical mode." The simultaneous assertion and denial of authority is the primary effect of *Diary of a Bad Year's* rhetoric: authority of opinion, authority of social position, authority of genre, authority of language.

The deconstructive force within the form of *Diary of a Bad Year* works to add resistance to all of its textual moves, but it does so while also insisting on an awareness of the contexts that make writing and reading possible, what Lear calls the book's *spectacle of embedding*:

> That is, we see how the moral stances that are officially to be presented in the book form are embedded in the fantasies, happenings, musings, and struggles of the author's day-to-day life. It is that from which a normal book of moral essays would be cut off. I suggest that this imaginary embedding is meant to draw along parts of the reader's soul that would not be led by argument alone. (2010: 75)

Along with Stuart J. Murray, I am not convinced by "Lear's claim that *Diary's* sections are designed to reflect the three different parts of the Platonic soul (one could just as easily propose psychoanalytic or semiotic topographies)" (2014: 5), but Lear nonetheless identifies significant ways the text makes an appeal beyond straightforward argument and shows the limits of argument divorced from context. Johnson reaches a similar conclusion when discussing Paul de Man, deconstruction, and feminism: "While de Man's writing is haunted by the return of personification, feminist writing is haunted by the return of abstraction. The challenge facing both approaches is to recognize these ghosts not as external enemies but as the uncannily familiar strangers that make their own knowledge both possible and problematic" (1989: 46).

Those ghosts haunt *Diary of a Bad Year*, a book that recognizes and dramatizes just how much the disavowal of authority is not a straightforward task. Of de Man, Johnson writes: "Testimonials repeatedly assert that it was precisely his way of denying personal authority that engendered the unique power of his personal authority" (1989: 45). This is not necessarily the case for JC, but it is very much a bind J.M. Coetzee was in at the time he wrote *Diary of a Bad Year*— he was not simply an eminent writer and academic, but also the first person to win a second Booker Prize, an internationally best-selling writer, a Nobel laureate. Discussing Solzhenitsyn in *Giving Offense*, Coetzee stated that when he won the Nobel, Solzhenitsyn acquired "a degree of invulnerability" (1996: 137). Much of Coetzee's writing and public speaking from the beginning of his career onward demonstrate attempts to question the invulnerable authority of the author figure, but such attempts enter the foreground with *Elizabeth Costello, Slow Man, Diary of a Bad Year,* and *Summertime*. The critical and commercial success of *Disgrace* and then the award of the Nobel Prize added an inescapable, unrenounceable weight to the byline *J.M. Coetzee*. No matter how difficult it may have been before for Coetzee to deny or lessen his personal authority—to create vulnerability—after *Disgrace* it became nearly impossible.

As Johnson points out, there is a gender element to the inability to disavow authority, for she notes that "de Man's discourse of self-resistance and uncertainty has achieved such authority and visibility, while the self-resistance and uncertainty of *women* has been part of what has insured their lack of authority and their invisibility." (A simple thought experiment is worthwhile here: Would Nadine Gordimer or Toni Morrison have won the Nobel Prize if they expressed as much discomfort with making authoritative statements and issuing opinions as Coetzee did? Certainly, patriarchy punishes women for speaking out more than men, but this does not mean that patriarchy rewards self-resistance and uncertainty in women, even as it may desire those traits. White, heterosexual men's silence is readable as wise and enigmatic; women's silence stays silent.) For people already in a position outside of power, disavowal of authority only confirms the dominant discourse and strengthens forces of erasure. "It would seem," Johnson writes, "that one has to be positioned in the place of power in order for one's self-resistance to be valued. Self-resistance, indeed, may be one of the few viable postures remaining for the white male establishment" (1989: 45). With *Diary of a Bad Year*, it appears that Coetzee came to appreciate that, like humane values, self-resistance by the white male may be necessary, but it also may not be sufficient. The solution to such a problem was to create texts where the reader cannot take for granted either the authority of the text's content, or, more importantly, the authority of the byline. *Diary of a Bad Year* is still a book by J.M. Coetzee, but in reading it we learn how perilous it is to ascribe an authority to authorship beyond the brute fact of a byline.

Like Woolf's *Three Guineas*, *Diary of a Bad Year* is a fundamentally anti-authoritarian text, but it is differently so because it is written by someone with some of the greatest privileges of authority—the most privileged gender, sexuality, skin color; a man of international renown; a man whose work has made him wealthy.[13] Most of the world's newspapers, magazines, and book publishers would be happy to host Coetzee's opinions. He would be perfectly positioned for ersatz ethics, no matter what debates he entered or what side he took in the debate.

While Coetzee could see (and admire) that Dostoyevsky's dialogism increased the realism of his novels and made his characters convincing, straightforward

---

[13] By the time she wrote *Three Guineas*, Woolf had accumulated significant privilege and authority (she'd recently been on the cover of *Time* magazine), but the reception of her work, and *Three Guineas* in particular, proves the truth of Barbara Johnson's insight about women and self-resistance.

dialogism isn't enough to render ethics real. Jonathan Lear notes a weakness of the dialogue form made famous by Plato and, in a different way, used by Elizabeth Costello. Such dialogue "can encourage in the reader a sense that he is in the audience, watching the characters debate as though they were up on stage. Rather than being thrown into philosophy's midst, challenged to examine one's beliefs, one can feel like an arbiter, able to choose one's position from among the many presented according to taste" (2010: 72). Being *thrown into philosophy's midst* may be, then, one goal for the reader of *Diary of a Bad Year*, a goal supportive of actual ethical thinking. It is the form of the book that allows such thinking, because "there is no easy way for a reader to take on the strong opinions simply by taking Coetzee's or JC's word for it. If we think of ethical thought as something that cannot be accepted on authority, then this is a literary form that defeats a typical way in which ethical thought is itself defeated" (81). This destabilizing form moves beyond an absence of authority (a pedagogy seeking to teach readers to rely on their own insights rather than those of an intruding narrator) and creates a pedagogy that makes authority itself the focus of analysis. Such a pedagogy requires readers to learn both to do their own ethical thinking and to be aware of the seductions of authority.

Good infinity: *Summertime*

In the fall of 1997, J.M. Coetzee was in residence at Stanford University, where, less than a month after the Tanner Lectures at Princeton, he read his *Lives of Animals* lectures ("The Philosopher and the Animals," "The Poets and the Animals"). In addition, he gave a reading from his newly released book, *Boyhood: Scenes from Provincial Life*. The Stanford Humanities Center website reported that "Coetzee began his reading from *Boyhood* with the question his publisher asked him: 'Is this fiction or memoir?' Coetzee answered, 'Do I have to choose?'"[14]

The choice was one that seems to have annoyed him as he was writing. Kannemeyer reports that Coetzee began writing *Boyhood* in the first person point of view, then switched to third person early in the process. During the writing in August 1993, he made a note to himself: "Not a memoir but a novel, a slim novel"

---

[14] The web page is now defunct, but is available via the internet archive here: https://web.archive.org/web/20020817083443/http://shc.stanford.edu:80/shc/1997-1998/events/coetzee.html. The passage is also quoted by Sheila Collingwood-Whittick in "Autobiography as *Autre*biography" (2001: 14).

and then in September: "Think about all I did not do in this memoir: bring the atmosphere to life, tell anecdotes" (Kannemeyer 505). Nonetheless, despite the distancing effect of the third-person viewpoint, most readers seem to have read *Boyhood* and its sequel, *Youth*, as relatively unproblematic memoirs, and Kannemeyer himself considered them generally reliable sources of biographical information.

With *Summertime*, the problem of genre became a central concern of the book itself, because what was published as the third of the *Scenes from Provincial Life* could not in any way be read uncomplicatedly as memoir. Not only does most of the text consist of interviews with characters who knew a character named John Coetzee in the 1970s, but the John Coetzee of *Summertime* is dead. The death of this author is one key to the book's purposes, as Spivak says: "All texts lay out desires. Some make it their topic. All texts can give you the practices of the ethical reflexes. Some texts present those practices. This text presents the desiring character, about whom truth can be told because he is dead" (2014: 136).

Though published recently, *Summertime* has already received significant, insightful critical attention, and my purpose here is not to reiterate what has already been said, but to consider how *Summertime* develops our understanding of Coetzee's relationship to aesthetics, fiction, fictionality, pedagogy, and didacticism. *Elizabeth Costello* and *Diary of a Bad Year* push fiction perhaps as far from fictionality as it can go when the reader enters the text expecting a novel (or, at least, fiction); *Summertime* pushes from the opposite direction, showing what traces survive when what is assumed to be nonfiction is infused with fictionality. Of the three books, *Summertime* is by far the least polemical in its content—there is nothing like Elizabeth Costello's lectures or JC's "Strong Opinions." The primary focus of *Summertime* is the personal and intimate, which is exactly what Julia, at the end of her interview with Mr. Vincent, identifies as "what novels are about" (Coetzee 2012: 348). Coetzee's work from its beginning has shown that the personal is embedded within contexts that are social, political, and historical; furthermore, he has insisted that these contexts are also often textual. It is unsurprising that a man who is not only a novelist but a scholar of language and literature should value an analysis of textual inflections of power. Such an interest is highly Modernist—certainly, one of the shared qualities in the work of Woolf, Delany, and Coetzee is a persistent concern with inflections of power via language—even as it stands in opposition to certain Modernist tendencies that idealize an abstraction of the text from everything but itself. That opposition unites the otherwise often different inflections of Modernism that Coetzee, Delany, and Woolf deploy. Their ideas of the autonomy of art emphasize the freedom of the artist, not the separation of the work from the cares and crises of the world.

In an interview in *Doubling the Point*, Coetzee says he has "lost interest in Nabokov" because though Nabokov suffered the loss of his homeland and a beloved Old World culture, he "balked at facing the nature of his loss in its historical fullness" (1992: 28). Before he ever published a novel, and in the same year Nabokov published a book titled *Strong Opinions*, Coetzee was already criticizing Nabokov for an ideal of artistic autonomy at odds with his own: "The ideal of *Pale Fire*," Coetzee wrote in 1974, "is a Symbolist ideal: a state of being in which, having incorporated into itself all possible interpretations of itself, the work of art has, like a closed system of mirrors, shut itself off forever from interpretation and become a monument of unageing intellect" (Coetzee 1974: 6). Such an ideal is not Coetzee's: though he clearly desires that art be autonomous from socio-political determinism, his idea of autonomy does not require the work of art to be hermetic. That vision of art is apparent in his 1974 essay as an opposition to what Coetzee calls the "bad infinity of exegesis" that Nabokov attempts to contain in his novels (6). In his analysis of Nabokov (both in his remarks on *Pale Fire* and his more general comments in *Doubling the Point*), Coetzee sets himself against what he sees as Nabokov's desire for a self-contained text, a text stabilized by the authority of the text itself. In *Diary of a Bad Year*, JC's own "Strong Opinions" seem to aim to be "a monument of unageing intellect," and the anti-authoritarian force of the book shows the delusion of such a goal.

Summertime presents even more voices than *Diary of a Bad Year*, and it repeatedly emphasizes the historical and geographical locations of its characters, not only via their own words but also via the places and dates listed at the end of each of the interviews. It is only at the end of the book that we encounter anything undated (the final notebook of "undated fragments"). By the end, though, there is less need for situating: readers should by this point be able to situate the text for themselves. Once again, the progress of the book is away from outside authority (in this case a biographer) and toward the good infinity of the unstable text.

An unstable text is not, though, a text outside of "historical fullness"; quite the opposite, as history itself is not a stable text. *Summertime* begins with news that has become historical: First, a diaristic date ("22 August 1972") and then the opening sentence: "In yesterday's *Sunday Times*, a report from Francistown in Botswana." This fragment from John's notebook begins shortly after his return to South Africa, and immediately he is confronted with brutality outside South Africa that nonetheless originated there: "The killers appeared to be black, but one of the neighbours heard them speaking Afrikaans among themselves and was convinced they were whites in blackface. The dead were South Africans, refugees who had moved into the house mere weeks ago" (Coetzee 2012: 287). Not only that, but the killers' car was "a white American model." John's own identities and movements are mirrored in this act, his own bind clear: If he ever thought of himself as a refugee, he would now have to confront his use of such a term for himself, because whatever hardships he faced did not include hit squads. Regardless of his origins, he has arrived in South Africa like a white American vehicle, an item designed and built in white America. His challenge, as a white South African returned from America and with an Afrikaans name (if not exactly an Afrikaner identity), is how to avoid replicating violence, a violence that here is likely committed by murderous minstrelsy. Again and again, John must acknowledge white state violence against perceived enemies at the margins of the state—and must acknowledge it not as a general, abstract tendency, but as daily news items both horrifying and numbing: "So they come out, week after week, these tales from the borderlands, murders followed by bland denials. He reads the reports and feels soiled" (287).

His father, who dislikes "on the one hand, thugs who slaughter defenceless women and children, and, on the other, terrorists who wage war from havens across the border," avoids the news by reading cricket scores. "As a response to a moral dilemma it is feeble; yet is his own response—fits of rage and despair—any better?" The violence of "the men who dreamed up the South African version of public order" is not, as he says he once thought, a misreading of history, but rather an absolute ignorance and denial of history: "to say they had misread history was itself misleading. For they read no history at all" (288). The Afrikaner Nationalists "erected their fortress state and retreated behind its walls; there they would keep the flame of Western Christian civilization burning until finally the world came to its senses" (289). Building a fortress against public criticism, denying history, insisting on one's own rightness—John reads the violence of the Afrikaners as resulting from a closed epistemology, a denial of any reality outside the feedback loop of narrow ideology, the creation of a hermetic text that contains all its own answers and bends the world to its own shape, regardless of the misery and terror that result.

Each fragment ends with notes that the biographer later calls "memos addressed to himself," written in 1999 or 2000, "when he was thinking of reworking his diaries as a book" (299). The memo after the first fragment reads: "To be expanded on: his father's response to the times as compared to his own; their differences, their (overriding) similarities" (289). The memos incite a ghost text in readers' minds by pointing toward unexplored directions and unwritten pages. The final fragment links the personal and political physically, reflecting on the nearness of Pollmoor Prison to John's own home. "It is of course an irony that the South African *gulag* should protrude so obscenely into white suburbia[…]," leading him to wonder, "What does one do with the brute fact of Pollsmoor once the irony is used up?" The memo that follows states: "Continuation: the Prisons Service vans that pass along Tokai Road on their way from the courts; flashes of faces; fingers gripping the grated windows; what stories the Truscotts tell their children to explain those hands and faces, some defiant, some forlorn" (296–297). If we as readers pause here before turning the page, if we imagine the continuation that is sketched, then we must take a moment to reflect on how we tell stories to cover up unpleasant truths; how we reconcile the way we live with what we know; how, in other words, we use stories to help us get through our days and escape the crushing, debilitating guilt that might attend true contemplation of the gulag at the end of our street. What tales do we tell ourselves to make it possible to walk through town without looking in the eyes of the faces that glance our way through grated windows? And perhaps most importantly: What imprisoned eyes look out at us in our own world, separate from the world of the book? What streets do we walk down with conscience walled away?

The reader who comes to *Summertime* after *Boyhood* and *Youth* is primed for such work because the earlier books have set up expectations of form and meaning. Each reader has had to learn how to answer the question of what the words are trying to do, and then readers must reconcile their own reading practice with what these texts have given them to read. *Boyhood* and *Youth* are similar enough in form and effect that they create a gravitational field of expectations. The pedagogy of *Summertime* builds on the knowledge and habits the reader accumulated with the earlier books, expanding on the techniques each reader has developed to make sense of those texts while also, and quite quickly, challenging those techniques, complicating them, contradicting them. That reader is used to the third-person point of view and has probably come to think of the work nonetheless as a memoir, since aside from the point of view there is nothing in either text to undermine that assumption of genre and there is much to support it. These opening pages of *Summertime* are in the same style as the earlier memoir-novels, thus setting readers up for an expectation of continuity, an expectation first unsettled by the memos and then shattered with the Julia interview that replaces the notebook fragments after about ten pages. Considering the works together in the single volume of *Scenes from Provincial Life* makes the effect stark: After nearly 300 pages, the reader must learn new reading strategies for the rest of the almost-500-page book. (On a purely pedagogical level, we might consider this like the leap between high school and college.) The shift is likely less jarring for a reader who came to the texts as separate books, particularly if they read them as they were published, and so had years between reading each. Nonetheless, *Summertime* was always labeled and marketed as the third of the series, so the likelihood of the reader expecting it to be a continuation of *Boyhood* and *Youth* was always there, even if the reading experience may have been a bit different.

While the memos gently break the continuity with *Boyhood* and *Youth*, they create a continuity with *Diary of a Bad Year*, adding an overtly dialogic element to the text in much the same way as JC's diaries do. The texts are not parallel on the page, however, and once the first notebook section ends, the book is given over to other (mostly female) voices, much as JC's diary section at the end of that book is given over to Anya. In *Summertime*, though, the white male author's text is not present; the author is dead, his authority open not only to contestation but also to obliteration.

Though the shift from the notebook fragments to the interview with Julia is the most abrupt and radical jump in the text, readers must continue to adjust their strategies with each interviewee. Julia's interview is set up in a standard, familiar Q&A interview format, with the interviewer's questions and comments italicized and the interviewee's responses in standard font. The next interview, with John's cousin Margot, is exactly the opposite: the interviewer (Mr. Vincent) speaks at length and in standard font, while the brief responses from Margot are italicized. Or so it seems at first. After a few paragraphs, the text proves to be more complicated: What we are reading is a transcript of Mr. Vincent reading an edited interview with Margot back to her for her comment. He has "fixed up the prose to read as if it were an uninterrupted narrative spoken in your voice" (350). Within the diegesis, then, much of the substance of this section is a work of prose created from an original text to which we have no access. Instead, we read the edited-interpreted prose and the commentary by the original interviewee and the interviewer who edited her words. (The levels of voice and situation are quite complex, but the presentation is straightforward and not especially confusing.)

What this fiction stages is difficulties of biography, memoir, history, and interpretation. These difficulties will raise questions for any readers, but they will raise particular questions for readers of *Boyhood* and *Youth*—not because Margot necessarily contradicts any of the content of those books (her recollections often cover the time period that those books themselves do), but because they force us to consider to what extent Coetzee's own smooth, third-person texts are far from simple transcriptions of experience. Margot says to Mr. Vincent, "When I spoke to you last year, I was under the impression you were simply going to transcribe our interview. I had no idea you were going to rewrite it completely," to which he responds, "I have not actually rewritten it, I have merely recast it as a narrative, giving it a different form. Giving it new form has no effect on the content" (353). If Coetzee had written a "raw" transcript alongside the narrative Mr. Vincent reads, we could have judged for ourselves, but that would have undermined the effect, because we have no access to the raw material of life that he shaped into *Boyhood* and *Youth*. We must reflect on the question of to what extent the reworking of material (such as memories) into narrative reconfigures that material. Though we know from all of his critical writings that Coetzee does not agree with Mr. Vincent that form has no effect on content, Coetzee, the author of *Summertime*, does not intrude to contradict him, instead leaving us to come to our own conclusions. That the question is raised is what matters.

After the Margot chapter, *Summertime* returns to the traditional interview form, though the book now moves us to a character, Adrianna, who is mostly negative toward the character of John. While Julia and Margot both presented unappealing aspects of John's personality and behavior, they still maintained a generally positive assessment of him overall. Adrianna does not. She says she "detested him" and told him so, that he "forced me to detest him" (425). She calls him "disembodied" and asks "How could this man of yours be a great man when he was not human?" (436). She is aware of the desires of the biographer regarding the subject: "This is not the story you wanted to hear, is it? You wanted a different kind of story for your book" (425), a statement that not only implicates the biographer but also echoes out to readers generally, because the word Adrianna uses is *story*—bringing our thoughts back to the "tales of the borderlands" and the "stories the Truscotts tell their children" from the very first pages of *Summertime*. After the first notebook section, *Summertime* is mostly (though not completely) concerned with personal questions, but because it begins as it does, the personal questions are inevitably shadowed by their historical situation.

Following Adrianna, Martin provides a more generally positive view of John. This interview also brings us toward a different sort of personal, intimate world: that of male academic colleagues. The topic of white South African identity appears when the interviewer raises it as something John would not write about, at least regarding other people's identity: "When he gets to your white South Africanness he stops and writes no more. Have you any idea why he should have stopped just there?" Martin suggests the topic was either too complex for what John was writing or that he grew bored with writing about academic life. Martin himself suspects it was the former. "Broadly speaking, he and I shared a common stance towards South Africa, namely that our presence there was illegitimate. [...] Whatever the opposite is of *native* or *rooted*, that was what we felt ourselves to be" (442). Sophie, discussed at the beginning of this chapter, rounds out the interviews with a wide-ranging exploration of writing, politics, utopia, South Africa, language, and, ultimately, John as both a person and a personage. "He was just a man," Sophie says, "a man of his time, talented, maybe even gifted, but, frankly, not a giant" (467).

The notebook of "Undated Fragments" that closes *Summertime* is significantly less political or social in its concerns than the notebook at the beginning. Now, the concerns are memories of friends and family and of certain works of art, particularly music, especially the works of Schubert and Bach. Music plays a meaningful role in the book. Axel Englund sees the music in *Summertime* (and in *Diary of a Bad Year*) as expressing John's desire to escape the Cartesian duality of mind and body, a desire that he can never fulfill, even as he appears to know it is based on a false dichotomy—the dichotomy is too deeply culturally embedded for him to escape it, and in any case his body doesn't much want to cooperate with his mind. But there is a further purpose to the use of music, one visible elsewhere in *Summertime*, especially in the final notebook:

> Coetzee's evocation and self-conscious questioning of the clichés attached to these composers and genres reveal his awareness that music, even when it raises claims to spiritual transcendence, is given its meaning in the realm of discourse that it supposedly bypasses. It is culturally embedded discourse that ascribes to music the capacity to reach beyond language, either into pure spirit or bodily pleasure. (Englung 2017: 102)

A desire to reach beyond language is common to Coetzee's novels from early in his career through to its later stages. As early as his 1974 essay on *Pale Fire*, Coetzee identifies Nabokov as inferior to Beckett because "That art is radical which, facing the abyss between language and the world, turns toward silence and the end of art" (5). That sort of radicalism is clearly a type the flesh-and-blood Coetzee values, perhaps not as an absolute goal, but at least as a temptation. The desire to face the abyss between language and world is not a merely literary or artistic desire. As Coetzee's many discussions of Afrikaans (in and out of *Summertime*) show, language is political and politics is a linguistic activity as much as it is a bodily activity, not only because of the ideas, instructions, laws, etc. that get communicated via a language, but also because of what sort of language is valued and rewarded, the social role of particular ways of speaking and writing, the official validation of some languages over others. (We must not forget that the Soweto uprising of June 1976 was a protest against the mandating of the Afrikaans language in schools. At least 176 people were killed by the police during the uprising.) Language may be a matter of life and death. The desire to go beyond language is similar to the desire to go beyond politics: an impossible dream, perhaps, but more clearly a self-annihilating desire—a desire for silence, the end of art, the end of history, society, culture, politics. The death of the author.

A pedagogy for liberation

To cede authority one must first assert it. This is a dilemma that Coetzee's novels between *Disgrace* and *The Childhood of Jesus* wrestle with. If Coetzee simply wanted to get rid of his authority, he would stop writing and wield whatever legal power possible to reclaim the rights to his books and prevent them from being reprinted and distributed. He would refuse all public events, all lectures, all interviews, all awards. Obviously, that is not what he wants. From the evidence of his texts, Coetzee seems to want to use his situation to illuminate the forces, desires, and assumptions that make his situation possible. That his situation is unique in many of its features does not mean the forces that formed that situation are unique, and it is those forces that these novels make visible and, in making visible, render open to analysis and critique. As author, Coetzee is taking on the authority of the pedagogue, the didact, but he does so in a way that tries to mitigate the didactic power of his authority, thus infusing his books with what we might call, borrowing from Paulo Freire, a pedagogy of liberation. Such a pedagogy is a process for both knowledge production and knowledge analysis.

In *A Pedagogy for Liberation*, Freire identifies some of the elements necessary for the production of knowledge as "action, critical reflection, curiosity, demanding inquiry, uneasiness, uncertainty" (Freire and Shor 1987: 8). These are good virtues for the reader of Coetzee, as well, especially given how often his work leaves us uneasy and uncertain. The narratives are so full of gaps and ambiguities that they scream out for interpretation, yet the narratives refuse to interpret themselves.

Some authority remains, however: the authority of the pedagogy. Freire repeatedly says that a pedagogy of liberation is anti-authoritarian but not anti-authority in the sense of being "anything goes": "When I criticize manipulation, I do not want to fall into a false and nonexistent nondirectivity of education. For me, education is always directive, always. The question is to know towards what and with whom is it directive" (Freire and Shor 1987: 109). A perfectly anti-authoritarian book would either be one of blank pages or one filled with random words. While either may be of use to the writer—who may assert the authority to make a mark on the blank page or to rearrange the random words—neither is much good for readers. The writer's arrangement of words, sentences, and paragraphs directs the reader's thoughts, but in texts like Coetzee's (and Woolf's and Delany's), direction doesn't need to be determining. This is ultimately the difference within a Freirian paradigm between authority and anti-authority: a Freirian pedagogy directs learners via the authority of the teacher toward open ways of thinking—ways of thinking that (potentially) allow the thinker to recognize and analyze the dominant ideology. The teacher's authority, Freire says, must be mobile, flexible, and itself open to learning, and he agrees with his interlocutor Ira Schor, who says that "the teacher's authority must always be there, but it changes as the students and the study evolve, as they emerge as critical subjects in the act of knowing. The teacher also is recreated if the process is working" (92). Since the text is separate from the writer, it's impossible to say whether the writer is "recreated in the process" of writing, but certainly in *Diary of a Bad Year* and *Summertime*, Coetzee uses recreations of himself and his public image to spur readers on toward new ways of thinking and knowing the texts.

Such flexible ways of thinking and knowing—and of teaching and learning—are valuable during a crisis. Countless examples of hasty thinking and bad knowledge are available from the history of crises, and piles of texts grown gangly with good intentions bear testament to the ill effects of crisis on writing. The immediacy of a crisis tempts us to respond quickly and to shrink thinking into slogans, to march over nuance and bury contradictions beneath barricades. These dangers are well documented. But the effect of a crisis lingers, not only in graveyards and ruins, but in stagnated thought and ersatz ethics. Furthermore, the world is not utopian, and one crisis may end just as ten others begin. The novels Coetzee wrote after the end of apartheid show the necessity for careful thinking after a crisis, a time when relief at the end of immediate suffering may turn to complacency.

"Reality," Freire says, "is a becoming, not a standing still" (Freire and Shor 1987: 182).

6

Conclusion

Virginia Woolf, Samuel R. Delany, and J.M. Coetzee are significantly different writers, but they have each drawn from various strains of Modernism to create texts in which the structure and aesthetics of the text itself contribute to an experience whereby receptive readers will be challenged to think in new ways. Though they are not writers who have been discussed together before, there are notable similarities in how their pedagogical forms have been received by critics and common readers.

In *Woolf's Ambiguities*, Molly Hite describes the effect of Woolf's novels in a manner reminiscent of descriptions of Coetzee's work by Carol Clarkson (2009), Jonathan Lear (2010), Jan Wilm (2016), and others:

> In Woolf's fiction, attitudes that appear to have the author's sanction and that counsel us to think and act in particular ways arise only to be undercut, within prose that scrupulously refrains from endorsing a single position as the one that Woolf "wants us to see" or "means" or "is showing us" (or "assumes" or "cannot see beyond") or other such critical locutions.

Hite goes on to contrast Woolf's work both with that of other Modernists and with polemical writers in a way that fits with Coetzee's relationship to writers such as Nadine Gordimer: "The writing is radically experimental in ways that other modernist fiction writers did not attempt and stands in explicit contrast to a tradition of feminist polemical fiction that critics are only beginning to bring into dialogue with Woolf's work." While I prefer to stick with ideas of dialogism and polyphony rather than Hite's "tonal complexity" (productive in her study, but too much of a catch-all for my purposes), she describes well the effect of such texts, whatever label we apply to them:

> When we pay attention to their tonal complexity, her novels emerge as disorienting and difficult in original and positive ways: full of unfamiliar and disconcerting effects, resisting translation into other idioms, embodying a newness that remains strange despite long acquaintance, and raising the possibility of further revelations the more profound because unanticipated—revelations of precisely what readers have not always thought and felt. (Hite 2017: xi)

Newness that remains strange is common to all three writers I have discussed, and it is central to their texts' pedagogies because such newness is what fuels the possibility that readers will experience revelations beyond what they have already thought and felt. In that sense, then, the "Make it new!" of Modernism is not a command that fetishizes newness for its own sake, but rather is a fundamental technique of critical pedagogy.

In describing his work in Brazil, Paulo Freire wrote that he and his collaborators sought to create

> an education which would lead men to take a new stance toward their problems—that of intimacy with those problems, one oriented toward research instead of repeating irrelevant principles. An education of "I wonder," instead of merely, "I do." Vitality, instead of insistence on the transmission of what Alfred North Whitehead [in *The Aims of Education*] has called "inert ideas—that is to say, ideas that are merely received into the mind without being utilised, or tested, or thrown into fresh combinations." (2005: 32–33)

What is made new via critical pedagogy is the student's perception of something in the world; learning is not a matter of received, inert ideas, but of research born from intimacy with the problems of life and society. The fundamental value in a stance of "I wonder … " is congruent with Modernist and metamodernist texts that spurn propaganda and preaching and seek instead a pedagogy that requires an active, thinking, critical, questioning reader.

In *A Pedagogy for Liberation*, Freire argues that it is not general techniques that differentiate the liberating teacher from the non-liberating (or even oppressive) teacher; rather, it is the stance toward reality and the object of the pedagogy. Switching from lecturing to class discussions, for instance, is no guarantee that a pedagogy is liberating because "traditional teachers will make reality opaque whether they lecture or lead discussions. A liberating teacher will illuminate reality even if he or she lectures. The question is the content and dynamism of the lecture, the approach to the object to be known. Does it critically reorient students to society? Does it animate their critical thinking or not?" (Freire and Shor 1987: 40). Such a perspective is a helpful one when we think of how Woolf, Delany, and Coetzee navigate the genres of the essay and the novel, because, as Hite says of Woolf, "her antipathy toward 'teachers and preachers' extended in her own writing practice only to works of fiction, and in particular to the novels 'of vision' that we associate with her great middle period. She was a master of teaching and preaching in essays intended to instruct and persuade" (2017: 172).[1] The same is true of Delany. For Woolf and Delany, the essay form is often like a particularly talented teacher's lecture: full of ideas, analyses, demonstrations, quotations, and, not infrequently, didacticism. Yet Woolf is also often like Coetzee in that her dislike of "preaching" leads her toward particularly ironic and polyphonic styles for her essays, styles that in both writers' works complicate any simple representation of an authorial self. In Woolf, this was a feminist practice, as Lisa Low has described: "Instead of writing that expresses the personality, the voracious need for the assertion of self, Woolf strives to find a writing that expels the self" (1997: 265). While I think a case can be made for Coetzee as an at-least-occasionally feminist writer, his striving for a writing "that expels the self" comes from other motivations, as discussed in Chapter 3.[2]

Delany works differently; in stark contrast to Woolf and (especially) Coetzee, he has embraced an authoritative authorial stance in his essays and interviews, conveying a pose of confidence in his own opinions, knowledge, and perception of the world that has been remarkably consistent since his teenage journals. This brings us back to Barbara Johnson's notion that self-resistance is a viable mode for members of the white male establishment but not others. The authoritative stance seems to me necessary given Delany's context(s). Imagine it otherwise: What would be the effect if the first black, gay writer to gain any prominence within the field of science fiction—a field often considered juvenile, subliterate, and unserious—wrote essays in which he consistently undermined his own authority? While Woolf's gender certainly set her below men in the social hierarchy, and because of her gender she was denied many of the routes

---

[1] Hite quotes the "teachers and preachers" phrase from the drafts of *The Waves*, where Rhoda says, "Teachers & preachers I have always thought the lowest of mankind" (Hite 2017: 51). Woolf's own feelings on teachers were complicated, depending on the institutions to which the teachers were affiliated and the assumptions about learning and society that the teachers held. It seems to me that Hite is correct in saying that "Woolf herself clearly objected to 'preaching'—and 'teaching,' if we construe this word to connote its literary form, didacticism" (52).

[2] Such an expulsion of self is also central to numerous writings on Coetzee and autobiography, including my own essay "Intentional Schizophrenia," which is why I do not belabor it here.

to cultural authority, she nonetheless wrote for highly respected publications and was soon seen as part of the most serious literary and social communities. And though Coetzee's identity as a South African did not lend him the cultural authority that citizenship with a more powerful country would, his identity as a white heterosexual male (with a PhD) marked him from the beginning of his career with privileges unavailable to either Woolf or Delany.

Therefore, we could see these writers as existing on a spectrum of access to hegemonic power, and that spectrum coincides with the strategies of authorial authority within their nonfiction: Coetzee, the least marginalized, continuously works to undermine the authority in his texts; Woolf's nonfiction, particularly in its longer forms, grows more polyphonic as her reputation solidifies (with *Three Guineas*, published less than a year after her appearance on the cover of *Time* magazine, at the apex); Delany, the most marginalized in both a social and literary position, writes nonfiction that rarely undermines its authoritative stance.[3]

Nonetheless, when writing fiction, even Delany tends toward a complex, unsettling, de-stabilizing dialogism, and the differences in the ways these writers approach narrative authority in nonfiction compared to the similarity with which they approach narrative authority in fiction suggest a shared view of how to approach the task of writing around (before, during, after) crisis: that, in fact, it is nonfiction that is limited, while fiction, in all its heteroglossic glory, offers a wider range of possibilities for the writer who wants to do something other than preach.

What we have discovered, then, is not that these writers pushed fiction to the limits of its fictionality for the sake of inserting polemic in a disingenuous way, but that by pushing against fiction's fictionality, these writers of very different backgrounds, geographies, privileges, situations, tastes, and styles created texts that do the pedagogic work of liberating the reader toward a critical, ethical thinking that less Modernist, less polyphonic, and more traditionally fictional texts do not—even if those texts are more explicitly committed to particular socio-political visions. Monologic, preaching, propagandistic texts may *present* ethical thought, but they are less likely to *stimulate* it than the polyphonic pedagogies practiced by Woolf, Delany, and Coetzee in their fiction. These

---

[3] A good argument could be made that Delany's memoir *The Motion of Light in Water* undermines its authority by highlighting the vagaries of memory. I think there is justice to such a view, but the authorial voice in that book still sounds to me quite confident and monologic. The (often-biting) self-critiques that Delany writes under the pseudonyms as K. Leslie Steiner and S. L. Kermit are almost entirely associated with his fiction (mostly the Return to Nevèrÿon series), making Steiner and Kermit characters within his fictional universe, not dialogic functions within his nonfiction.

texts work against the ersatz ethical thought Jonathan Lear describes, a kind of thought which may offer information and ideas, but which nonetheless is overwhelmed by "the sense that the space for ethical thought [is] already filled" (2010: 69). Such ersatz ethical thinking is similar to Freire's "banking concept of education," where "knowledge is a gift bestowed by those who consider themselves knowledgeable upon those whom they consider to know nothing. Projecting an absolute ignorance onto others, a characteristic of the ideology of oppression, negates education and knowledge as processes of inquiry" (2000: 72). Against the banking concept of education stands critical, liberatory education, an approach that bell hooks describes as one that "makes education the practice of freedom" by encouraging a type of "teaching that enables transgressions—a movement against and beyond boundaries" that will "open our minds and hearts so that we can know beyond the boundaries of what is acceptable, so that we can think and rethink, so that we can create new visions" (1994: 12). Woolf, Delany, and Coetzee never fall into the oppressive ideological trap of assuming an absolute ignorance in their readers, and so their texts demonstrate a practice of freedom and enable—indeed, demand—transgressions against settled boundaries of accepted genres and accepted opinions.

Fictionality, through its serious games of make-believe, stimulates ethical thought in a way nonfictionality can't, because fictionality allows an added level of rhetorical and conceptual distance through which to reimagine the world. Iser describes this quality well in *The Fictive and the Imaginary*:

> As the represented world is not a world, but the reader imagines *as if* it were one, clearly the reader's reaction must be guided by that representation. Thus the "as-if" triggers acts of ideation in the recipient, causing him or her to conceive what the world of the text is meant to bring about. This activity eludes qualification as either subjective or objective, for the stimulated conceivability is patterned by the world represented, the surpassing of which opens up a dimension to be imaginatively concretized. In this very process of ideation, once again boundaries are overstepped: the world of the text is exceeded and the diffuseness of the imaginary assumes form. Triggering an imaginative reaction to the world represented in the text proves to be the function of the "as-if" construction, which comes to fruition through the attitudes the reader is induced to adopt to the world exemplified by the text. (Iser 1993: 16)

Iser describes here a particular way of reading, one that relies on the sense of the work of fiction as fiction, and so makes clear the value of foregrounding a text's fictionality. However, conventionality is equally important to consider, because settled techniques of any sort are less likely to encourage an active reading than techniques that first incite and then frustrate readers' expectations.

The unsettling of fictionality and nonfictionality is one set of such techniques, but as *The Years* and *The Mad Man* both make clear, readers' expectations of genre may be just as effective for a pedagogy of liberation. Different crises require different approaches to fictionality if authentic ethical thought is to be possible. Fictionality has a complex relationship to ideas of truth, and crises may not only be crises of society or politics, but also crises of the discourse of truth. Delany could have kept writing about a fantasy plague in a fantasy land and trusted that many readers would have read the text as an allegory of AIDS, but he chose to break through the fictionality in "The Tale of Plagues and Carnivals" because he was in a crisis where, as Coetzee said in his Jerusalem Prize Acceptance Speech, there was "too much truth for art to hold, truth by the bucketful, truth that overwhelms and swamps every act of the imagination" (1992: 99). By alternating between the truth of his everyday experience and the fantasy of Nevèrÿon, Delany was able to bring in bucketfuls of truth without swamping every act of his imagination. Later, while the crisis continued but had become subject to multiple discourses, he could return to a less problematized fictionality with *The Mad Man*, but here through the liberating pedagogy of "pornotopic fantasy" rather than sword & sorcery fantasy.

Coetzee's most sustained and beguiling experiments with fictionality began after the crisis of the apartheid state was resolved and the new reality of the new South Africa (with a new set of crises) emerged. It was then that he seems to have judged it appropriate to tie the pedagogy of his novels to a problematization of fictionality because now the risk of that problematization of fictionality becoming a problematization of truth was lower, the stakes less stark—now, there might be just enough truth for art to hold it without artfulness becoming overwhelmed or, alternately, without the idea of truth itself getting scared to death by the specter of relativism. (No-one who seeks liberation from authoritarianism can afford to be a relativist, because relativism risks equating freedom with slavery, ignorance with strength, war with peace.) This is not to say that Woolf, Delany, and Coetzee are relativists—they are not—but that any unsettling of fictionality inevitably runs the risk of being perceived as relativistic simply because of the complex historical and discursive relationship between ideas of fictionality and truth.

These writers cannot risk relativism because the crises they face are real to the point of being life-threatening. ("Reality," Philip K. Dick said, "is that which, when you stop believing in it, doesn't go away" [1987: 4]. The threat of a crisis killing you may make reality suddenly quite vivid to anyone less committed to relativism than Dr. Pangloss.) It is for this reason that Modernism remains attractive. Mazzoni points out in *Theory of the Novel* that for

> many of the great authors born between the 1870s and 1880s—for Proust, Woolf, Forster, or Lawrence—the task of the novel was still that of telling about the existence of people like us, and not of creating fantastic worlds, stylistic games, metaliterature, *écriture*, or pure lies. The critical vocabulary that dominated during the years of modernism was very different from the critical lexicon used by the avant-garde movements of the 1950s and 1960s to justify their works. The basic reason was that, although conceived in different terms, a majority of modernist novelists remained faithful to the same project we find in the critical writings of the authors who were born around 1840 (Zola, James), and even before that in the critical writings of Balzac or Stendhal: to properly, realistically represent everyday life. (Mazzoni 2017: 288)

There is plenty to quibble with in Mazzoni's details (Woolf's *Orlando* is nothing if not metaliterature) and many details that are not applicable here (Delany spent much of his career creating fantastic worlds; *écriture* could describe most of Coetzee's work), but his valuable insight is that the writers from Flaubert up through the Modernists shared a commitment to an idea of reality that many post-Second World War avant-garde writers and critics did not; this insight explains why such writers as Delany and Coetzee, both born in the early 1940s, so often refer in their nonfiction to Modernist touchstones and so rarely to, for instance, John Barth or Thomas Pynchon. There is reason to believe that Delany and Coetzee share a general belief that the task of the novel is "to properly, realistically represent everyday life" (which includes, of course, the way the mind works in everyday life, the way we experience everyday life—the complaint of the Modernists, including Woolf, was *not* that the nineteenth-century social novels were realistic, but that they were not realistic enough). Their commitments are to a particular way of structuring reality via fiction that is more congruent with the assumptions of the Modernists than with many later avant-garde writers. Mazzoni, who (as Ben Parker has astutely criticized) squeezes the novel into an anti-transcendent teleology, can't account for this, but David James can in his description of metamodernists in *Modernist Futures*. For James, metamodernist writers are different from other contemporary writers in "their capacity to articulate modes of ethical and political commentary precisely through a sincere rather than self-parodic dedication to rendering perceptual experience" (2012: 13).

What James calls metamodernist writers' attention to the "participatory nature of form" (16) is what leads me to read the works I have discussed here as having a pedagogy. Woolf, Delany, and Coetzee each identify ways that form may affect readers' participation with the text, but identification is not enough—they also put that participatory nature of form to work. The methods by which they do so, and the ends toward which they aim, are the pedagogy. That each is a liberatory pedagogy is clear from the demands they place on readers: demands to be active and thoughtful, to think beyond the authority of the writer, the writer's reputation, or even the text itself.

Whether such thinking can carry over into the world outside the text is not within the writer's ability to determine any more than a teacher is able to determine if students will all transfer their experience of the classroom to the world beyond its walls. But if the writer is able to encourage authentic ethical thought, and to provoke the reader toward recognizing and analyzing ersatz ethical thought, then there is every possibility for imaginations to be activated and for certain habits of reading to transfer into habits of thinking that then affect habits of being.

CODA

Throughout the summer of 1940, Virginia and Leonard Woolf endured numerous air raids while at their country home in Rodmell, Sussex. Then in the fall, bombs destroyed their London home in Mecklenburgh Square. Asked by Americans to write something about "what should be the attitude of women towards war and peace," Virginia Woolf created the essay "Thoughts on Peace in an Air Raid," in which she said that though war is male ("The defenders are men, the attackers are men"), if a woman believes this is a fight for freedom, then she might fight on the side of the English. "But there is another way of fighting for freedom without arms; we can fight with the mind. We can make ideas that will help the young Englishman who is fighting up in the sky to defeat the enemy" (*E* 6: 242). The difficulty is that men hold all the positions of power in government and society. But women must be willing to think and express themselves. She quotes William Blake: "I will not cease from mental fight," and adds: "Mental fight means thinking against the current, not with it" (243).

To demonstrate thinking against the current, Woolf echoes an idea from *Three Guineas*: "Let us try to drag up into consciousness the subconscious Hitlerism that holds us down. It is the desire for aggression; the desire to dominate and enslave" (243).

She insists on thinking beyond the immediate moment, even as the bombs fall. The mind needs to create, the imagination needs to continue, and even now, Woolf says, we must think about the world the men in the airplanes will return to once the battle is over. Masculine violence must end, but the desire for it can't be ignored. Young men love glory, they find glory in guns, and if society takes away that glory, then what will such men do?

> Therefore if we are to compensate the young man for the loss of his glory and of his gun, we must give him access to the creative feelings. We must make happiness. We must free him from the machine. We must bring him out of his prison into the open air. But what is the use of freeing the young Englishman if the young German and the young Italian remain slaves? (245).

The sound of guns interrupts her thinking. A German plane lands and the pilot, relieved that the fight is over, is captured by English soldiers, who give him a cigarette and a cup of tea. There may be hope in such shared humanity, Woolf suggests.

But then it is just a quiet summer night, and she must send her fragmentary notes off to America, "to the men and women whose sleep has not yet been broken by machine-gun fire" (245). Perhaps the fragments can be shaped into something useful. Now, though, "in the shadowed half of the world," she must sleep.

References

Aggleton, Peter, and Richard Parker. 2015. "Moving beyond Biomedicalization in the HIV Response: Implications for Community Involvement and Community Leadership among Men Who Have Sex with Men and Transgender People." *American Journal of Public Health* 105 (8): 1552–8.

Ai, Walter Abish, Claribel Alegria, M.F. Beal, J.M. Coetzee, Samuel R. Delany, William Eastlake et al. 1984. "Forum: Writing and Politics." *Fiction International* 15 (1): 1–24.

Allen, Judith. 2010. *Virginia Woolf and the Politics of Language*. Edinburgh: Edinburgh University Press.

Altman, Lawrence K. 1982. "New Homosexual Disorder Worries Health Officials." *The New York Times*, May 11, 1982, C1.

Amin, Kadji. 2017. *Disturbing Attachments: Genet, Modern Pederasty, and Queer History*. Durham, NC: Duke University Press.

Anders, Charlie Jane. 2009. "Samuel Delany Answers Your Science Fiction Questions!" Io9. June 20, 2009. http://io9.com/5295779/samuel-delany-answers-your-science-fiction-questions.

Andrews, Charles. 2017. *Writing against War: Literature, Activism, and the British Peace Movement*. Evanston, IL: Northwestern University Press.

Attridge, Derek. 2004. *J.M. Coetzee & the Ethics of Reading: Literature in the Event*. Chicago: University of Chicago Press.

Attwell, David. 2010. "Mastering Authority: J.M. Coetzee's *Diary of a Bad Year*." *Social Dynamics* 36 (1): 214–21. https://doi.org/10.1080/02533950903562575.

Attwell, David. 2011. "Coetzee's Postcolonial Diaspora." *Twentieth Century Literature* 57 (1): 9–19.

Attwell, David. 2015. *J.M. Coetzee and the Life of Writing: Face to Face with Time*. New York: Viking.

Auster, Paul, and J.M. Coetzee. 2013. *Here and Now: Letters 2008–2011*. New York: Penguin.

Beebe, Maurice. 1972. "Ulysses and the Age of Modernism." *James Joyce Quarterly* 10 (1): 172–88.

Bellin, Roger. 2012. "Pornotopia." Los Angeles Review of Books. May 21, 2012. https://lareviewofbooks.org/article/pornotopia/.

Berman, Jessica. 2011. *Modernist Commitments: Ethics, Politics, and Transnational Modernism*. New York: Columbia University Press.

Berry, Paul, and Mark Bostridge. 1995. *Vera Brittain: A Life*. London: Chatto & Windus.

Berthoff, Ann E. 1987. "Foreword." In *Literacy: Reading the Word and the World*, edited by Paulo Freire and Donaldo Macedo, xi–xxiii. Hoboken, NJ: Taylor & Francis.

Boehmer, Elleke. 2011. "J.M. Coetzee's Australian Realism." In *Strong Opinions: J.M. Coetzee and the Authority of Contemporary Fiction*, edited by Chris Danta, Sue Kossew, and Julian Murphet, 3–17. New York: Continuum.

Booth, Wayne C. 2008. *The Rhetoric of Rhetoric: The Quest for Effective Communication*. Malden, MA.: Blackwell Publishing.

Bottome, Phyllis. 1938. *The Mortal Storm*. New York: Little, Brown.

Briggs, Julia. 2005. *Virginia Woolf: An Inner Life*. Orlando: Harcourt.

Brittain, Vera. (1936) 2000. *Honourable Estate: A Novel of Transition*. London: Virago.

Brooks, Peter. 2008. "The Ethics of Reading." *Chronicle of Higher Education* 54 (22): B5.

Cartwright, Justin. 2007. "Diary of a Bad Year, by J M Coetzee." *The Independent*, September 2, 2007. http://www.independent.co.uk/arts-entertainment/books/reviews/diary-of-a-bad-year-by-j-m-coetzee-463604.html.

Chan, Evelyn T. 2010. "Professions, Freedom and Form: Reassessing Woolf's *The Years* and *Three Guineas*." *The Review of English Studies* 61 (251): 591–613. https://doi.org/10.1093/res/hgq013.

Charles, Ron. 2005. "Limping to Love." *The Washington Post*, September 25, 2005. http://www.washingtonpost.com/wp-dyn/content/article/2005/09/22/AR2005092201021.html.

Chekhov, Anton. 1973. *Anton Chekhov's Life and Thought*. Edited by Simon Karlinsky. Translated by Michael Henry Heim and Simon Karlinsky. Berkeley: University of California Press.

Cheney, Matthew. 2007. "Night and Day: The Place of *Equinox* in Samuel R. Delany's Oeuvre." Strange Horizons. December 17, 2007. http://strangehorizons.com/non-fiction/reviews/night-and-day-the-place-of-equinox-in-samuel-r-delanys-oeuvre/.

Cheney, Matthew. 2009. "Intentional Schizophrenia: J.M. Coetzee's Autobiographical Trilogy and the Falling Authority of the Author." Quarterly Conversation. December 7, 2009. http://quarterlyconversation.com/intentional-schizophrenia-j-m-coetzees-autobiographical-trilogy-and-the-falling-authority-of-the-author.

Cheney, Matthew. 2016. "On Samuel R. Delany's 'Dark Reflections.'" Los Angeles Review of Books. October 9, 2016. https://lareviewofbooks.org/article/on-samuel-delanys-dark-reflections/.

Cheney, Matthew, Craig Laurance Gidney, Geoffrey H. Goodwin, Keguro Macharia, Nick Mamatas, Njihia Mbitiru, Lavelle Porter, Ethan Robinson, and Eric Schaller. 2014. "Samuel R. Delany: Another Roundtable." The Mumpsimus. March 24, 2014. https://mumpsimus.blogspot.com/2014/03/samuel-r-delany-another-roundtable.html.

Chernaik, Warren. 2018. "Milton's 'Fit Audience.'" *Milton Studies* 60 (1–2): 108–33. https://doi.org/10.1353/mlt.2018.0014.

Clarkson, Carrol. 2009. *J.M. Coetzee: Countervoices*. New York: Palgrave Macmillan.

Coetzee, J.M. 1974. "Nabokov's Pale Fire and the Primacy of Art." *University of Cape Town Studies in English* (6): 1–7.

Coetzee, J.M. 1992. *Doubling the Point: Essays and Interviews*. Edited by David Attwell. Cambridge, MA: Harvard University Press.

Coetzee, J.M. 1996. *Giving Offense: Essays on Censorship*. Chicago: University of Chicago Press.

Coetzee, J.M. 1997. "Voice and Trajectory: An Interview with J.M. Coetzee." By Joanna Scott. *Salmagundi* (114/115) (April): 82–102.

Coetzee, J.M. 1999. *The Lives of Animals*. Princeton, NJ: Princeton University Press.

Coetzee, J.M. 2004. *Elizabeth Costello*. New York: Penguin Books.

Coetzee, J.M. 2006. "J.M. Coetzee in Conversation with Jane Poyner." By Jane Poyner. In *JM Coetzee and the Idea of the Public Intellectual*, edited by Jane Poyner, 21–4. Athens: Ohio University Press.

Coetzee, J.M. 2008. *Diary of a Bad Year*. New York: Viking.

Coetzee, J.M. 2012. *Scenes from Provincial Life: Boyhood, Youth, Summertime*. New York: Penguin.

Coetzee, J.M. 2016. "J.M. Coetzee [2 Interviews, 1991/2000]." In *The Best of Writers and Company*, edited by Eleanor Wachtel, 223–38. Windsor, Ontario: Biblioasis.

Cole, Sarah. 2012. *At the Violet Hour: Modernism and Violence in England and Ireland*. New York: Oxford University Press.

Collingwood-Whittick, Sheila. 2001. "Autobiography as *Autre*Biography: The Fictionalisation of the Self in J.M. Coetzee's *Boyhood: Scenes from Provincial Life*." *Commonwealth: Essays and Studies* 24 (1): 13–23.

Collinson, Diané. 1985. "Ethics and Aesthetics Are One." *The British Journal of Aesthetics* 25 (3): 266–72. https://doi.org/10.1093/bjaesthetics/25.3.266.

Craven, Peter. 2007. "Diary of a Bad Year." *The Age*. August 28, 2007. http://www.theage.com.au/news/book-reviews/diary-of-a-bad-year/2007/08/28/1188067098779.html?page=fullpage.

Crewe, Jonathan. 2015. *In the Middle of Nowhere: J.M. Coetzee in South Africa*. Lanham, MD: University Press of America.

Daiches, David. 1942. *Virginia Woolf*. The Makers of Modern Literature. New York: New Directions Books.

Daugherty, Beth Rigel. 1997. "Readin', Writin', and Revisin': Virginia Woolf's 'How Should One Read a Book.'" In *Virginia Woolf and the Essay*, edited by Beth Carole Rosenberg and Jeanne Dubino, 159–75. New York: St. Martin's.

Davis, Ray. 1996. "Delany's Dirt." In *Ash of Stars: On the Writings of Samuel R. Delany*, edited by James Sallis, 162–88. Jackson: University Press of Mississippi.

Dean, Tim, and Steven Ruszczycky. 2014. "AIDS Literatures." In *The Cambridge History of Gay and Lesbian Literature*, edited by E.L. McCallum and Mikko Tuhkanen, pp. 712–731. Cambridge: Cambridge University Press. http://universitypublishingonline.org/ref/id/histories/CHO9781139547376.

Delany, Samuel R. 1989. *The Straits of Messina*. Seattle: Serconia Press.

Delany, Samuel R. (1983) 1993. *Neveryóna, or: The Tale of Signs and Cities—Some Informal Remarks towards the Modular Calculus, Part Four*. Middletown, CT: Wesleyan University Press.

Delany, Samuel R. (1979) 1993. *Tales of Nevèrÿon*. Middletown, CT: Wesleyan University Press.

Delany, Samuel R. (1973) 1994. *Equinox*. New York: Rhinoceros.

Delany, Samuel R. (1985) 1994. *Flight from Nevèrÿon*. Middletown, CT: Wesleyan University Press.

Delany, Samuel R. (1987) 1994. *Return to Nevèrÿon*. Middletown, CT: Wesleyan University Press.

Delany, Samuel R. 1994. *Silent Interviews: On Language, Race, Sex, Science Fiction, and Some Comics : A Collection of Written Interviews*. Middletown, CT: Wesleyan University Press.

Delany, Samuel R. 1995. *Atlantis: Three Tales*. Middletown, CT: Wesleyan University Press.

Delany, Samuel R. 1996. *Longer Views: Extended Essays*. Middletown, CT: Wesleyan University Press.

Delany, Samuel R. 1999a. *Shorter Views: Queer Thoughts & the Politics of the Paraliterary*. Middletown, CT: Wesleyan University Press.

Delany, Samuel R. 1999b. *Times Square Red, Times Square Blue*. New York: New York University Press.

Delany, Samuel R. 2000. *1984: Selected Letters*. Rutherford, NJ: Voyant.

Delany, Samuel R. (1988) 2004. *The Motion of Light in Water: Sex and Science Fiction Writing in the East Village*. Minneapolis: University of Minnesota Press.

Delany, Samuel R. 2004. *Stars in My Pocket Like Grains of Sand*. Wesleyan University Press.

Delany, Samuel R. 2005. "The Gamble." *Corpus*: An HIV Prevention Publication, Fall 2005.

Delany, Samuel R. 2007. *Dark Reflections*. New York: Carroll & Graf Publishers.

Delany, Samuel R. 2009. *Conversations with Samuel R. Delany*. Edited by Carl Freedman. Literary Conversations Series. Jackson: University Press of Mississippi.

Delany, Samuel R. (1978) 2011. *The Jewel-Hinged Jaw: Notes on the Language of Science Fiction*. Middletown, CT: Wesleyan University Press.

Delany, Samuel R. (1976) 2011. *Trouble on Triton: An Ambiguous Heterotopia*. Middletown, CT: Wesleyan University Press.

Delany, Samuel R. 2012. "For Big Other on William H. Gass's Birthday." Big Other. July 30, 2012. https://bigother.com/2012/07/30/for-big-other-on-william-h-gasss-birthday-by-samuel-r-delany/.

Delany, Samuel R. (1984) 2012. *Starboard Wine: More Notes on the Language of Science Fiction*. Rev. ed. Middletown, CT: Wesleyan University Press.

Delany, Samuel R. 2013. *About Writing: Seven Essays, Four Letters, & Five Interviews*. Middletown, CT: Wesleyan University Press.

Delany, Samuel R. (2004) 2013. *Phallos*. Edited by Robert Reid-Pharr. Enhanced and Rev. ed. Middletown, CT: Wesleyan University Press.

Delany, Samuel R. (1978) 2014. *The American Shore: Meditations on a Tale of Science Fiction by Thomas M. Disch—"Angouleme."* Middletown, CT: Wesleyan University Press.

Delany, Samuel R. 2015. *A, B, C: Three Short Novels*. New York: Vintage.

Delany, Samuel R. (1994) 2015. *The Mad Man: Or, The Mysteries of Manhattan*. Kindle. New York: Open Road Media.

Delany, Samuel R. 2016. *In Search of Silence: The Journals of Samuel R. Delany*. Edited by Kenneth R. James. Vol. 1. Middletown, CT: Wesleyan University Press.

Delany, Samuel R. 2017. "Ash Wednesday." *Boston Review*. May 8, 2017. https://bostonreview.net/literature-culture/samuel-r-delany-ash-wednesday.

Delany, Samuel R., and Mia Wolff. (1999) 2013. *Bread & Wine: An Erotic Tale of New York*. Seattle: Fantagraphics Books.

Dick, Philip K. (1985) 1987. "Introduction: How to Build a Universe That Doesn't Fall Apart Two Days Later." In *I Hope I Shall Arrive Soon*, edited by Mark Hurst and Paul Williams, pp. 1–26. New York: St. Martin's Press.

Empson, William. 2006. *Selected Letters of William Empson*. Edited by John Haffenden. New York: Oxford University Press.

Englund, Axel. 2017. "Intimate Practices: Music, Sex, and the Body in J. M. Coetzee's *Summertime*." *Mosaic: An Interdisciplinary Critical Journal* 50 (2): 99–115.

Ercolino, Stefano. 2014. *The Novel-Essay, 1884–1947*. New York: Palgrave Macmillan US.

Falcato, Ana. 2017. "The Ethics of Reading J. M. Coetzee." *Studies in the Novel* 49 (2): 250–75. https://doi.org/10.1353/sdn.2017.0019.

"Fiction Book Review: *The Lives of Animals*." 1999. *Publishers Weekly* 246 (6): 193.

Foucault, Michel. (1972) 2009. "Preface." In *Anti-Oedipus: Capitalism and Schizophrenia*, edited by Gilles Deleuze and Félix Guattari, translated by Robert Hurley, Mark Seem, and Helen R. Lane, xi–xiv. Penguin Classics. New York: Penguin Books.

Freire, Paulo. (1970) 2000. *Pedagogy of the Oppressed*. Translated by Myra Bergman Ramos. New York: Continuum.

Freire, Paulo. 2005. *Education for Critical Consciousness*. Bergman Ramos. New York: Continuum.

Freire, Paulo, and Donaldo Macedo. 1987. *Literacy: Reading the Word and the World*. Hoboken: Taylor & Francis.

Freire, Paulo, and Ira Shor. 1987. *A Pedagogy for Liberation*. London: Macmillan Education UK.

Friedman, Susan Stanford. 2015. *Planetary Modernisms: Provocations on Modernity across Time*. New York: Columbia University Press.

Froula, Christine. 2005. *Virginia Woolf and the Bloomsbury Avant-Garde: War, Civilization, Modernity*. New York: Columbia University Press.

Furlani, Andre. 2007. *Guy Davenport: Postmodern and After*. Avant-Garde & Modernism. Evanston, IL: Northwestern University Press.

Gallagher, Catherine. 2006. "The Rise of Fictionality." In *The Novel*, edited by Franco Moretti, 1: 336–63. Princeton: Princeton University Press.

Giroux, Henry A. 2013. "When Schools Become Dead Zones of the Imagination: A Critical Pedagogy Manifesto." Truthout. August 13, 2013. https://truthout.org/articles/when-schools-become-dead-zones-of-the-imagination-a-critical-pedagogy-manifesto/.

Goldstone, Andrew. 2013. *Fictions of Autonomy: Modernism from Wilde to de Man*. New York: Oxford University Press.

Gordimer, Nadine. 1984. "The Idea of Gardening." *The New York Review of Books*, February 2, 1984.

Gottlieb, Michael S., Howard M. Schanker, Peng Thim Fan, Andrew Saxon, Joel D. Weisman, and Irving Pozalski. 1981. "Pneumocystis Pneumonia–Los Angeles." *MMWR. Morbidity and Mortality Weekly Report* 30 (21): 250–2.

Gould, Deborah B. 2009. *Moving Politics: Emotion and ACT UP's Fight against AIDS*. Chicago: University of Chicago Press.

Grady, Constance. 2017. "The New Novel from Nobel Prize Winner J.M. Coetzee Is Aggressively Dry and Obscure." Vox. February 21, 2017. https://www.vox.com/culture/2017/2/21/14669550/schooldays-of-jesus-jm-coetzee-review.

Guiguet, Jean. 1965. *Virginia Woolf and Her Works*. Translated by Jean Stewart. New York: Harcourt, Brace & World.

Haule, James. 2009. "Reading Dante, Misreading Woolf: New Evidence Of Virginia Woolf's Revision of *The Years*." In *Woolf Editing/Editing Woolf: Selected Papers from the Eighteenth Annual Conference on Virginia Woolf*, edited by Eleanor Jane McNees and Sara Veglahn, 232–54. Clemson, SC: Clemson University Digital Press.

Head, Dominic. 2009. "A Belief in Frogs: J.M. Coetzee's Enduring Faith in Fiction." In *J.M. Coetzee and the Paradox of Postcolonial Authorship*, edited by Jane Poyner, 100–17. Athens: Ohio University Press.

Hirsch, Pam. 2012. "Authorship and Propaganda: Phyllis Bottome and the Making of The Mortal Storm (1940)." *Historical Journal of Film, Radio and Television* 32 (1): 57–72. https://doi.org/10.1080/01439685.2012.648053.

Hite, Molly. 2017. *Woolf's Ambiguities: Tonal Modernism, Narrative Strategy, Feminist Precursors*. Ithaca, NY: Cornell University Press. http://www.jstor.org/stable/10.7591/j.ctt1w0db2c.

Hollander, Rachel. 2007. "Novel Ethics: Alterity and Form in 'Jacob's Room.'" *Twentieth Century Literature* 53 (1): 40–66.

Holleran, Andrew. (1983) 1984. *Nights in Aruba*. New York: New American Library.

Holtby, Winifred. (1932) 2007. *Virginia Woolf: A Critical Memoir*. New York: Continuum.

Hong, Jeesoon. 2004. Review of *Lily Briscoe's Chinese Eyes: Bloomsbury, Modernism and China* by Patricia Laurence. *The China Quarterly* 178: 534–5.

hooks, bell. 1994. *Teaching to Transgress: Education as the Practice of Freedom*. New York: Routledge.

hooks, bell. 2010. *Teaching Critical Thinking: Practical Wisdom*. New York: Routledge.

Iser, Wolfgang. 1993. *The Fictive and the Imaginary: Charting Literary Anthropology*. Baltimore: Johns Hopkins University Press.

James, David. 2012. *Modernist Futures: Innovation and Inheritance in the Contemporary Novel*. New York: Cambridge University Press.

James, David, and Urmila Seshagiri. 2014. "Metamodernism: Narratives of Continuity and Revolution." *PMLA* 129 (1): 87–100. https://doi.org/10.1632/pmla.2014.129.1.87.

James, Kenneth R. 2000. "An Introduction to the Letters of Samuel R. Delany." In *1984: Selected Letters*, edited by Samuel R. Delany, pp. ix–xxvi. Rutherford, NJ: Voyant.

Johnson, Barbara. 1989. *A World of Difference*. Baltimore: Johns Hopkins University Press.

Johnson, Barbara. 2014. *The Barbara Johnson Reader: The Surprise of Otherness*. Edited by Melissa Feuerstein, Bill Johnson González, Lili Porten, and Keja Valens. Durham, NC: Duke University Press.

Johnston, Georgia. 2003. "From the Margins of Derrida: Samuel Delany's Sex and Race." *Oxford Literary Review* 25: 219–38.

Jones, Christine Kenyon, and Anna Snaith. 2010. "'Tilting at Universities': Woolf at King's College London." *Woolf Studies Annual* 16: 1–44.

Kannemeyer, J.C. 2012. *J.M. Coetzee: A Life in Writing*. Translated by Michiel Heyns. Melbourne: Scribe.

Kenner, Hugh. 1984. "The Making of the Modernist Canon." *Chicago Review* 34 (2): 49–61. https://doi.org/10.2307/25305247.

Kohlmann, Benjamin. 2014. *Committed Styles: Modernism, Politics, and Left-Wing Literature in the 1930s*. Oxford: Oxford University Press.

Krutch, Joseph Wood. 1933. "Literature and Propaganda." *The English Journal* 22 (10): 793. https://doi.org/10.2307/804175.

Kutz, Eleanor, and Hephzibah Roskelly. 1991. *An Unquiet Pedagogy: Transforming Practice in the English Classroom*. Portsmouth, NH: Boynton/Cook Heinemann.

Lapointe, Grace. 2018. "Teacher-Student Relationships: A Dangerous Trope." Book Riot. August 15, 2018. https://bookriot.com/2018/08/15/teacher-student-relationships-in-books/.

Lear, Jonathan. 2010. "The Ethical Thought of J.M. Coetzee." *Raritan* 28 (1): 68–97.

Lee, Hermione. 2003. Review of *Elizabeth Costello* by J.M. Coetzee. *The Guardian*, August 30, 2003, sec. books. https://www.theguardian.com/books/2003/aug/30/bookerprize2003.highereducation.

Lind, L. Robert. 1939. "The Crisis in Literature: II: Propaganda and Letters." *The Sewanee Review* 47 (2): 184–203.

López, María J. 2011. *Acts of Visitation: The Narrative of J.M. Coetzee.* Cross Cultures: Readings in Post/Colonial Literatures and Cultures in English 140. New York: Rodopi.

Low, Lisa. 1997. "Refusing to Hit Back: Virginia Woolf and the Impersonality Question." In *Virginia Woolf and the Essay*, edited by Beth Carole Rosenberg and Jeanne Dubino, 257–73. New York: St. Martin's Press.

Lowry, Elizabeth. 2016. Review of *The Schooldays of Jesus* by J.M. Coetzee. *The Guardian*, August 18, 2016. http://www.theguardian.com/books/2016/aug/18/the-schooldays-of-jesus-jm-coetzee-review.

Macharia, Keguro. 2014a. "Benign Perversion." Gukira. April 13, 2014. https://gukira.wordpress.com/2014/04/13/benign-perversion/.

Macharia, Keguro. 2014b. "Rough Notes on Delany." Gukira. April 12, 2014. https://gukira.wordpress.com/2014/04/12/rough-notes-on-delany/.

Majumdar, Robin, and Allen McLaurin. 1997. *Virginia Woolf: The Critical Heritage.* New York: Routledge.

Malzberg, Barry. 1976. "Books." *The Magazine of Fantasy and Science Fiction* 51 (3): 30–6.

Man, Paul de. 1979. *Allegories of Reading: Figural Language in Rousseau, Nietzsche, Rilke, and Proust.* New Haven: Yale University Press.

Marcus, Jane. 1988. *Art & Anger: Reading Like a Woman.* Columbus: Ohio State University Press.

Mazzoni, Guido. 2017. *Theory of the Novel.* Cambridge, MA: Harvard University Press.

McDonald, Peter D. 2010. "The Ethics of Reading and the Question of the Novel: The Challenge of J. M. Coetzee's *Diary of a Bad Year*." *Novel* 43 (3): 483–99. https://doi.org/10.1215/00295132-2010-026.

Moi, Toril. 1985. *Sexual/Textual Politics: Feminist Literary Theory.* New York: Methuen.

Muñoz, José Esteban. 2009. *Cruising Utopia: The Then and There of Queer Futurity.* New York: New York University Press.

Murphet, Julian. 2011. "Coetzee and Late Style: Exile within the Form." *Twentieth Century Literature* 57 (1): 86–104.

Murray, Stuart J. 2014. "Allegories of the Bioethical: Reading J.M. Coetzee's *Diary of a Bad Year*." *Journal of Medical Humanities* 35 (3): 321–34. https://doi.org/10.1007/s10912-014-9273-9.

Nelson, Emmanuel S., ed. 1993. *Contemporary Gay American Novelists: A Bio-Bibliographical Critical Sourcebook.* Westport, CT: Greenwood Press.

North, Michael. 2013. "The Making of 'Make It New.'" Guernica. August 15, 2013. https://www.guernicamag.com/the-making-of-making-it-new/.

Obaldia, Claire de. 1995. *The Essayistic Spirit: Literature, Modern Criticism, and the Essay.* New York: Oxford University Press.

Olszewski, Tricia. 2008. "Funny Games and the Witnesses: The Pain Event." *Washington City Paper.* March 14, 2008. https://www.washingtoncitypaper.com/arts/film-tv/article/13035048/funny-games-and-the-witnesses-the-pain-event.

Orwell, George. (1968) 2000. "The Frontiers of Art and Propaganda." In *My Country Right or Left, 1940–1943*, edited by Sonia Orwell and Ian Angus, 4: 123–7. The Collected Essays, Journalism, & Letters of George Orwell. Nonpareil Books: David R. Godine.

Packer, George. 1987. "Blind Alleys." *The Nation* 244 (12): 402–5.

Parker, Benjamin. 2017. "What Is a Theory of the Novel Good For?" *Boundary 2* (blog). June 14, 2017. http://www.boundary2.org/2017/06/benjamin-parker-what-is-a-theory-of-the-novel-good-for/.

Patton, Cindy. 1986. *Sex and Germs: The Politics of AIDS*. Montreal: Black Rose Books.

Patton, Cindy. 2002. *Globalizing AIDS*. Theory out of Bounds, v. 22. Minneapolis: University of Minnesota Press.

Peach, Linden. 2000. *Virginia Woolf*. New York: St. Martin's Press.

Pearl, Monica B. 2013. *AIDS Literature and Gay Identity: The Literature of Loss*. Routledge Studies in Twentieth-Century English Literature 29. New York: Routledge.

Periyan, Natasha. 2018. *The Politics of 1930s British Literature: Education, Class, Gender*. Historicizing Modernism. New York: Bloomsbury Academic.

Poyner, Jane. 2009. *J. M. Coetzee and the Paradox of Postcolonial Authorship*. Athens: Ohio University Press.

Radin, Grace. 1981. *Virginia Woolf's* The Years: *The Evolution of a Novel*. Knoxville: University of Tennessee Press.

Rainey, Lawrence, ed. 2005. *Modernism: An Anthology*. Hoboken, NJ: John Wiley & Sons.

Ravela, Christian. 2016. "'Turning Out' Possessive Individualism: Freedom and Belonging in Samuel R. Delany's *The Mad Man*." *MFS Modern Fiction Studies* 62 (1): 92–114.

Richter, Harvena. 1970. *Virginia Woolf: The Inward Voyage*. Princeton, NJ: Princeton University Press.

Robinson, Spider. 1976. "Galaxy Bookshelf." *Galaxy*, October 37 (7): 121–33.

Robinson, Spider. 1980. "The Reference Library." *Analog*, May 50 (5): 165–74.

Robinson, Lillian S., and Lise Vogel. 1971. "Modernism and History." *New Literary History* 3 (1): 177–99. https://doi.org/10.2307/468387.

Rose, Phyllis. (1978) 1987. *Woman of Letters: A Life of Virginia Woolf*. New York: Harcourt Brace Jovanovich.

Saint-Amour, Paul K. 2015. *Tense Future: Modernism, Total War, Encyclopedic Form*. New York: Oxford University Press.

Saloman, Randi. 2012. *Virginia Woolf's Essayism*. Edinburgh: Edinburgh University Press.

Scott, Darieck. 2010. "Porn and the N-Word Lust, Samuel Delany's *The Mad Man*, and a Derangement of Body and Sense(s)." In *Extravagant Abjection: Blackness, Power, and Sexuality in the African American Literary Imagination*, 204–55. New York: New York University Press.

Shaviro, Steven. 2006. "The Mad Man." The Pinocchio Theory. November 30. http://www.shaviro.com/Blog/?p=528.

Shore, Daniel. 2012. *Milton and the Art of Rhetoric*. New York: Cambridge University Press.

Siskin, Clifford. 1996. "The Rise of Novelism." In *Cultural Institutions of the Novel*, edited by Deidre Lynch and William B. Warner, 423–40. Durham, NC: Duke University Press.

Snaith, Anna. 2000. *Virginia Woolf: Public and Private Negotiations*. New York: St. Martin's Press.

Spencer, Kathleen L. 1985. "Deconstructing *Tales of Nevèrÿon*: Delany, Derrida, and the 'Modular Calculus, Parts I–IV.'" *Essays in Arts and Sciences* 14 (May): 59–89.

Spiro, Mia. 2013. *Anti-Nazi Modernism: The Challenges of Resistance in 1930s Fiction*. Evanston, IL: Northwestern University Press.

Spivak, Gayatri Chakravorty. 2003. *Death of a Discipline*. The Wellek Library Lectures in Critical Theory. New York: Columbia University Press.

Spivak, Gayatri Chakravorty. 2012. *An Aesthetic Education in the Era of Globalization*. Cambridge, MA: Harvard University Press.

Spivak, Gayatri Chakravorty. 2014. *Readings*. London: Seagull Books.

Taylor, Rod C. 2014. "Narrow Gates and Restricted Paths: The Critical Pedagogy of Virginia Woolf." *Woolf Studies Annual* 20: 55–81.

Tidwell, Joanne Campbell. 2008. *Politics and Aesthetics in the Diary of Virginia Woolf*. New York: Routledge.

"Timeline of HIV/AIDS." 2016. HIV.Gov. 2016. https://www.hiv.gov/hiv-basics/overview/history/hiv-and-aids-timeline.

Transue, Pamela J. 1986. *Virginia Woolf and the Politics of Style*. Albany: SUNY Press.

Treichler, Paula A. 1987. "AIDS, Homophobia and Biomedical Discourse: An Epidemic of Signification." *Cultural Studies* 1 (3): 263–305. https://doi.org/10.1080/09502388700490221.

Tucker, Jeffrey A. 2004. *A Sense of Wonder: Samuel R. Delany, Race, Identity and Difference*. Middletown, CT: Wesleyan University Press.

Wachter-Grene, Kirin. 2015. "'On the Unspeakable': Delany, Desire, and the Tactic of Transgression." *African American Review* 48 (3): 333–43.

Walsh, Richard. 2007. *The Rhetoric of Fictionality: Narrative Theory and the Idea of Fiction*. Theory and Interpretation of Narrative. Columbus: Ohio State University Press.

Watson, Stephen. 1986. "Colonialism and the Novels of J. M. Coetzee." *Research in African Literatures* 17 (3): 370–92.

Wheare, Jane. 1989. *Virginia Woolf: Dramatic Novelist*. London: Palgrave Macmillan UK.

Wilkins, Alasdair. 2012. "The Fake Chemical Compound Isaac Asimov Invented to Punk Science Writers." Io9. February 23, 2012. https://io9.gizmodo.com/the-fake-chemical-compound-isaac-asimov-invented-to-pun-5887014.

Williams, Zoe. 2011. "No Time for Novels—Should We Ditch Fiction in Times of Crisis?" *The Guardian*. November 19, 2011. http://www.theguardian.com/theguardian/2011/nov/19/read-serious-books-zoe-williams.

Willis, J.H. 1992. *Leonard and Virginia Woolf as Publishers: The Hogarth Press, 1917–41*. Charlottesville: University Press of Virginia.

Wilm, Jan. 2016. *The Slow Philosophy of J.M. Coetzee*. London: Bloomsbury.

Winterhalter, Teresa. 2003. "'What Else Can I Do but Write?' Discursive Disruption and the Ethics of Style in Virginia Woolf's *Three Guineas*." *Hypatia* 18 (4): 236–57.

Wollaeger, Mark. 2008. *Modernism, Media, and Propaganda: British Narrative from 1900 to 1945*. Princeton: Princeton University Press.

Wood, Alice. 2013. *Virginia Woolf's Late Cultural Criticism: The Genesis of* The Years, Three Guineas *and* Between the Acts. Historicizing Modernism. London: Bloomsbury.

Wood, James. 2007. Review of *Diary of a Bad Year* by J.M. Coetzee. *The New Yorker*, December 24, 2007.

Wood, Robin. 2018. *Robin Wood on the Horror Film: Collected Essays and Reviews*. Edited by Barry Keith Grant and Richard Lippe. Contemporary Approaches to Film and Media Series. Detroit: Wayne State University Press.

Woodhouse, Reed. 1998. *Unlimited Embrace: A Canon of Gay Fiction, 1945–1995*. Amherst: University of Massachusetts Press.

Woods, Gregory. 1998. *A History of Gay Literature: The Male Tradition*. Yale University Press.

Woolf, Virginia. 1975–1980. *The Letters of Virginia Woolf*. Edited by Nigel Nicolson and Joanne Trautmann Banks. 6 vols. New York: Harcourt Brace Jovanovich.

Woolf, Virginia. 1977–1984. *The Diary of Virginia Woolf*. Edited by Anne Olivier Bell and Andrew McNeillie. 5 vols. New York: Harcourt Brace Jovanovich.

Woolf, Virginia. 1978. *The Pargiters: The Novel-Essay Portion of The Years*. Edited by Mitchell Leaska. A Harvest/HBJ Book. New York: Harcourt Brace Jovanovich.

Woolf, Virginia. 1986–2011. *The Essays of Virginia Woolf*. Edited by Stuart N. Clarke and Andrew McNeillie. 6 vols. London: Hogarth Press.

Woolf, Virginia. 1990. *Congenial Spirits: The Selected Letters of Virginia Woolf*. Edited by Joanne Trautmann Banks. New York: Harcourt Brace Jovanovich.

Woolf, Virginia. (1937) 1992. *The Years*. Edited by Hermione Lee. Oxford World's Classics. Oxford: Oxford University Press.

Woolf, Virginia. (1938) 2006. *Three Guineas*. Edited by Jane Marcus. Orlando: Harcourt.

Woolf, Virginia. (1937) 2008. *The Years*. Edited by Eleanor McNees. Orlando: Harcourt.

Woolf, Virginia. (1937) 2012. *The Years*. Edited by Anna Snaith. The Cambridge Edition of the Works of Virginia Woolf. Cambridge: Cambridge University Press.

Woolf, Virginia. (1929) 2015. *A Room of One's Own*. Edited by Susan Gubar. Houghton Mifflin Harcourt.

Yadav, Alok. 2010. "Literature, Fictiveness, and Postcolonial Criticism." *Novel* 43 (1): 189–96. https://doi.org/10.1215/00295132-2009-081.

Yao, Steven. 2009. "A Rim with a View: Orientalism, Geography, and the Historiography of Modernism." In *Pacific Rim Modernisms*, edited by Mary Ann Gillies, Helen Sword, and Steven Yao, 3–33. Toronto: University of Toronto Press.

Zinos-Amaro, Alvaro. 2014. "Roundtable on Samuel R. Delany, Grand Master." Locus Online. March 11, 2014. http://www.locusmag.com/Roundtable/2014/03/roundtable-on-samuel-r-delany-grand-master/.

Index

aesthetics 14, 39, 59–60, 73, 91, 112, 135
   and education 69
   and ethics 33–6, 61, 162
   and propaganda 16, 65, 72, 142, 153
   see also Modernism
AIDS/HIV 86, 119 n.5, 132 n.11
   and fiction 86, 90–1, 117
   and metaphor 98–100
   tragic narrative 117–18
   transmission 119
   see also Delany, Samuel R.
Allen, Judith 8
ambiguity 6, 15, 17, 37, 45–6, 58, 102, 104 n.17, 141, 154, 171
Amin, Kadji 124
Anand, Mulk Raj 34
Andrews, Charles 71, 72
art-for-art's-sake. *See* autonomy
Asimov, Isaac 85
Attridge, Derek 136, 152 n.10
Attwell, David 11, 139, 143 n.6
Auden, W. H. 43, 74, 79
Auerbach, Eric 46
Auster, Paul 141
authoritarianism 4, 17, 29, 53, 59, 155, 161, 164, 171
authority 62, 170–1
   Coetzee and 54, 139, 152, 155–7, 159–62, 167, 176
   Delany and 175–6
   and gender 161, 175
   and pedagogy 171
   Woolf and 61–2, 175–6
autonomy 1, 3–4, 5 n.1, 14, 18, 30 n.19, 82, 156, 164

Bakhtin, Mikhail 22, 86
Barnes, Djuna 13, 74, 80
Beard, Jo Ann 24 n.15
Beckett, Samuel 12, 55, 80, 136
Beebe, Maurice 6
Bell, Clive 39

Bell, Julian 39, 43
Bellin, Roger 114, 125 n.8
Benjamin, Walter 12
Bennett, Arnold 41, 57
Berman, Judith 10 n.4, 33–4
Berthoff, Ann 69
Biko, Steve 149 n.9
Black, Naomi 48 n.6
Blake, William 180
Bloch, Ernst 19
Boehmer, Elleke 138 n.2
Booth, Wayne 17
Bottome, Phyllis 64–5, 72
Bradbury, Malcolm and James McFarlane 8
Briggs, Julia 57
Brittain, Vera 12, 41, 62–5
Broch, Herman 69
Broderick, Damien 21 n.12
Brooks, Peter 153–4
Buchan, John 65

Cartwright, Justin 142
Cervantes, Miguel de 136, 144
Chan, Evelyn T. 46
Charles, Ron 142
Chekhov, Anton 37
Chile 149
Clarkson, Carol 173
Coetzee, J. M. 21–2, 62, 135–72, 173–81
   and allegory 22, 151–2
   as apolitical 135–6
   and Australia 138, 142–3
   and colonialism 138–9
   and crisis 4, 143, 145–52
   Diary of a Bad Year 18, 22, 35, 37, 84 n.9, 146–7, 152–62, 171
      conclusion 149–51
      as destabilized text 153
      and *Disgrace* 155
      form 35 n.20, 153–5, 157
      genre 141, 142, 154

Index

narrators 154
pedagogy 154, 157
and polemic 153
and readers 154–5
reviews 142, 143, 153–4
and Woolf, *The Pargiters* 35
and Woolf, *Three Guineas* 161
Elizabeth Costello 22, 34–5, 37, 84 n.9, 160
"At the Gate" 152
conclusion 148–9, 150–1
genre 141–2, 144
and *Lives of Animals, The* 145–7
reviews 141–2
essays and nonfiction prose
Boyhood 21, 146, 147, 162–3
"Confession and Double Thought" 157
Doubling the Point 11, 164
Elizabeth Costello (*see under* Coetzee, J. M.)
Giving Offense 145, 154, 160
"Jerusalem Prize Acceptance Speech" 137, 144, 178
Lives of Animals, The 22, 145–7, 162
Scenes from Provincial Life 144 n.7, 167
Summertime (*see under* Coetzee, J. M.)
Youth 21, 138, 146, 147 n.8, 163
fiction
Childhood of Jesus 22, 26, 141, 143
Death of Jesus 22, 26
Diary of a Bad Year (*see under* Coetzee, J. M.)
Disgrace 26, 54, 137, 139–41, 150, 160
Dusklands 21, 34, 139, 143 n.6
Elizabeth Costello (*see under* Coetzee, J. M.)
Foe 141, 143 n.6
In the Heart of the Country 143 n.6
Life and Times of Michael K 152
Master of Petersburg, The 141
Schooldays of Jesus 22, 26, 141
Slow Man 35, 84 n.9, 141, 160

Waiting for the Barbarians 154, 159
and language 169–70
and metafiction 143
as metamodernist 12–13, 82, 136–7
and Modernism 11, 12, 136–7, 179
and Nobel Prize 160
and novel form 141–2
and propaganda 16
reviews of 26–7, 141–3
and South Africa 135, 136–9, 178
Summertime 21, 22, 35, 37, 84 n.9, 135–6, 138, 147, 155, 162–70, 171
and *Boyhood* and *Youth* 147–8, 166–8
conclusion 148, 150–1, 169–70
and *Diary of a Bad Year* 164, 167
and *Disgrace* 139–40
form 164–7
genre 141, 163, 166–7
and history 164–5
and *Lives of Animals, The* 145
music in 169
narrators 139–40, 164, 167–9
pedagogy 166
South Africa in 165–6, 169
see also authority, fictionality
Cole, Sarah 71–2
Conrad, Joseph 12
Crane, Hart 13, 80, 81
Craven, Peter 143
crisis 1, 4, 7, 39–40, 72, 73, 113, 133, 152, 172
and pedagogy 147, 157, 171–2
and propaganda 13–18
and queerness 74
see also Coetzee, J. M.; Delany, Samuel R.; fictionality; form; Modernism; Woolf, Virginia
critical pedagogy. *See* pedagogy

Daugherty, Beth Rigel 28, 29, 61
Davenport, Guy 80
Davis, Ray 111, 125 n.8
Dearmer, Geoffrey 63
deconstruction 84, 157–60
DeFoe, Daniel 85, 136
Delany, Samuel R. 19–21, 54, 173–81
as activist 107–8
and AIDS 21, 77–9, 89–90, 99–100, 107–8, 119 n.5

and autobiography 87–90
as black, gay male writer 77
consistency of concerns 75–9
and crisis 4, 73–5, 110, 178
essays and nonfiction prose
   About Writing 11
   "Atlantis Rose … " 80
   "Aversion/Perversion/Diversion" 88
   "Gamble, The" 89, 119, 120 n.6
   Heavenly Breakfast 88, 90
   journals 77, 79, 82–3, 87
   Longer Views 90
   Motion of Light in Water 77, 79, 88, 90, 111–13, 120 n.6, 176 n.3
   1984: Selected Letters 110, 120 n.6, 130
   "Rhetoric of Sex/The Discourse of Desire, The" 89–90
   "Scorpion Garden, The" 114, 116
   "Scorpion Garden Revisited, The" 114
   "Shadows" 83 n.8, 90
   Shorter Views 90
   Times Square Red, Times Square Blue 93, 116
fiction
   "Atlantis: Model 1924" 21, 73 n.1, 81
   Atlantis: Three Tales 108
   Dark Reflections 21 n.13
   Dhalgren 19, 76, 79, 108
   Einstein Intersection, The 82–3
   Equinox (aka *Tides of Lust*) 77, 108, 110, 115
   Flight from Nevèrÿon 19, 74, 88, 92–8
   Hogg 77, 78 n.3, 79, 108, 110, 114, 115, 116, 125 n.8
   Jewels of Aptor 19
   Mad Man, The (see under Delany, Samuel R.)
   Neveryóna 19, 85
   Phallos 108
   Return to Nevèrÿon (book) 19, 108, 110
   Return to Nevèrÿon (series) 19–20, 74, 83, 84, 92, 101 n.16, 104
   Splendor and Misery of Bodies, of Cities, The 109 n.2, 110
   Stars in My Pocket Like Grains of Sand 21, 109
   "Tale of Plagues and Carnivals, The" (see under Delany, Samuel R.)
   Tales of Nevèrÿon 19, 74, 92–3
   Tides of Lust (see under *Equinox*)
   They Fly at Çiron 108 n.1
   Through the Valley of the Nest of Spiders 76, 77, 111, 114, 125 n.8
   Trouble on Triton (aka *Triton*) 19, 83, 93
interviews
   Conversations with Samuel R. Delany 11
   Silent Interviews 11
   "Thomas L. Long Interview, The" 99, 130 n.9
Mad Man, The 20–1, 36, 91, 110–33
   and AIDS 116–21, 125
   and death 117
   and didacticism 117
   and economics 120–1, 128
   and epistemology 121
   as fictional autobiography 128–30
   and fictionality 129–30, 131–2
   genres 111, 128, 130
   letters in 130 n.10
   metafiction 128–9
   as pornography 110, 111, 131
   and pornotopia 114–16, 128, 132–3
   and race 122–4, 126–8
   and the reader 29
   as subversive novel 111, 122
   and tragedy 117
   pedagogy 21, 111, 115, 123, 178
   see also pedagogy
and Modernism 11, 12–13, 74–5, 179
modular calculus 83–6
and pornography 110
and propaganda 16
and science fiction 34, 75–7, 80–1, 101 n.16, 108–9, 130–1, 151

sexual activity 88–9
sexuality as communism 117, 128
"Tale of Plagues and Carnivals, The"
   18, 20, 34, 36, 73–106, 108, 110,
   119, 128, 143, 178
   and AIDS 86–7
   and fictionality 86, 95–7, 101,
      105–6
   and metaphor 100–1
   and Modernism 104
   and readers 103–5
   as appendix 92–8
   narrators 102–3
   numbering of sections 98,
      104 n.17
   pedagogy 92, 97–8, 101, 105–6
   writing of 86–7
   see also nonfiction, pedagogy
   and Woolf 13, 73–4, 80, 82
   writing career 75–9
   see also authority, fictionality
Deleuze, Gilles and Félix Guattari 52
de Man, Paul 157–8, 160
Derrida, Jacques 77, 93, 128
Dick, Philip K. 178–9
didacticism 1, 15–17, 26, 30, 33, 142, 175
   and Brittain, *Honourable Estate* 63–4
   and crisis 24, 75, 137, 152
   and the novel 17, 22, 30–1, 139, 156
   see also pedagogy; pornography;
      propaganda; Woolf, Virginia
Dirda, Michael 108–9
Dostoyevsky, Fyodor 136, 141, 150, 161

Empson, William 43, 81 n.7
Ercolino, Stefano 69 n.20
essays 18, 24 n.15, 34, 153, 157, 159, 175
   and novel form 25, 35 n.20, 49, 64,
      69–70, 142, 144, 146
   and Woolf, *The Pargiters* 44–6
   see also nonfiction
estrangement 32, 114–15
ethics 5, 17, 162, 176, 178, 180
   ersatz 33, 59, 155, 177
   see also aesthetics
Eurocentrism 9

Falcato, Ana 156
fascism 2, 4, 39, 48, 51–2, 55, 65, 66, 70

Faulkner, William 79, 80
feminism 7, 12 n.6, 34, 60 n.16, 156–7,
   159, 160, 173, 175
fiction 22–7, 35, 142–3, 151
   and crisis 73
   definition 22–3
   vs. fictionality 23 n.14
   and paratexts 24, 144
   see also nonfiction
fictionality 23, 33, 84 n.9, 176, 177–8
   Coetzee and 139, 141–5, 150–1, 163,
      178
   and crisis 69–71, 86, 143, 145–52, 178
   Delany and 85–7, 90, 100, 105, 129–30,
      132, 178
   and form 25
   Woolf and 49, 69–70
   see also fiction, rhetoric
Ford, Ford Madox 12, 136
form 7, 14, 42, 49, 69, 84, 180
   and crisis 36, 73–4
   the novel 25, 29–31, 33, 50–5, 142, 179
   pedagogy and 19, 27, 28, 33, 53, 61, 72,
      92, 162, 176
   see also aesthetics, essays, fictionality
Foucault, Michel 20, 52, 77
Freire, Paulo 27, 31–2, 56 n.12, 61, 69,
   170–2, 174–5, 177
Friedman, Susan Stanford 9–10
Froula, Christine 47 n.4
Furlani, Andre 10, 81

Gallagher, Catherine 32
Galsworthy, John 41
Gay Men's Health Crisis 92, 103
George, W. L. 5
Gilbert, Stewart 79
Giroux, Henry 27, 69
Goethe, Johann Wolfgang von 30
Gordimer, Nadine 135, 140, 152, 173
Gould, Deborah B. 117–19, 122
Grady, Constance 26–7
Guiguet, Jean 60

Hacker, Marilyn 79
Hafley, James 58
Haneke, Michael 140
Haule, James 59
Head, Dominic 146, 152

Hite, Molly 47 n.4, 58–9, 69, 173–4, 175
Hitler, Adolf 43
Hogarth Press 12, 40, 43
Hollander, Rachel 61
Holleran, Andrew 86
Holtby, Winifred 12 n.6, 63
Hong, Jeesoo 10 n.4
hooks, bell 27, 30, 177
Howard, Robert 74

imagination 25, 27, 57, 59, 60–1, 69, 72, 104–5, 133, 151, 177, 180
influence 9–10, 11–12, 79, 81–2
Iser, Wolfgang 24–5, 151, 177
Isherwood, Christopher 43

James, David
  Modernist Futures 81, 136, 179–80
  and Urmila Seshagiri 9, 10, 81, 136
James, Kenneth 82–3, 90
Johnson, Barbara 77, 157–9, 160, 175
Johnston, Georgia 88
Joyce, James 5, 10, 12, 41, 79, 107

Kafka, Franz 12, 136, 152
Kalliney, Peter 9 n.3
Kannemeyer, J. C. 27 n.17, 137 n.1, 138, 163
Kaprow, Allan 111–13
Kenner, Hugh 12 n.6
Kermit, S. L. 84 n.9, 103
Kohlmann, Benjamin 39
Kristeva, Julia 20, 77
Krutch, Joseph Wood 14–15
Kutz, Eleanor and Hephzibah Roskelly 32, 104

Latham, Sean and Gayle Rogers 8
Laurence, Patricia 10 n.4
Lear, Jonathan 33, 155, 160, 162, 173, 177
Leaska, Mitchell 45, 58, 59
Lee, Hermione 34, 141
Lehmann, John 41, 43–4
Lind, L. Robert 14–15
literature 37, 80, 131
  gay 91
  and propaganda 14–16, 73
Lopéz, María J. 138, 148
Low, Lisa 175

Lowry, Elizabeth 26, 142
Lukács, György 34

Macharia, Keguro 125 n.8
Malzberg, Barry N. 19 n.11
Mansfield, Katherine 40
Marcus, Jane 57
Mazzoni, Guido 22, 30, 179
Metamodernism 9, 10–11, 31, 39 n.1, 82, 136, 179–80. *See also* Coetzee, J. M.; Delany, Samuel R.; Woolf, Virginia
Milton, John 28–9
Modernism 5–13
  and aesthetics 7, 152
  as apolitical 6–7
  and crisis 13–14, 74–5
  definition 8–10
  global/planetary 8–10
  vs. modernism 8–10
  New Modernist Studies 7, 35
  and the novel 31, 179
  and objects 80
  and power 163
  and propaganda 14, 153
  and readers 152
  see also Coetzee, J. M.; Delany, Samuel R.; pedagogy; Woolf, Virginia
Moi, Toril 7–8
Moore, G. E. 33–4
Moten, Fred 157
Muir, Edwin 58
Muñoz, José Esteban 111–12, 132
Murphet, Julian 152 n.10
Murray, Stewart J. 152 n.10, 160
Musil, Robert 12, 69

Nabokov, Vladimir 91, 156 n.11, 164
newness 32–3, 39, 41, 174
Ngugi wa Thiong'o 9 n.3
Nicolson, Benedict 2–3, 137
nonfiction 23–4, 175
  and Delany, "The Tale of Plagues and Carnivals" 94, 97
  and fiction 82–6, 146, 163
  and readers 144
  see also essays
novel. *See* form
novelism 54, 72, 115

Obaldia, Claire de 25
Oppen, George 4
Orientalism 10 n.4
Orwell, George 73

Packer, George 143 n.6
parataxis 31, 66–9
Parker, Ben 179
Patton, Carol 118
Pawlowski, Merry 48 n.6
Peach, Linden 59 n.15
Pearl, Monica B. 91
pedagogy 17, 27–33, 180
    critical 27, 29–30, 53, 61, 132, 174
    vs. didacticism 18, 28–9
    failed or rejected 26, 53–4, 140, 143
    and Modernism 31
    and propaganda 57–65, 174
    and the reader 28, 143, 180
    see also authority, crisis, form
Periyan, Natasha 61
Plato 5, 50, 57, 162
pornography 91, 114–17, 123–4
    and didacticism 107, 116
    see also Delany, Samuel R.
postcolonialism 11, 34
postmodernism 10, 82, 179
Pound, Ezra 39
Poyner, Jane 146–7, 151
propaganda 7, 14–17, 53, 59, 65, 73, 82, 158, 176
    and didacticism 16–17
    and information 16
    and literature 14–15, 135
    and the novel 142
    and Woolf, *Three Guineas* 62
    see also crisis, didacticism, pedagogy, readers
Proust, Marcel 12, 79

queer studies 11, 34, 124–5

Radin, Grace 45, 47 n.4, 48 n.5, 58, 59, 69
Rainey, Lawrence 8
Ravela, Christian 120–1
reader-response criticism 25 n.16

readers 82, 104, 151, 177–8, 180
    active vs. passive 31–3, 46, 62, 72, 74–5, 153, 158
    didacticism, propaganda, and 16–17, 49–50, 174
    and expectations 18, 25–6, 29, 51, 65–6, 97, 111, 143, 144 n.7
    and fictionality 23–5, 27
    and pornography 114–16, 123–4
    see also pedagogy, Modernism
Reed, Paul 86
rhetoric 17, 28, 130, 159
    and ethics 33
    and fictionality 23–4, 27, 87, 143, 146, 151, 153, 154, 177–8
Richardson, Dorothy 5, 41
Richter, Harvena 60 n.16
Rilke, Rainer Maria 87, 130
Robinson, Lillian S. and Lise Vogel 6
Robinson, Spider 19 n.11
Rose, Phyllis 53–4

Saint-Amour, Paul K. 70–1
Saloman, Randi 34
Scott, Darieck 121 n.7, 123–4, 125–6, 127–8
Scott, Joanna 142
Selincourt, Basil de 57–8
Shaviro, Steven 117, 128
Sinclair, May 5
Sinclair, Upton 1, 17 n.9
Singer, Peter 145–6
Siskin, Clifford 54
Smyth, Ethel 42
Snaith, Anna 12 n.7, 48–9, 55, 59
Solzhenitsyn, Aleksandr 160
Sontag, Susan 20, 98, 99–100, 131
Spencer, Kathleen 74, 92–3
Spender, Stephen 43
Spiro, Mia 74
Spivak, Gayatri 27, 60, 66, 69, 139, 158, 163
Stein, Gertrude 50
Steiner, K. Leslie 84 n.9, 103, 114–15
Stonewall riots 78
sword & sorcery stories 20, 74, 128, 178

Taylor, Rod C. 56 n.12, 61
Tidwell, Joanne Campbell 8

Toomer, Jean 13
Transue, Pamela J. 53–4, 69
Treichler, Paula 90 n.10, 108
Tucker, Jeffrey Allen 107, 119, 122

utopia 66, 112, 117, 132, 135, 172

Wachter-Grene, Kirin 122
Wagner, Richard 80, 81
Walsh, Richard 22–4, 142–3
war 16, 36, 51, 61, 62, 70, 137, 180–1
Watson, Stephen 138
Williams, William Carlos 80
Williams, Zoe 73
Wilm, Jan 11, 154, 173
Wilson, Romer 5
Winterhalter, Teresa 62
Wisor, Rebecca 48 n.6
Wittgenstein, Ludwig 34, 98
Wollaeger, Mark 14, 16
Wood, Alice 48, 59
Wood, James 35 n.20
Wood, Robin 140
Woodhouse, Reed 91, 111
Woods, Gregory 90–1
Woolf, Leonard 43, 180
Woolf, Virginia 18–19, 39–72, 173–81
    and Coetzee 35, 161, 175
    and crisis 1, 4, 70
    and Delany 13, 73–4, 82, 175
    and didacticism 46, 48, 57, 153
    and education 27 n.17, 28, 61
    essays and nonfictional prose
        "How Should One Read a Book" 28, 60
        "Leaning Tower, The" 16, 41
        "Letter to a Young Poet, A" 41, 43–4, 56 n.13
        "Modern Fiction" 80
        "New Biography, The" 44
        "On Not Knowing Greek" 50
        "Poetry, Fiction, and the Future" 43
        Room of One's Own, A 40, 49, 62, 84 n.9, 156
        "Thoughts on Peace in an Air Raid" 180–1
    Three Guineas 18–19, 29, 45, 48, 49, 51, 60, 61–2, 84 n.9, 116, 181
        "Why Art Today Follows Politics" 1–2, 14, 16, 64
    and essay-novel 18–19, 34, 45–6
    fiction
        Between the Acts 19, 49
        Flush 49, 84 n.9
        Jacob's Room 18, 42, 59 n.15, 66
        "Mark on the Wall, The" 39, 40, 42
        Mrs. Dalloway 18, 40, 42, 54
        Night and Day 40, 41, 42, 45, 47
        Orlando 18, 40, 49, 59 n.15, 84 n.9, 179
        Pargiters, The 18–19, 34, 44–7, 48, 53, 57, 58, 64, 69
        To the Lighthouse 18, 40, 54
        "Unwritten Novel, An" 42
        Voyage Out, The 40
        Waves, The 1, 18, 40, 41, 44, 45, 47, 49, 54–5, 58, 66, 175 n.1
        Years, The (see under Woolf, Virginia)
    and Lawrence, D. H. 12
    as metamodernist 12, 41
    and Modernism 11–12, 12 n.6, 42
    and propaganda 15–16, 65
    and war 62
    Years, The 18–19, 36, 39–72, 82, 103, 111, 116, 157
        characters 51–2, 53
        compared to Bottome, *The Mortal Storm* 64–5
        compared to Brittain, *Honourable Estate* 62–5
        and ethics 52–3
        and family novel genre 51
        and historical events 51
        narrator 55–6
        neglected by scholars 58 n.14
        and novel form 49–50, 55, 57–8
        pedagogy 21, 53–4, 55, 56 n.12, 59–61, 66, 70, 72
        and propaganda 52, 59, 72
        publication and sales 43
        and the reader 29, 46, 49–50, 52–5, 57, 59, 66

reception 58–9
repetition within 52, 56
as science fiction 80–1
themes 48
titled *Here and Now* 50
unity within 56

and violence 71–2
see also authority, essays, fictionality, propaganda

Yadev, Alok 22–3
Yao, Stephen 10 n.4

www.ingramcontent.com/pod-product-compliance
Lightning Source LLC
Chambersburg PA
CBHW052042300426
44117CB00012B/1943